Hopes and Expectations

Hopes and Expectations

The Origins of the Black Middle Class in Hartford

Barbara J. Beeching

Cover illustration: (Top) Carrington family members in an automobile. Accession number 1981.136.47, the Connecticut Historical Society. (Bottom) *View of the City of Hartford, Connecticut* by the British artist William Havell, c. 1841.

Published by State University of New York Press, Albany

© 2017 State University of New York

For information, contact State University of New York Press, Albany, NY
www.sunypress.edu

Production, Eileen Nizer
Marketing, Anne M. Valentine

Library of Congress Cataloging-in-Publication Data

Names: Beeching, Barbara J.
Title: Hopes and expectations : the origins of the black middle class in
   Hartford / Barbara J. Beeching.
Description: Albany : State University of New York Press, 2016. | Includes
   bibliographical references and index.
Identifiers: LCCN 2015036648 | ISBN 9781438461656 (hardcover : alkaline paper)
   | ISBN 9781438461649 (pbk. : alkaline paper) | ISBN 9781438461663 (e-book)
Subjects: LCSH: African Americans—Connecticut—Hartford—Social conditions.
   | African Americans—Connecticut—Hartford—Economic conditions. | Middle
   class—Connecticut—Hartford—History. | Community life—Connecticut—
   Hartford—History. | Primus, Nelson, 1842–1916. | Primus, Rebecca, 1836–1932. |
   Brown, Addie. | African Americans—Connecticut—Hartford—Biography. | Hartford
   (Conn.)—Economic conditions. | Hartford (Conn.)—Race relations.
Classification: LCC F104.H3 B44 2016 | DDC 305.896/07307463—dc23
LC record available at http://lccn.loc.gov/2015036648

10 9 8 7 6 5 4 3 2 1

In memory of Marie Walker Simpson
who told me about it

Contents

Illustrations   ix

Acknowledgments   xiii

Introduction   xv

PROLOGUE

Chapter 1   Migrant of Necessity   3

Chapter 2   Growing Up with the Community   19

EXPECTATIONS RISING

Chapter 3   Family Life amid Racial Turmoil   31

Chapter 4   Beyond Uplift: A New Spirit of Resistance   45

Chapter 5   A Black Middle Class Takes Shape in Time of War   65

EXPECTATIONS AT WORK

Chapter 6   Nelson Primus: The Artist in Boston   85

Chapter 7   Rebecca Primus: The Teacher in Royal Oak   107

Chapter 8   Addie Brown: The Working Girl in Hartford   135

EXPECTATIONS DEFERRED

Chapter 9   Growth and Decline   163

Chapter 10   Loss and Persistence   175

Epilogue   195

Appendix A. Blacks in Hartford 1830–1880   197

Appendix B. Primus Timeline with Pertinent Historical Events   199

Notes   205

Bibliography   241

Index   255

Illustrations

Images

1.1   Jeremiah Asher, minister and memoirist.   4

1.2   Hartford, 1836, Lithograph.   13

1.3   Hartford's Federal Style State House, 1830s.   14

2.1   The Talcott Street Congregational Church, Hartford's first black religious institution.   22

3.1   Prudence Crandall, schoolmistress and breaker of precedent.   33

3.2   Holdridge Primus, porter, stands streetside in front of the store he served for more than forty years.   39

4.1   James Mars, quiet but effective advocate of civil rights.   46

4.2   The Reverend James W. C. Pennington, fugitive slave, ordained minister, educator, first pastor of the Talcott Street Congregational Church.   48

4.3   Broadside announcing Augustus Washington's Daguerrean Gallery.   54

5.1   James Williams, longtime janitor and handyman at Trinity College, known to the students as "Professor Jim, Professor of Dust and Ashes."   69

5.2   The Twenty-Ninth (Colored) Regiment Connecticut Volunteer Infantry. In Beaufort, South Carolina, 1864, before seeing action in Virginia.   78

6.1 Typical flourish with which Nelson Primus closed his letters home. 86

6.2 Boston's first African American meetinghouse, and the former homes of David Walker and Maria Stewart would have drawn Nelson Primus to explore Joy Street, shown here from Beacon Street. 100

7.1 Sample page from one of Rebecca Primus's "home weeklies." 108

7.2 Hartford's Railroad Station, where Rebecca Primus boarded the train for her trip to Baltimore and ultimately Royal Oak, Maryland. 111

8.1 Sample page of an Addie Brown letter to Rebecca Primus. 136

8.2 Hartford's Main Street in the late 1860s, looking north from Central Row, showing tracks of the horse trolleys, with a mix of former homes converted to commercial use and newer structures built to accommodate business concerns and apartments. 137

9.1 By 1880 Connecticut had a grand new capitol building, and the former state house, now Hartford's City Hall, shared its former front yard (facing the river) with a grandiose Post Office. The side of the building that faced Main Street became its main entrance. 164

9.2 Main Street, 1880, had fewer of the old homes in place; the gaslights were gone. Notice the electric wires. 165

10.1 Stunned San Franciscans make their way through the rubble after the earthquake and fire of 1906. 187

10.2 Sometime after 1900, a smartly dressed Nelson Primus, right, worked in a San Francisco delicatessen by day, painted at night. 191

10.3 Like the Primus letters, this dress worn by Rebecca was preserved as a family keepsake. In the style of the 1870s, beautifully made, it may have been her wedding dress. 192

10.4 With the church building as background, the members of Hartford's Talcott Street Church assembled for this wide-angle

depiction of the survival and the solidarity of their
congregation. Rebecca Primus, with the large hat, is at the
center of the cutout, second row.   193

E.1   One of a series of Harris/Primus family gatherings in and
        around Boston, this one, around 1900, includes Rebecca
        Primus (Aunt Beckie).   196

Maps

1.1   Connecticut, 1800.   5

5.1   The Primus Family's Hartford.   73

7.1   Royal Oak and other destinations Rebecca mentions in her
        letters.   113

Plates

follow page 188

10.1   Nelson Primus, *Lizzie Mae Ulmer*. Boston, 1876.

10.2   Nelson Primus, *Unknown Woman*. Boston, 1881.

10.3   Nelson Primus, *Unknown Man*. Seattle or San Francisco, 1899.

10.4   Nelson Primus, *Going to Meet Papa*. San Francisco, 1908.

10.5   Nelson Primus, *Fortune Teller*. San Francisco, 1898.

10.6   Nelson Primus, Unnamed. San Francisco, 1900.

Acknowledgments

Individuals and organizations, libraries and museums, scholars, friends, relatives, and strangers have helped put this work together. I thank them all. First of course, those who preceded me in "discovering" the Primus Papers: the late David White, who told me about them; Farah Jasmine Griffin, who edited the letters of the two women; and Karen Hansen, who analyzed the friendship between them. All three generously shared their findings. I also note the happy discovery of a descendant of the Primus family, Jesse Harris, who supplied a hitherto unknown picture of an early twentieth-century family reunion.

Then the data banks: over the years I spent so much time in the Connecticut State Library that some of the employees thought I worked there. The History and Genealogy staff was generous with suggestions and guidance, as were state archivists Mark Jones and Bruce Stark. My second home away from home was the State Historical Society, home of the treasured letters. Judith Johnson was an outstanding source of ideas and facts, and more recently Tasha Caswell and Sierra Dixon have been equally accommodating.

I found help as well at the New-York Historical Society Museum and Library and in the public libraries of Boston, San Francisco, Seattle, and in those closer to home in Waterbury, Branford, North Branford, and Guilford. Luckily for me, the Hartford History Center in the Hartford Public Library opened its doors in time to supply additional help and a rare document. I found important material at the Beinecke Rare Book and Manuscript Library, Yale University, Mystic Seaport Library, and the National Archives in Washington. The Harriet Beecher Stowe Center Library yielded significant sources, as did the Homer Babbidge Library, University of Connecticut.

My deep thanks to Altina Waller, who patiently marked up reams of ragged early drafts. Other benefactors are Kaz Kazlowski at the Prudence

Crandall Museum; Karin Peterson, Connecticut State Historic Preservation Office; Stacey Stachow at the Wadsworth Atheneum; and art historians Hildegarde Cummings, William Hosley, and E. J. Montgomery. Dr. Walter Evans and Linda Evans; and Harmon and Harriett Kelley, collectors of African American art, have been generous and unfailingly helpful.

Anyone who studies local history finds company and help from the public historians who know where to dig and what to do with their findings. Diana Ross McCain has answered many questions in person and through her writings. Ted Groom shared his work, as did Christopher Webber. Elizabeth Oldham and Frances Kartunnen of the Nantucket Historical Society supplied critical local data, and Colleen Cyr, genealogical historian and nurse, proved a brilliant researcher. Historians Yvonne McGregor and the late Lessie Jackson of the Faith Congregational Church welcomed my questions.

My late husband, Paul Q. Beeching, instigated the entire project; my children provided assistance and/or diversion as needed. Friends Carol Fine and Mims Butterworth rescued me from a number of blunders. My apologies to those whose names should be here and are not. I am in debt to many, but claim all mistakes as my own.

Earlier versions of material in Chapters 6, 9, and 10 appeared in "Nelson A. Primus, African American Artist 1842–1916," *The International Review of African American Art* 18, no. 4 (2002): 46–50.

Earlier versions of material in Chapters 7 through 10 appeared in "Rebecca Primus and Addie Brown," in Elizabeth J. Normen, ed., *African American Connecticut Explored* (Middletown, CT: Wesleyan University Press, 2013), 198–206.

Earlier versions of material in Chapters 7 through 10 appeared in "Remembering Rebecca Primus," in *Twain's World: Essays on Hartford's Cultural Heritage* (Hartford, CT: *Hartford Courant*, 1999), 34–47.

An abbreviated early version of the major argument appeared in "Reading the Numbers: Census Returns as Key to the Nineteenth Century Black Community in Hartford, Connecticut," *Connecticut History* 44, no. 2 (Fall 2005): 224–247.

Introduction

It was the three voices that pulled me into this study, and I found them almost by chance. Shortly after retiring I began work on an advanced degree in American Studies, and for a course on the Gilded Age I went looking for examples of life in Hartford in the late nineteenth century. A friend advised me to go to the Connecticut Historical Society and take a look at the Primus Papers. These turned out to be three cardboard boxes of what collectors call ephemera—invitations, postcards, semiofficial documents, receipts—the memorabilia of an African American family in Hartford before, during, and after the Civil War into the so-called Gilded Age. The great find they contained was more than two hundred personal letters written mostly in the 1860s by three interrelated individuals pursuing three different ambitions in three different locations. The letters open up lives far removed from the world of J. P. Morgan, the Hartford native more closely associated with the period, but once I started reading, I was hooked.

In November 1865, a twenty-eight-year-old schoolteacher, Rebecca Primus, began a series of "home weeklies" to her parents in Hartford. She described for them her days on the Eastern Shore of Maryland, where she founded a Freedmen's Bureau school. At about the same time, her brother Nelson began writing home about his new life in Boston with his wife and infant daughter as he set out to make a name and a career for himself as an artist. The third writer, Addie Brown, was a young domestic worker in Hartford who wrote voluminously to Rebecca, lamenting their separation and describing her own struggle to achieve a semblance of security and stability.

The writers touch on race, class, gender, religion, politics, news events, fashions, music, books, food, and weather. They describe their friends and associates and reveal their overlapping networks. They catalog incidents of discrimination and tell how they responded. Some of their statements assume information today's reader does not have, and of course each tailors his or her letters to the recipients, but in their separate voices the writers come alive. We see the rooms they inhabit, hear how they spend their time, learn of their hopes for the future, and notice their close ties to the Hartford they knew. They were real people with real problems, grappling with prejudice, exclusion, and worse; occasionally surprised, often amused, sometimes angry. In their dailiness, the letters build suspense, for today's readers, along with the writers, want to know what would happen next.

I was not the first to find the Primus letters fascinating. In the 1970s, David White, the independent historian who directed me to them, described the Hartford Addie Brown inhabited and wrote about it. In the 1990s, Karen Hansen examined the close relationship between Addie Brown and Rebecca Primus, and Farah Griffin edited the letters of the two women.[1]

The three Primus writers introduce not just themselves, but also a family, and a black world within a white one. A web of relatives, friends, and associates had come together in a hostile environment to create a community of its own—but what kind of family; what sort of community? How typical were the two ambitious professionals, teacher and artist, and the energetic, unskilled young woman bent on betterment? How did they fit in? What was the community like—size, origins, makeup, social life, institutions? And what did happen next? What changed over time, and why? How did the Civil War and Emancipation affect the African Americans in Hartford? After Reconstruction, in the economic turmoil and the rise of the robber barons, what became of the three letter writers and their ambitions?

I set out to trace three lives and found myself examining the particular world they inhabited through more than eighty years. The search took me through two academic degrees and twenty years of my life. It led from descriptions of slavery in New England to studies of black communities in the antebellum North to more recent examinations of individual black lives. It led to the public records—local newspapers, the US Census, city directories, birth, marriage and death notices, real estate holdings, court proceedings, probate documents, and estate inventories for African Americans in the lifetime of the Primus family members.

Following family and community through the decades reveals the connection between the struggle for a decent life and the goal of securing full citizenship and equal rights. That effort was shaped in part by local demographics. Until the Civil War ended, Hartford's African Americans were overwhelmingly Northern born and raised. They were Black Yankees, although their grandparents had been slaves. Connecticut's early economy was tied to the triangle trade, based on capturing, transporting, selling, and feeding Africans, and some inevitably were brought home by Connecticut merchants and ship captains. Most of those held in the North were isolated singly or in small numbers in the homes of white masters, but, as was true in the South, their status was at the very bottom of the ladder: they were property. Indifferently fed and clothed, they slept in the cellar or the attic and were subject to the discipline routinely meted out to inferiors. The early census recorded only their numbers and referred to them, along with Native Americans, as Others, never by name.

Slaveholding gradually waned in New England during and after the Revolutionary War, but freedom proved a hollow gift. In white minds, Africans and Native Americans were seen and treated as servants and inferior beings. Race prejudice was firmly in place. In Hartford, their numbers were small, but by 1820 free local blacks had begun a long slow march toward inclusion in the culture that surrounded them. One step at a time, they built a community that enjoyed years of promise, however faint, and progress, however modest, which reached its high point during the Civil War years, followed by a decline as steep as the rise had been gradual. At the top of the arc is the discovery of a black middle class in Hartford. Holdridge and Mehitable Primus, parents of Rebecca and Nelson, took part in the rise of black fortunes in Hartford and endured the dénouement. What lasted over time was the middle class way of life they adopted on the way up.

The existence of a class of black strivers aiming for equality is not in question, but my calling it a "middle class" requires definition and defense, because some historians reject it. Historian Glenda Gilmore, for example, writes that "the concept of a middle class, as historians use it, seems too rigid to describe this group of leading black men and women. It is a term they never used; instead, they called themselves the 'better' classes." Douglas Daniels agrees, writing, "It is a mystery to me that scholars can use a term [black middle class] derived from analysis of white Europeans and Americans, making it inapplicable in discussion of a people who experience race segregation and job discrimination to a degree that is unique in history."[2]

Others accept the term without comment. Leon Litwack, for one, simply assumes its existence, writing "many lower-class Negroes attempted to improve their position by obtaining regular employment and an education, virtual prerequisites for . . . admission into the middle class." Nick Salvatore applies the term to a group much like that in Hartford: "Although working-class by every economic criteria, [they] were functionally more akin to the emerging white middle class in their concern for social order and personal rectitude." And Gary Nash writes of " 'respectable' black families . . . who had achieved something close to a bourgeois style of life, even if their occupations did not connote middle-class status in the eyes of white neighbors."[3] Leslie Harris, summarizing New York City's antebellum years, finds that "[t]he fate of the black middle class or aspiring middle class was bound inextricably with that of the black working class in a society that saw all blacks as inferior and defined that inferiority partially in terms of class." Even more recently, Carla Peterson states that antebellum leaders in New York City, "[m]uch like white middle-class Americans, . . . placed emphasis on education, a Protestant ethic of hard work, and strict adherence to a code of respectability."[4]

Members of Hartford's black middle class embraced the qualities of respectability, reform, and refinement, but added an active interest in community welfare, expressed in support of efforts to reinforce black unity and at the same time promulgate the image of African Americans as capable, educated, informed citizens—as *equals*.

Hartford's black community was unique in some ways, but in its formation and development it follows a pattern found in other Northern cities. The first step was founding a black house of worship. To have a church of their own brought members a range of new freedoms—to meet, to speak freely, to worship according to their beliefs, to plan, to set goals, to cooperate to help the needy, and to speak with one voice to the white world around them. The black church was the seedbed for black schools, black reform, black outreach, and black protest.

Alongside the overall picture of a citizenry united by color and background, differences and disagreements surface, sometimes addressed openly, sometimes masked. Echoed in the letters, this finding creates a complex picture of a population searching for a way to obtain simple justice in a century of turmoil.

What follows is what happened next and also what came before. It is a story of individuals, family, and community over time; of expectation and disappointment, loss and endurance, change and continuity—a new look at African American life in the nineteenth-century North.

THE ASHER/PRIMUS FAMILY

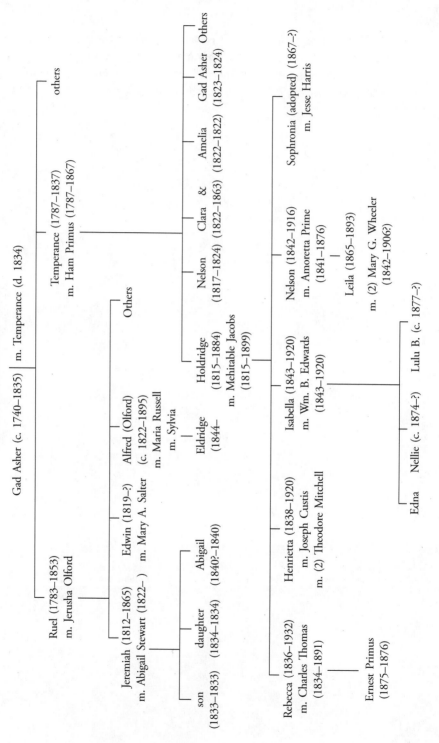

PROLOGUE

1

Migrant of Necessity

Growing up in New England thirty-odd years after the American Revolution, Holdridge Primus would have heard family stories of slavery and tales of black soldiers' battlefield heroics. More than likely, he heard the stories from his maternal grandfather, Gad Asher. The events of Asher's life embody a past that underlay the identity of many African Americans in the Northern states at the time. Jeremiah Asher, a cousin of Holdridge, preserved their grandfather's recollected experience in two memoirs.[1] Filtered by time and undoubtedly altered in its details, the story linked Holdridge and Jeremiah and all of Gad Asher's progeny to the founding of the Republic and reinforced their claim to citizenship. Later, as an activist Baptist minister, Jeremiah wrote the story of his life twice, and in both works he emphasized the importance of his grandfather's experiences as a slave, a soldier, and a free man.

According to Jeremiah, Gad Asher was born on his father's farm in Guinea, West Africa. From the age of four he was sent to the fields with an older brother, charged with scaring off the birds.[2] Keeping watch on their raised platform one day, the boys saw two white men approaching. Alarmed, the youngsters ran for home. The older boy got away, but his young brother did not. The kidnappers gagged the child and carried him to the coast, where he was put aboard a slave ship. Frightened and confused, he was nevertheless spared "many of the worst horrors of the middle passage."[3] The crew treated him kindly—possibly out of sympathy, but also to make sure that a saleable bit of the cargo was not lost. When the ship reached its destination, the boy was put up for sale.

The destination, we are told, was Guilford in the colony of Connecticut. This would have been somewhat unusual, because slave traders generally

FIGURE 1.1. Jeremiah Asher, minister and memoirist. *Credit:* Jeremiah Asher portrait, from *An Autobiography*, with details of a visit to England: and some account of the history of the Meeting Street Baptist Church, Providence, RI, and of the Shiloh Baptist Church, Philadelphia, PA. BX6455.A84 A3 1862; neg. #90375d, New York Historical Society Museum Library.

made their first stop in the West Indies. Still, it was possible. In the 1740s, when Gad Asher was seized, Guilford had two harbors equipped to handle slave vessels of forty to fifty tons.[4] The ship that carried the young African was part of the so-called "triangle trade," a three-cornered exchange variously described but involving lumber, livestock, and farm produce from the North American colonies; sugar and molasses from the West Indies; and slaves from Africa. For the sum of forty pounds, the small captive became the property of an East Guilford ship's carpenter named Bishop. He took the boy home, named him, and "became remarkably fond of him."[5]

Gad Asher was not the only slave in Guilford. In 1756, a report to the British crown numbers the town population at 2,322, including 59 blacks, few or none of them free.[6] By that time, slavery in New England was a century old. In 1634, after John Winthrop's Puritans, in league with the Narragansetts, destroyed the Pequot settlement near what is now Mystic, Connecticut, the few who were not brutally slaughtered were enslaved. Seventeen were sent to the West Indies and traded for "cotton, tobacco, and a group of Africans," who were returned to Winthrop's colony.[7] When Bishop bought the young captive, the pastor of the East Guilford Congregational Church owned eight slaves.[8] The practice of slaveholding was not uncommon in the North, even though some New England clergymen expressed a growing unease over it.[9]

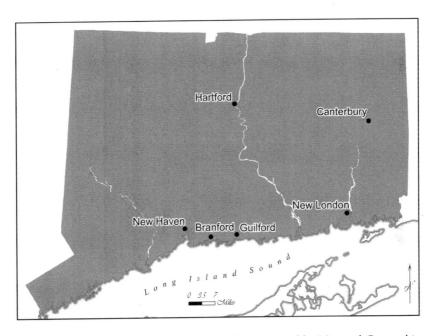

Map 1.1. Connecticut, 1800. *Credit:* Prepared and created by Map and Geographic Information Center (MAGIC) at the University of Connecticut Libraries, Storrs, CT. University of Connecticut, 2015. Data sources: MAGIC at University of Connecticut Library, Storrs, CT. Minnesota Population Center, National Historical Geographic Information System: Version 2.0 Minneapolis, MN. University of Minnesota, 2011.

Possibly related to these doubts, the naming of slaves in both North and South betrayed some reservation about the concept of one human being owning another. Historian Ira Berlin characterizes as a "cosmic jest" the custom of assigning heroic names—Pompey, Jupiter, Cato, Hercules—to slaves, mocking their lowly status.[10] Whether in this spirit or simply taking note of the boy's forced migration, his owner chose for him the names of two of the tribes of Israel.[11] Gad and Asher were the sons of Jacob and Zilpah, servant of Jacob's first wife, Leah. Young Gad Asher was somewhat unusual in having two names—the second of which came to be used as his surname.[12]

Slavery persisted in the North because of the need for workers.[13] Unlike plantation slaves in the South, most in Connecticut were isolated, with no more than two or three in a household. As was true in the South, some were trained in specific skills, some served aboard ships, and others worked in the master's house or in the fields.[14] Venture Smith, a contemporary of Gad Asher, was also captured as a child in Guinea. His narrative details his experiences as a slave on Long Island and later in Stonington, Connecticut.[15] In his youth, Venture carded wool, pounded corn, and served as waiter and "cup bearer." As an adult, he worked at different trades: boatman, all-round farmhand, and trusted tradesman. Gad Asher may have worked as a domestic servant, or he could have served as a carpenter's apprentice, learning the trade of his owner. What is clear in the lives of both Venture Smith and Gad Asher is that in seeking their freedom and then living as free men they embraced the ways and to some extent the ideas of white men. Whether joining a church, buying property, or naming and educating their children, both assumed that they were entitled to the opportunities available to citizens.

Jeremiah offers no details of his grandfather's upbringing, but Gad Asher would not have been treated as a member of the Bishop family. As for claims that Northern slavery was milder than that in the South, Ira Berlin notes that masters, Northern or Southern, "treated their slaves with extreme callousness and cruelty at times because this was the way they treated all subordinates, whether indentured servants, debtors, prisoners-of-war, pawns, peasants, or simply poor folks."[16] This provides ample explanation for the fact that, however "fond" Bishop may have been of the small boy he had bought, he later treated him less than honorably.

When the Revolutionary War was going badly for the colonists, Gad's owner was called up for military service. "Preferring the comforts of home to the dangers and hardships of a campaign," he made use of a Connecticut law that enabled an owner to free a slave and "allow" him to volunteer as substitute in the Army or Navy.[17] Gad Asher enlisted in May 1777 for the duration of the war.[18] He told Jeremiah that he "fought side by side with white men in two or three important battles."[19] When he returned to Guilford in 1783, he learned that Bishop now demanded repayment of the forty pounds Asher had cost him.[20]

Gad had already paid a price for his freedom. The source, nature, and extent of his injury remain unknown, but the Revolution had cost him his sight. Jeremiah said the old man attributed the loss to the combination of "intense heat, and inhaling the dense smoke of gunpowder, and exposure to the dew of heaven by night."[21] A double-edged piece of luck, the disability qualified him for a government pension, so that he was able to save the amount necessary to buy his freedom. This experience again resembles that of Venture Smith, who was tricked into buying himself several times over.[22] Both men achieved freedom through their own efforts.

Starting his life as a free man, Gad would have been at least forty years old and, according to Jeremiah, already married to a free woman named Temperance.[23] Little is recorded about Temperance—not even her maiden name—but a contemporary white man wrote that in June 1823 she was called to the bedside of a dying pastor, showing that the community recognized her as a healer.[24] The practice of medicine was largely in the hands of housewives in the eighteenth century. The uses and application of herbs were handed down from mother to daughter, so Temperance probably had learned from her mother, who was most likely a slave. African remedies may well have been among those she used.

Once freed, slaves tended to move away from the oversight of their former owners, and not surprisingly one of Gad's first acts as a free man was to settle his family in the northern section of Branford, the town west of Guilford.[25] Because Temperance was not a slave, their children were free. Among those who lived beyond infancy, the following have been identified: Temperance (mother of Holdridge Primus), Ruel (father of Jeremiah Asher), Henrietta, Marietta, and Brunella.[26] Note that these are not African names. Rather, they conform to naming patterns common among white colonial New Englanders. These fell into four categories: biblical, hortatory, traditional English, and "other"—a category that reflected secularization and other influences of the Enlightenment.[27] Based on naming practices of the time, we might guess that young Temperance, named for her mother, was the firstborn daughter. Ruel is biblical (Moses's father-in-law), and the others may have been named after relatives or friends. Henrietta is a feminine form of Henry; Marietta is a diminutive of Maria; and Brunella's name could be a reminder that some of the German troops had not returned home after the Revolutionary War. These Asher names suggest a New England identity, reflecting the adoption, reluctant or willing, of the dominant culture.

If Gad Asher was trained in his youth as a carpenter, blindness made such work impossible. He turned to farming, the most common occupation of all Connecticut householders in the eighteenth and early nineteenth centuries. By 1792, no doubt with the help of his pension, he bought two and a half acres of land in North Branford.[28] His son Ruel and other members of the family lived and worked on the farm. Ruel's son, Jeremiah, born in 1812, became the old man's "eyes" and the audience for many repetitions of his life story. Jeremiah's autobiography emphasizes the importance of the Revolutionary cause to his generation of African Americans and ties his own lifelong quest for equality to Gad Asher's military service.

Two other black veterans who lived in North Branford often visited Gad Asher, and the three told and retold their experiences in the "terrible and never-to-be-forgotten battle for American Liberty."[29] Young Jeremiah "became so accustomed to hear these men talk, until I almost fancied to myself that I had more rights than any white man in the town . . . Thus, my first ideas of the right of the colored man to life, liberty and the pursuit of happiness, were received from those old veterans and champions for liberty." Such beliefs led him to "resist" the insults of whites as a youth, a habit that "gave my parents much trouble."[30] To imagine he had more rights than whites was dangerous in a black youth, although in Jeremiah's case that conviction shaped the course of his ministry in later life. Inequality, the residue of slavery, was already fixed in the culture, so that black parents had no power to protect their own. The oppression of blacks, slave or free, was well established, even as Northern states began to distance themselves from slaveholding.[31] Connecticut, for example, passed a law abolishing slavery in 1784, just a year after the end of the Revolution. Still, as one scholar cautions, not only did it provide a gradual emancipation, it may have passed only because it was one item in a list of revised laws submitted by Roger Sherman and Richard Law. The implication is that the lawmakers, trusting their colleagues, approved the bundle of bills without discussing or perhaps even examining them.[32] The law, passed on January 8, 1784, provided that all children born after March 1 of that year would be free at the age of twenty-five. Others, including Gad Asher, would have been freed only by death.

Young Holdridge must have heard Gad Asher's story any number of times, and no doubt he knew of his cousin's challenges to race prejudice based on the conviction that those who fought with the colonists had earned rights of citizenship. In the years following the Revolution, the link between military service and full citizenship encouraged many Northern blacks to press for their rights.[33] Connecticut historian David White points out that the "children and grandchildren of the blacks of the Revolution were the first in Connecticut to make their feelings known to an apathetic white society . . . It was the James Mars, Amos Bemans, and Jeremiah Ashers who challenged Connecticut's conscience."[34] All three men later figured in the development of Hartford's black community.

Jeremiah nowhere discussed his grandfather's specific views with regard to rights of citizenship, but Gad Asher certainly made use of the culture in which he grew up. He may never have met Venture Smith, but both men displayed the same sense of entitlement. In spite of the duplicity of their masters, and fully aware of the racial climate around them, both accepted the ways of New England. Moreover, Gad Asher, along with many other slaves, participated in the war that promised "certain unalienable rights." In securing his freedom, naming his children, buying land, and apprenticing his son Ruel to a skilled tradesman, Gad Asher helped himself to the opportunities available to citizens of the new Republic.[35]

Another aspect of this acceptance is church membership. After moving to Branford as a free man, Gad Asher joined the Congregational Church and remained a member until his death—an act not wholly typical of African Americans at the time.[36] Aside from those who could benefit from membership, "slaves viewed Christianity with all of the suspicion and hostility due the religion of the owning class."[37] How then to account for Gad's faithful church attendance over some forty years? Recall that he came to New England and to slavery as a very young child, arriving in the 1740s along with the Great Awakening and its urgent message of salvation. In the custom of the times, he would have been taken to church along with members of the Bishop household. Certain aspects of Christianity may have appealed to him, and he could have blended it with the religion he had known in Guinea. Certainly it is possible that as a free man Gad joined the church to gain the favor of whites or at least to avoid criticism, and yet the difficulties and hardships he encountered in his life suggest the possibility that he found comfort in Christianity, or at least the prospect of a better hereafter.

In Gad's here and now, home ownership was a step up, and he found ways to take that step. He had the help of his son Ruel, who with his wife and children lived and worked on the farm. In 1815, perhaps with more savings from Gad's pension, father and son together purchased another ten acres.[38] Was it enough to support the two families? Historian Charles Sellers estimates that in the early nineteenth century, a family could subsist on "as little as twenty improved acres, employing a labor force of father, mother, and six to eight surviving children out of eight or ten pregnancies."[39] As of 1820, the two Asher households—eleven individuals—depended on the produce of twelve and a half acres.[40]

In the meantime, the other children of Gad and Temperance had left home to start families of their own. In 1811, their daughter Temperance married and moved with her husband, Ham Primus, to Guilford.[41] A Seaman's Protection Certificate dated 1810, found in the Primus Papers, identifies Ham Primus as "an American seaman, aged 23 years or thereabouts, of the height of five feet eight inches and a half, being a man of color, born at Branford and . . . a citizen of the United States of America."[42] Seaman's Certificates, issued beginning in 1796 to safeguard American sailors against impressment by the British Navy, also served African American sailors in Southern ports as proof of free status. They did not confirm the holder's rights as a citizen, only his nationality. As a fugitive, Frederick Douglass escaped to freedom on the strength of a borrowed Seaman's Certificate. The American eagle printed on the document convinced the train conductor that Douglass was a sailor and a freeman.[43] Ham Primus's certificate was his own, and the fact that it was preserved shows its importance to his son, Holdridge. Throughout the antebellum period, the question of African American citizenship remained a point of contention, until in 1857 Supreme Court Chief Justice Taney declared in the Dred Scott decision that blacks were not citizens. Nevertheless, Ham Primus's certificate was a family keepsake—a link to the past, a record of his occupation, and in hindsight an ironic affirmation of his own, and his children's, citizenship.

In Guilford, Ham had access to docks where short-haul coastal runs originated.[44] W. Jeffrey Bolster writes that "coasting became the job of choice for black mariners with dependents" since such work "allowed seamen with families to stay closer to home."[45] Ham obviously chose coastal runs since his wife, Temperance (Asher), gave birth to at least eight children between 1815 and 1827.[46] The first of these was Holdridge, born January 25, 1815. The records of Guilford's Episcopal churches supply the dates of birth, baptism, and in some instances the deaths, of the couple's children, evidence that this branch of the family also maintained ties to organized religion.[47] Moreover, the names of the couple's children again suggest identification with the dominant culture. Gad Asher Primus was named for his grandfather; Marietta for an aunt, the sister of Temperance. The nonbiblical, nontraditional names given the other children—Holdridge, Nelson, Clara, Amelia, and Margetta—come from a "vastly expanded pool of new [names]" that showed parents "rethinking their own roles and their expectations for their children."[48] Did Ham and Temperance give some of their children "new" names in the expectation of better lives and better times in the new century?

If so, their hopes were only partially fulfilled. Eight was not an unusual number of births for the period, nor was it unusual that not all eight survived childhood. In 1822, when Holdridge was seven years old, his infant sister Amelia died within days of baptism, while her twin, Clara, survived.[49] In 1824, when he was nine, two of his brothers, twenty-two-month-old Gad Asher and seven-year-old Nelson, both died of typhus within a two-week period.[50] Years later, Holdridge named his own son Nelson in memory of the brother so near his own age, surely his companion and playmate. Lucky to survive childhood himself, he encountered grief at an early age.

For the parents, the loss of three children in two years was compounded by other problems, and by 1830 Ham and Temperance had moved their family from Guilford to Gad Asher's farm in North Branford.[51] The move inland, away from the harbors of Guilford and Branford, signals the end of Ham's seafaring career. The change may have been forced on him, as growing racism in the antebellum years made it increasingly hard for black sailors to find work.[52] In addition, the Panic of 1819 initiated the boom and bust cycles that became a hallmark of nineteenth-century life.[53] Especially for blacks, the 1820s brought not only hard times but also "hard feelings and hard money."[54] The downturn affected the Ham Primus family and in fact the whole Asher clan. Tightened credit and the demands of the growing cash economy burdened debtors in particular—and farmers by the nature of their occupation are debtors.

Reflecting these developments, by 1828 Ham Primus was working as a farmhand. Malachi Linsley, a white Branford farmer, wrote in his diary that on December 16, "Ham and his Father [in-law] Asher come and thrashed my rye for 3 days."[55] This was not a casual hire, for Linsley had formerly owned a slave called "Uncle Ham," a resident of Branford.[56] Freed at the age of twenty-one, Uncle Ham had three sons, one of them named Ham—Holdridge's father.[57] The three days' work in December initiated a series of day jobs for Ham during the next few years: clearing stones out of Linsley's orchard, threshing grain, and other farm chores.[58] Ham also would have helped work Gad's farm and likely found other day jobs in the area.

However Ham and Temperance viewed their move to Gad's farm, Holdridge and his sisters may have welcomed it, because they now had the companionship of their Asher cousins and closer contact with their venerable grandfather. Hard times notwithstanding, in 1832 Ham managed to purchase an acre and a half of Gad Asher's land and reportedly built a house on it.[59] This purchase may reflect Ham's wish to maintain an independent household, but it also pointed to a need for additional housing. Ham's family and Ruel's, along with Gad and his wife, brought to seventeen the number of mouths to feed on some twelve acres of New England's stony soil.[60] Such doubling up was a familiar strategy for hard-pressed families, but in this case the resulting numbers still overtaxed available resources.

Combining households offered one means of coping with hard times, and another was to separate some members from the family group. A study of Appalachia at the turn of the nineteenth century found that, "[f]or Appalachians, moving into an extended family household represented an initial strategy . . . but, like New Englanders, seeking work elsewhere was an additional option that many were forced to choose.[61] The Ham Primus family made that second choice in April 1829, when they took nine-year-old Clara, the surviving twin, to the Linsley farm, where she stayed for a year and a half.[62] This arrangement, a form of apprenticeship in housekeeping, was common among both blacks and whites of the time, providing housing and meals and sometimes schooling for the child of a hard-pressed family. In later years, Holdridge and his wife would make use of the same strategy.

Sending young Clara to the Linsleys may have helped, but it hardly solved the problems facing the extended Asher family. As it happened, the two boys, Holdridge Primus and his cousin Jeremiah Asher, had reached their teen years and were able to help on the farm, but they were redundant there, because Ruel and Ham could do the work. At the same time, local jobs were scarce because of the recession, so that separation again provided a solution. Indeed, between 1750 and 1840, a combination of overpopulation, soil exhaustion, and the coming of industrialization led to a massive exodus from New England farms.[63] Young men—and women—left in unprecedented numbers for better opportunities in nearby cities or greener pastures in the West. The two cousins joined the migration. Jeremiah wrote that in 1828, when he was sixteen years old, he left home to look for work in Hartford.[64] Holdridge left around the same time, although the date has not been established.[65]

What were the circumstances of their leaving? What arrangements were made for them in Hartford? We can only guess at answers. Families forced to send a son or daughter away would, if possible, arrange employment in the new location, or at least direct the migrant to a friend or relative.[66] What we do know is that setting out together or separately, Jeremiah and Holdridge both traveled to Hartford around 1830. They necessarily took along habits formed and lessons learned at home, memories of family life, and the story of their grandfather's journey from kidnapped child to slave, then soldier and finally free man and landowner. Old enough to understand the need that sent them away, they were young enough to welcome the prospect of adventure in a new setting. We cannot recapture their thoughts at leaving, but we can refer to findings on the internal migrations of that time. "Americans," we learn, "appear to have accepted with little anxiety the traumas involved in pulling up stakes and moving. Confidence in the future and their desire to share in the general improvement outweighed their local and familial attachments."[67] In their later lives, these two migrants showed a willingness to adapt to new circumstances as both continued to value religion, family life, and education.

While Jeremiah became a Baptist minister and an outspoken advocate of black rights, Holdridge took a different path. We can trace that path over time, but all we can recapture of his journey from Branford to Hartford is how he might have traveled and what he saw when he arrived.

If he made his way east to Old Saybrook and sailed up the Connecticut River to Hartford, he would have been greeted there by a panoramic view of maritime commerce: ships coming and going and the noisy docks "smelling of molasses and Old Jamaica," the odor of the triangle trade.[68] Steam power was coming into use, but sailing vessels still carried passengers and trade goods up the Connecticut River as far as Hartford.

FIGURE I.2. Hartford, 1836, Lithograph. *Credit:* Frontispiece, John Warner Barber, *Connecticut Historical Collections*, 1836, reprint, Library of Congress 99-62405, Connecticut State Library.

He would have seen horses and mules "corralled on [the] wharves by the hundred awaiting shipment" to the West Indies, from which they would return with molasses, sugar, rum, and salt. By 1830, African slaves were no longer being brought legally to Hartford, but the West Indies trade remained a vital element in the city's economy.[69] The produce and animals crowding the city docks still went to feed the slaves and maintain the sugar plantations.

Having spent his early years in Guilford as the son of a sailor, Holdridge would have recognized the sloops and schooners in the harbor, the scows and flatboats bringing lumber from northern ports, but the covered wooden toll bridge across the Connecticut River and the ferries that connected Hartford and East Hartford would have been new to him. Up from the docks, the city was a cluster of buildings forming a modest skyline that stretched perhaps three quarters of a mile along the river. Viewed from the deck of an incoming ship, the scene was punctuated by the steeples of two Congregational meeting-houses. If the boat docked at the foot of State Street, Holdridge would have looked up to see a Hartford landmark still in place, the Federal-style State House of 1796 designed by Boston's Charles Bulfinch.

STATE HOUSE, HARTFORD, CONNECTICUT. 1834.

FIGURE 1.3. Hartford's Federal Style State House, 1830s. *Credit:* The Connecticut Historical Society.

Alternatively, Holdridge could have traveled by stage overland on the New Haven and Hartford Turnpike—as of 1799 "the ultimate in intercity communication" and still in use.[70] He might have noticed the contrast between the rural vistas along the way and the relatively dense huddle of buildings that made up the city of Hartford (incorporated in 1784). In 1830, the population was just under 10,000, with 495 African Americans, all of them free. Main Street was unpaved and dusty or muddy depending on the weather; householders gathered each morning at the markets and down at the wharves to buy provisions and exchange the latest local news—daily newspapers had not yet appeared. Two watchmen patrolled the streets from 10:00 p.m. until just before sunrise.[71] Even so, the interests that would make Hartford a manufacturing, publishing, and insurance center were beckoning those in search of a better life than that afforded by the grudging soil of most Connecticut farms.

The two young migrants found their opportunities limited. Young, bright, and strong, but also black, they both secured predictably menial positions, fortunately for them with prestigious white families. Jeremiah Asher "went to Hartford, where a cousin who resided there had obtained for me a situation with Henry L. Ellsworth, Esq., for ten dollars per month."[72] Henry Ellsworth was a son of Oliver Ellsworth, a Founding Father who had served as a Connecticut delegate to the Constitutional Convention of 1787 and later as the first chief justice of the United States Supreme Court.[73] The helpful cousin was probably related to Jeremiah's mother, Jerusha Olford Asher, whom he describes as being "of the Indian extraction and . . . born in Hartford."[74] Sharing their status as Others, Native Americans and African Americans frequently intermarried.

Holdridge Primus's first job in Hartford was as a servant in the household of William Wolcott Ellsworth, twin brother of Jeremiah's employer.[75] Almost certainly he also found welcome with his aunt's Olford relatives and benefited from Jeremiah's connection with the Ellsworth family.[76] William W., a lawyer in the family tradition and like his brother a member of Hartford's elite, had married a daughter of Noah Webster. He served as a representative in Congress from 1829 to 1833, around the time when Primus came to Hartford.[77] Whether the young newcomer accompanied Ellsworth to Washington during legislative sessions or more likely stayed in Hartford with the family, the job gave him the opportunity to observe an educated, influential, wealthy gentleman and his family. At the same time, it gave him a chance to show his employer that he was an able and reliable worker; a serious and responsible young man. The fact that he and

Jeremiah both worked for members of the prominent Ellsworth family possibly brought them a degree of notice within the black community; at least it would have helped them get acquainted.

As a youngster, Holdridge had seen the advantages of establishing a connection with influential whites in his father's relationship with Malachi Linsley, and Jeremiah Asher had his own experience of such benefits. During his employment with Henry Ellsworth, Jeremiah contracted typhus, and Ellsworth's wife provided constant care: "My own mother could not have done more for me."[78] Such solicitude on the part of an elite white employer was not unusual. Historian Nick Salvatore, tracing the life of an African American worker in nineteenth-century Massachusetts, notes that Amos Webber's white employer provided "protection in the often hostile racial atmosphere in Worcester" and willingly accommodated his trusted employee's needs in scheduling his duties.[79] Robert Cottrol, in a study of the nineteenth-century black community in Providence, observes that "White Providence was somewhat prepared to reward the diligent black servant."[80]

Overall, in spite of their having found well-disposed employers, the two newcomers found a high level of racial tension in the city. Cambridge scholar Edward Abdy, touring Hartford in 1833, asked a black gardener "how his brethren were treated in the town." He learned that "they were insulted and annoyed in a very shameful manner. Frequent broils and fights were the consequence; and the bitter feeling of animosity . . . had much increased since the Colonization Society had become more active."[81] The American Colonization Society, founded in 1816, stated as its purpose the gradual emancipation of slaves, and—revealing the gap between abolition and racial equality—the subsequent "return" of the "Africans" to their "homeland." This strategy was designed to produce an all-white American citizenry, the ultimate goal of colonizationists.[82] By 1830, black leaders had begun to agitate for the abolition of slavery, and by the middle of the decade an increasingly vociferous Anti-Slavery Society with black and white membership underscored the effort with a barrage of pamphlets, flyers, and broadsides supporting abolition and opposing colonization.[83] Hostility grew as anti-abolitionists in turn stepped up their efforts; Abdy's informant was describing the effects of this escalating clash. In another passage, Abdy states his own opinion:

> Throughout the Union, there is, perhaps, no city, containing the same amount of population, where the blacks meet with more contumely and unkindness than at this place [Hartford,

Conn.]. Some of them told me it was hardly safe for them to be in the streets alone at night . . . To pelt them with stones, and cry out nigger! nigger! as they pass, seems to be the pastime of the place.[84]

As previously noted, race prejudice was already firmly planted in the North: as a youngster, Jeremiah Asher was granted the "privilege" of attending the district school in Branford, but as soon as he had mastered the rudiments of reading and arithmetic, his father (Ruel Asher) was advised to "take me out of school and bind me out to some good master and then I would be good for something."[85] This advice served the dual purpose of removing a black child from the schoolroom and impressing upon the family that education was of little use to African Americans. Frederick Douglass, hired as a caulker in New Bedford, quickly discovered that the skills he gained in slavery were useless, as white workers refused to work with him.[86] Hartford's racial climate appears to have been of a piece with that of Branford and New Bedford.

As a newcomer, Primus would have spent long days with his white employer's family, but for companionship and guidance, he turned to the black community. Raised in a churchgoing family, he would have found his way to the African Religious Society, a nondenominational meetinghouse and gathering place, where he very likely met young Mehitable Jacobs, for there or elsewhere the two, still in their teens, became acquainted. We know nothing of the growing mutual interest between the two, but as a newcomer to the city, Holdridge Primus had made fortunate connections—in his first employer and in his blossoming friendship with Mehitable, daughter of a prominent local black family.

2

Growing Up with the Community

Mehitable Esther Jacobs was baptized in Hartford on November 26, 1815. Although the date of her birth is unknown, she was born into what her eldest daughter would later call a "venerable and famous" black family.[1] Mehitable's paternal grandfather, Reece Jacobs, came to Hartford from Long Island with his family around 1769, at the age of fourteen. While many blacks in Connecticut were still slaves at the time, Reese was free.[2] He later married Mabel (diminutive of Mehitable), a woman from nearby Wethersfield. Their three sons were Aaron, Jeremiah, and James. The middle son, Jeremiah, was one of the city's early black entrepreneurs, a maker of boots and shoes. With a clientele of both white and black residents, he was one of the few African Americans who owned a home.[3] The family's "venerable" status was based on Reece's early arrival as a free man, Aaron's position as a founding member of Hartford's first black church, and Jeremiah's double distinction as a tradesman and homeowner.[4]

Jeremiah's children were born and raised in the "small wooden house opposite the South Green," which also served as his shop. The Jacobs family, like the Ashers and Primuses, subscribed to New England naming traditions: Mehitable, the firstborn, was named for Reese's wife, Mabel, (the child's grandmother), and Esther for her own mother.[5] Her younger siblings included two girls, Bathsheba and Emily, and a boy, Jeremiah, named for his father: two biblical references and one contemporary name. Of Mehitable's childhood we know only that she learned to read and write and mastered the skill of dressmaking. By the time she reached her mid-teens, her father had died and her mother, Esther, had become the head of the family, which included the four children and their grandmother, Mabel. With young Jeremiah the only male, this mostly female household offered the example of a capable woman coping with responsibility in a time of loss.

Mehitable's early years coincide with the beginnings of a recognizable black community in Hartford, and members of her family played a part in establishing the city's first black institution. At the age of four, she would not have grasped the importance of the event, but in November 1819, Hartford's "people of colour, tiring of the custom of being assigned seats in the galleries of the white churches, began to worship by themselves."[6] In established churches blacks did not worship side by side with whites, but were confined "either in an 'African corner,' a 'Nigger Pew,' seats marked 'B.M.' (Black Members), or aloft in 'Nigger Heaven.' "[7] The specifics differed from one church to another, but Jeremiah Asher describes the "negro pew" in Hartford's white Baptist Church as "the most objectionable one I had ever seen."[8] There were in fact two enclosures for blacks, one in either corner of the gallery "about six feet square, with the sides high enough that worshippers could hardly see the minister or the rest of the congregation, and calculated to accommodate about fifteen or twenty persons."[9] Hartford's black protesters, along with Jeremiah Asher, found such enclosures insulting.

The description of Hartford's African Americans "tiring of the custom of being assigned seats in the galleries" first appeared in the church history published in 1944.[10] The phrase soft-pedals the affront, as it mutes the resentment that motivated these first protesters. Repeated in every succeeding historical account published by the congregation, the sentence became scripturelike, putting dignity above anger. Was it copied from an earlier, lost account that reflected the style and thinking of the original protesters, or was it written in 1944, reflecting the climate of race relations at that time?

We know only that in 1819, a group of Hartford blacks met with Joel Hawes, pastor of Hartford's First Congregational Church, to state their objections. No record of the meeting exists, but we can assume a civil exchange, because Hawes proposed that the African Americans worship in a separate space on First Church property, and they accepted.[11] Because the Congregational Church was Connecticut's established religion until 1818, these early protesters were most likely raised in that faith. And yet the first clergyman to serve the new African Religious Society was a black Baptist preacher, Asa Goldsborough, who served a congregation in Providence, Rhode Island, not long afterward.[12]

This modest protest of 1819, a first step taken by local blacks to affirm their rights, presents a paradox. A group of believers withdrew from the very institution in which they sought equal standing. Denied inclusion, they resorted to separation. Indignant at being crowded into discriminatory seating, a brave few stated their objections, but the result was not the dismantling of the "negro pews," and indeed it is not clear that they expected it to be, for separation brought its own benefits. Meeting on their own, they could speak freely on political and religious matters and decide a variety of questions independent of white oversight. They may have been inspired by the example of blacks in larger cities, where community-building efforts were already under way. Philadelphia and Boston, for example, with larger black populations, had organized their own religious societies in 1787 and 1796, respectively.[13] Philadelphia's black population then was 7,582; Boston's 1,687.[14] Hartford, with a black population of just 355 in 1820, had nevertheless produced a group of activists willing to voice dissent. The result of their action probably pleased white church members as much as it did the protesters. The Reverend Hawes's solution removed them from segregated seating, from the nave of the church, and in fact from the congregation.

Thereafter the assistance of the white power structure proved similarly two-edged: in several instances it enabled blacks to achieve their goals and at the same time further separated them from whites. Historian Leonard Curry observes that white support was "sporadic and usually available only in the initiatory stages of church development. The black church in urban America," he emphasizes, "was overwhelmingly the vision of the black spirit, organized by black minds, built by black hands, and the solace of black souls."[15]

Subsequent events in Hartford confirm the accuracy of Curry's assessment: in 1820, the year following the protest, the new black congregation took a second step toward community formation, requesting its own Sunday School. White Hartford's Sunday School Union provided funds for the black congregation to rent a meeting place and hire an instructor. The location selected, in a sail loft, was near the docks in a neighborhood where many blacks lived.[16] The third step came in 1826, when the black congregation organized itself as the African Religious Society of Hartford. Shortly afterward, its members, including Mehitable's grandfather Reese Jacobs, took a fourth step, appealing for help in securing land on which to build a dedicated meetinghouse.[17] Contributions from blacks and whites enabled the African Religious Society to purchase land at the corner of Talcott and Market Streets and build a two-story brick meetinghouse, the cost estimated at $2,500.[18] Members took pride in the fact that ministers of white Baptist and Congregational churches participated in the opening ceremonies.[19] Thus by 1827, just eight years after the initial protest, Hartford blacks had created their own religious center, founded a Sunday school for

TALCOTT STREET CONGREGATIONAL CHURCH.

FIGURE 2.1. The Talcott Street Congregational Church, Hartford's first black religious institution. *Credit:* The Connecticut Historical Society.

their children, and built their own meetinghouse, confirming the presence of an active black community.

One further step connects Mehitable's family to the city's early black leadership. Hartford schools, underfunded and in decline, admitted but did not welcome black students.[20] For their parents, the remedy again was to separate. In 1830, local black leaders circulated a petition requesting city funding for a school for black children. The first name on the petition was that of Mehitable's uncle, Aaron Jacobs.[21] Again with black and white cooperation, the effort succeeded, and the first district school for blacks was opened in the basement of the African Religious Society meeting house on Talcott Street.

When we attempt a closer look at Hartford's black population in Mehitable's early years, we note that because of its relatively small size, all of its residents would have been acquainted with one another, at least on sight. In 1819, all 355 of Hartford's blacks would have known the identity of those who approached the Reverend Hawes. We are not so lucky. The earliest records have been lost, and church pamphlets supply only the names of church officers as of 1826, along with a list of some who were "among the active members" at the time.[22] Below are names that appear nowhere in the standard histories of Hartford, but they were the early leaders of Hartford's emerging black community.[23]

Asher, Jeremiah
Babcock, Primus
Blackstone, John
Cook, Joseph
Daniels, William W.
Foster, Henry
Freeman, Mason
Garrison, George
Jacobs, Aaron
Magira, Ishmael
Mason, William
Sheen, T. W.
Swan, Prince
Swere, Edmund
Wells, Thomas

Mehitable's uncle, Aaron Jacobs, was a member, as was Holdridge Primus's cousin Jeremiah Asher. Reconstructed church records describe members of the African Religious Society as "free people and natives of New England, some of Indian Blood. Nearly all could read and write."[24] No women are named, but members' wives and children would have attended services and certainly took part in charitable and educational activities. The reference to Indian heritage connects with Jeremiah Asher's statement that his mother, Jerusha Olford Asher, a Hartford native, had Indian blood.[25] While a few of those on the list had mastered skills, for the most part they were ordinary working men holding menial jobs, trying to provide for their families and avoid or withstand the rancor of abusive whites. It is doubtful that any had higher education or professional training, but they understood the importance of solidarity as they sought to counteract the oppression that limited their lives. Jeremiah Asher, Ishmael Magira, and certainly others were descendants of Revolutionary War veterans.[26] Some would serve or send their sons to serve in the Civil War. Ten appear in the census for 1820 and/or 1830 as householders, meaning that they did not live in the homes or businesses of white employers. Several later represented Hartford at state and national black conventions. Some, including Prince Swan and Henry Foster, joined local temperance and other reform societies; Foster served as a local agent for William Lloyd Garrison's hard-line abolitionist newspaper *The Liberator*. He maintained a clothes-cleaning business of his own for a time and worked briefly for the black merchant tailor William Saunders, another agent for *The Liberator*. William Mason, formerly a manufacturer of wagons and cartwheels in Lyme, Connecticut, prospered in Hartford no doubt because of his occupation, which may have brought him more white clients than black.[27] Little is known about William W. Daniels except that some years later, after the death of his first wife, he married Clara Primus, Holdridge's younger sister whose twin died as a youngster. Over the years, other members of the extended Asher/Primus family found their way to the city and formed a supportive network.

These early members tended to be young. Of the twelve whose ages can be determined, eight were younger than thirty-five in 1830. The four who were older, Joseph Cook, William Mason, John Blackstone, and Aaron Jacobs, could have been among the protesters of 1819. Many on the list continued to support black improvement efforts and community advancement. Some cannot be traced, but it is safe to assume that most were as described—literate, free, and New England born.

Most, but not all. Two of these early activists exemplify the range of life experience represented in Hartford's black community. Joseph Cook was an unlettered native of Virginia in his late fifties, no doubt a former slave and possibly a fugitive. He made his way to Hartford shortly after the turn of the nineteenth century and became known among whites as a "very respectable colored man."[28] A white memoirist depicted him as a quaint local character and recalled overhearing him as he encouraged a group of blacks to contribute to the construction of the church for blacks. When a bystander remarked that he was not getting much response from his friends, Cook replied, "No sir, our folks are good to 'scribe, but poor [to] pay." In another instance, Cook chided his black friends, "Gentlemen, I don't doubt your good 'tentions, but I had rather see your names on this paper." However quaint his speech, Cook's *X* as signatory along with William Mason's in the purchase of the Talcott Street property for the African Religious meetinghouse shows his understanding of the importance of community building.[29] It shows as well the openness of the black community to newcomers willing to work for the general good.

John Blackstone, another senior member of the African Society, presents a different variation on the image of the black New Englander. His story is told in an anonymous 1843 pamphlet, probably written after his death. The author describes Blackstone as a former sailor who "lived most of his life in a poor hut."[30] He reportedly bought his first wife, Lilly, a "drunk," for a hogshead of molasses, and she bore three children: Tom, who ran away to sea and never returned, and Lois and Lucy, both of whom died early. After Lilly died, Blackstone married again, an unnamed woman who "kept a neat house" but also drank. According to the undoubtedly white author, religion proved Blackstone's "only solace."[31] After a life-changing conversion experience, he became an active supporter of the African Religious Society. He learned to read and at times hosted the Sabbath School in his lodging near the Meeting House on Talcott Street. He died of consumption in the early 1840s. By emphasizing the hardships Blackstone endured, the narrator seems to be imitating the slave narratives popular in the antebellum era, but—questions of accuracy aside—the narrative broadens our picture of the black community in Hartford. Blackstone maintained householder status in Hartford from 1800 to 1830 and appears to have shown remarkable persistence in his latter-day efforts to live a Christian life. Set beside a preponderance of Northern-born blacks in Hartford until 1870, the stories of Joseph Cook and John Blackstone show the presence and acceptance of diverse strands within the community and among its activists.

The absence of women's names in the above list of early members slights the contributions of a significant group. In the usage of the time, the name of a male on the church roster was understood to encompass others in his household, including his wife, who may well have attended church more faithfully and supported its functions more actively than did her husband. Thus the contributions as well as the names of individual women are largely lost, although the tale of one female church member shows a spirit of independence and provides an example of varied reactions within the church community.

Elizabeth (Betsy) Mars came to Hartford sometime in the 1820s and was joined later by her two brothers, James and John, who also figure in local history. All three were born slaves in Canaan, in northwest Connecticut, and all three developed strong ties to Christianity—Elizabeth as a missionary, James as a deacon, and John as a minister. Elizabeth's story was preserved because of her membership in a charitable association affiliated with the African Religious Society.[32] She was treasurer of the group in the late 1820s when the poetess Lydia Huntley Sigourney, the "Sweet Singer of Hartford," headed a campaign to send blacks as missionaries to Liberia. A leader of the Hartford Colonization Society, Mrs. Sigourney publicized the project as an opportunity to Christianize Africa—work purportedly best done by African Americans. Attracted by the possibility of devoting her life to that cause, Elizabeth Mars announced that she wished to become one of the missionaries. The local Colonization Society provided training and assistance, and by 1832 Elizabeth and her husband, William Johnson, sailed for Liberia. Widowed within weeks of her arrival, Elizabeth spent the rest of her life teaching in an Episcopal Missionary School there. After her first three difficult years, she wrote to a friend, "I have never regretted one moment coming to this place."[33] She returned to Hartford only once to visit. While most black leaders rejected the aims of the Colonization Society in the 1820s and 1830s, Elizabeth Mars and at least some women of the African Society felt otherwise—an example not only of diversity of opinion among Hartford blacks, but also of the self-confidence of many black women. Mehitable Jacobs was seventeen at the time, but her later life suggests that she could have seen in Elizabeth Mars some of the qualities she saw in her own mother: strength, dedication, and self-reliance.

The claim that women and their lives tended to disappear from the public record after marriage, like most generalizations, invites exceptions. If Elizabeth Mars was one woman whose story survived, another was Maria Stewart, a Hartford native who set nineteenth-century coverture on its ear. Born Maria Miller and orphaned at the age of five according to her own account, she was "bound out to the family of a clergyman [and] had the seeds of piety and virtue early sown in my mind." In her teens she left the family and went to Boston, where she married James W. Stewart, a friend of David Walker, whose 1829 pamphlet *Appeal to the Coloured Citizens of the World* called on slaves to rebel. Through that connection. Maria became an active abolitionist, and soon she added women's rights to her causes. Well before the Seneca Falls Convention of 1848—generally considered the inciting moment of the women's movement—Stewart seized the agency her gender was denied. She persuaded William Lloyd Garrison to publish her tracts and spoke forcefully on both subjects in public meetings before both men and women. Newspapers delightedly followed her contrarian career. Her views did not prevail in her lifetime, but Mehitable Jacobs, daughter of a self-sufficient mother, observer of the courage of Elizabeth Mars, could have seen in Maria Stewart a self-liberated, relentless campaigner, a woman to admire if not take as a life model.[34] Imagine young Mehitable reading Stewart's question "How long shall the fair daughters of Africa be compelled to bury their minds and talents beneath a load of iron pots and kettles?"[35] While she was never entirely free of what the pots and kettles represented, Mehitable was not buried under their weight. Part of her family legacy was her expertise as a dressmaker, which provided her income above what most women of color could command, and also the stature of a skilled entrepreneur.[36]

Elizabeth Mars saw emigration as an opportunity to spread Christianity, and some African Americans, doubting that equality could be achieved in this country, saw emigration as a chance to escape the prejudice that limited their lives. Still, in the cities of the North, majority black opinion at the time rejected colonization.[37] In Hartford, Sigourney's advocacy was not persuasive: African Americans recognized that the goal of the Colonization Society was simply to remove them from the country of their birth. Most Northern blacks had no direct ties with Africa, and many took seriously the promise of equality in the Declaration of Independence. Some claimed citizenship on the strength of relatives who had fought in the Revolution. Some believed that white prejudice could be overcome, and others lacked funds to pick up and move elsewhere. Some simply feared the unknown. Certainly the question would have been discussed and debated at the African Religious Society Meeting House.

Indeed, while the Meeting House brought together a group of individuals united in their objection to separate and unequal seating in white churches, its members developed strong and ultimately incompatible views on religious, political, and social questions. In a pattern repeated almost universally among Congregationalists, members of Hartford's African Religious Society held "spirited debates" on such matters as educational requirements for ministers, style of preaching, and the music used in services.[38] Jeremiah Asher remembered the Society meetinghouse as a place where "members of all denominations sometimes worshipped, sometimes quarreled."[39] He explained that those who favored Baptist teachings—himself included—were accused of thinking themselves "better than other Christians."[40] Eventually he left the African Society because of the "unprofitable harangues," but also because he "believed that immersion, and immersion of believers only, was Scriptural baptism."[41] Sources differ as to the causes of the harangues but agree that disagreement became chronic. Some, we are told, sought the order and restraint of the Congregational Church service while others, influenced by preachers of the Second Great Awakening, preferred less formal worship with spirited exhortation and singing.[42] Historian Stephen G. Ray maintains that "the differences and distinctions [among members of the Hartford African Religious Society] had more to do with issues of doctrine and polity than with liveliness of worship or the efficacy of political action."[43] In any event, by 1832, when Elizabeth Mars and her husband sailed for Liberia, it became clear that the African Religious Society did not satisfy all of its members. To resolve the dispute, members held a vote, and the majority favored union with the Congregational faith.

The resulting schism ended the African Religious Society as such. The choice of those who stayed was officially recognized in 1833 when the white pastors of Hartford's First and Second Congregational Churches, Joel Hawes and C. C. Vanarsdalen, joined to conduct a service that created the First Hartford Colored Congregational Church. Hartford's first black church thus joined a major white ecclesiastical institution. After adopting various names, in 1860 it became the Talcott Street Congregational Church.[44] The original meetinghouse was replaced in 1906, but in 1833 it exemplified the strength and purpose of Hartford's African American community. The new congregation, of which Mehitable Jacobs was "one of the original members," grew and prospered.[45] The young newcomer Holdridge Primus at some point became a member, again raising the possibility that he and Mehitable met in church.[46] We might even suggest that her presence at services helped secure his regular attendance.

Racial tension intensified in Hartford and elsewhere in the 1830s as a series of major incidents involving race and slavery kept those issues in the national spotlight. Hartford's African Americans had much to discuss wherever they gathered—in church, in barbershops and saloons, in living rooms, and perhaps in the Jacobs' small wooden house opposite the South Green.

At the same time, daily life went on, as it will: church services were held, ships came and went on the river, elections were contested, and teenaged Mehitable Jacobs finished her schooling. She learned her way around the black and white worlds that surrounded her, helped her mother with the younger children, and honed her skills—cutting patterns, hemming skirts, and binding buttonholes. Some evenings young Holdridge Primus, perhaps still working for the Ellsworth family, may have walked over to the Jacobs' place to call on her. All that is speculation, but a short entry in the city's vital records states that on July 27, 1835, the Primus family of Hartford had its beginnings, reported in a terse and not entirely accurate entry in the city's vital records: "Holdich Prium m. Mehitabel E. Jacob of Hartford."[47]

EXPECTATIONS RISING

3

Family Life amid Racial Turmoil

In June 1835, a three-day anti-black riot in Hartford shattered the white city fathers' visions of civic order. It also challenged some black activists' belief in the prospects for overcoming racial prejudice. A month later, the marriage of Holdridge Primus and Mehitable Esther Jacobs launched what the couple no doubt expected to be a long and satisfying life together. The contrast between the two events—public disorder and mutual affirmation—captures the contradictions and uncertainties that beset Hartford blacks in the antebellum period. More specifically, it prefigures the distance between the growing racial tension that would draw some Hartford blacks into active resistance and the family-centered, apolitical lives that Holdridge and Mehitable would create for themselves and their children. They started married life renting rooms in a working-class neighborhood and began to build a way of life that combined active support of church and community with the cultivation of cordial relationships with white elites.

At the time, Americans were reconsidering the significance of the Revolutionary War, reading with new eyes the claim that all men are created equal. As the growing population pushed West, "ordinary" white men rejected the old, class-based order and sought universal white suffrage. Free African Americans like Jeremiah Asher rejected the color-based order and sought recognition as citizens of the country of their birth.

By 1830, few blacks in Connecticut—and none in Hartford—were slaves, but all were well aware of a fixed division based on skin color. As a response, national black leaders devised the strategy of racial uplift as a blueprint for overcoming race prejudice. The first priority was to bring about the end of slavery, and black abolitionists were encouraged to find allies among whites. The second priority was in black hands. The theory proposed that African Americans could eventually break down barriers and achieve full citizenship by demonstrating their innate equality—by conspicuously adhering to the standards of the rising white middle class.[1] These standards were contained in the reforms that characterized the times: temperance, thrift, hard work, reliability, and Christian morality. This theory appealed to many blacks, including Holdridge and Mehitable, who quietly managed through thrift and careful planning to better their lives and those of their children. Jeremiah Asher, on the other hand, went beyond demonstrating his innate equality: he addressed the question directly, voicing to members of the white Baptist church his objection to the separate and unequal seating arrangements there. According to his memoir, the congregation invited him to speak on the subject, and as a result they did away with the enclosed areas and allowed African Americans to sit in any seats in the galleries.[2] The two cousins extracted quite different lessons from their shared years on Gad Asher's farm. They present two classic black responses to growing prejudice: accommodation in the careful life course of Holdridge Primus, and resistance as practiced by the outspoken Jeremiah Asher. In the 1830s, a series of events related to race questions, several of them centered in Connecticut, would paradoxically confirm each in his position.

The warning bell of what was to come sounded in 1829, just before Holdridge left Branford. In that year, Boston's David Walker published his *Appeal to the Coloured Citizens of the World*, spelling out in powerful prose the horrors of slavery and exhorting slaves to assert their manhood.[3] His blunt call for rebellion came just seven years after Denmark Vesey's slave rebellion in Charleston, South Carolina, had been narrowly averted. In 1831, in Southampton County, Virginia, Nat Turner's succeeded. *The Hartford Courant* carried detailed accounts of the initial carnage, the search for perpetrators, and their trials and executions. The revolt and its aftermath fixed national attention on the issue of slavery: abolitionists intensified their efforts, and slavery's defenders dug in to assure its continuance. The violence of Nat Turner's action underscored white fears that black men, enslaved or free, were dangerous.

That fear surfaced close to home in New Haven when Arthur Tappan, dedicated abolitionist, the Reverend Simeon Jocelyn, white minister of a black church in New Haven, and William Lloyd Garrison, editor of *The Liberator*, joined with other antislavery leaders to propose opening a school—a college—to prepare black men for skilled jobs in the mechanical and agricultural trades. They chose New Haven for the site "because of its literary and scientific fame, its central location, the relative liberality of state laws, and the 'friendly, pious, generous, and humane' character of the city's residents.' "[4] And yet the mayor and local newspapers denounced the proposal, claiming that such a school would provide a channel for spreading the doctrine of antislavery. It would attract unsavory blacks who would lower moral standards in the city and deter tourists as well as prospective students of Yale and other white schools.[5] Furthermore, founding a *college* for African Americans assumed that they were capable of higher learning and, worse, would encourage them to seek "social equality."[6] In a raucous town meeting, the generous and humane citizens of New Haven were badly outnumbered—the vote was seven hundred against, four in favor.[7] Part of the problem was the timing: the proposal was aired a month after the Nat Turner rebellion, when details of the massacre still dominated the news.

FIGURE 3.1. Prudence Crandall, schoolmistress and breaker of precedent. *Credit:* The Prudence Crandall Museum Collection, Connecticut Department of Economic and Community Development.

A year later, an incident in the town of Canterbury in eastern Connecticut again attracted statewide and national attention to questions of race and education. Schoolmistress Prudence Crandall accepted a young black woman, Sarah Harris, as a student in her seminary for young ladies.[8] Parents of the white students immediately withdrew their daughters from the school. Encouraged by William Lloyd Garrison, Crandall then advertised a seminary exclusively for "young misses of color." Her reward for reaching across the color line was a night in jail and nationwide coverage. Outraged whites threatened her students, her school, and her person. She endured attacks including attempted arson on her home, the site of her school. The state legislature passed a law prohibiting "the establishing of literary institutions . . . for the instruction of persons of Colour of other States."[9] The court case against the school was tried, appealed, and retried—with Attorney William Ellsworth leading the defense. If Holdridge Primus was still in Ellsworth's employ, he could have heard the matter discussed by whites in the family parlor as well as by blacks at the Talcott Street Church. Ellsworth did not prevail. Defeated, Prudence Crandall closed her school in 1834 and left the state. Hartford's black activists registered their protest by sending Mason Freeman to the 1833 National Negro Convention in Philadelphia to call for an investigation of the constitutionality of the law. It was a gesture only. Unable to hold office or even to vote, blacks had no political power.

The national notoriety surrounding the attempt to found a college for African Americans in Hartford and Prudence Crandall's attempt to school black women provides the background and probably the incentive for the Hartford riot of 1835, which preceded by a month the wedding of Holdridge and Mehitable. The three-day incident was one in an epidemic of major disturbances in New York City, Philadelphia, Boston, Utica, Cincinnati, Charleston, and elsewhere in the 1830s and 1840s.[10] The Hartford riot did not rank among the most violent, but it startled and alarmed the local citizenry. The sequence of events can be pieced together from newspaper articles and court records.[11] On Monday evening on June 9, 1835, a group of blacks met in a house on Front Street, not far from the Talcott Street Church. A mob of angry whites gathered outside, shouting threats and calling for those inside to come out. On the next night, a larger group of fifty or more whites appeared outside the Talcott Street Church, where a meeting of African Americans was again in progress. When the participants emerged, whites attacked them with clubs and other unnamed weapons. Christopher Cooper, a black man who lived nearby, ran home and returned with his gun. He reportedly shot William Peaster, one of the white rioters, in the side, back, and shoulder and wounded Lathrop Bliss in the right arm. With the butt of his weapon, he allegedly struck Edward Poble and several other white men. The rioters' response was to "pull down" the house where Cooper lived—said to be that of the convert John Blackstone. Cooper was arrested, as were several whites. On the third night, June 11, an even larger crowd gathered and pulled down two more black homes, those of Benjamin Flagg and William Gardner. The phrase "pulled down" is used repeatedly in the accounts: the method is not clear, but the effect certainly was to demolish the house. Because local law enforcement proved unable to stop or disperse the rioters, on the following day, Thursday, June 12, the county sheriff deputized a number of citizens and called on the Governor's Foot Guard for assistance. By then, either the riot had run its course or the presence of a larger force discouraged the troublemakers, for no further disturbance was reported.

The action was hardly spontaneous, because on the second night the white attackers brought clubs and other weapons, but those responsible remain unknown. The black shooter, Christopher Cooper, was tried in Superior Court and sentenced to six months in jail. Hartford City Court records identify eight white men charged with assault and six with disturbing the peace by pulling down Benjamin Flagg's house. Of the fourteen whites called into court, no record has been found of any being punished. A white memoirist writing fifty years later states that on the second and third nights, a group of "rafters" from Vermont who had come down the Connecticut River with loads of lumber joined the local white rioters.[12] This assertion, repeated in none of the other accounts, conveniently spread at least part of the blame to out-of-towners. And yet the court records identify all of those arrested as Hartford residents. None appear in the 1830 census, but three were listed in the City Directory: two as joiners (carpenters) and one—Lathrop Bliss, who sustained a gunshot wound—as proprietor of a "Segar" store. These three qualify as "gentlemen of property and standing," the phrase historian Leonard Richards used to describe key figures in the series of antiblack riots.[13] Aside from John Blackstone, the African Americans named in accounts of the affair have eluded further identification.

Newspaper accounts, the voice of the local bourgeoisie, expressed shock at the violence and focused on the breach of public order rather than the rancor that prompted the attacks. The *Hartford Review* headed its report "Disgraceful Riots" and estimated the number of rioters at about two hundred.[14] The Whig-leaning *Hartford Courant* referred to the "several riots which have disgraced our city in the past week" and expressed sympathy for "the colored people, several of whom have lost what little property they possessed, besides being subjected to lawless violence and exposure of life."[15] No blacks were interviewed or quoted in accounts of the riots, nor were their rights mentioned or defended. The rioters, most likely a mixture of working-class men, artisans, and entrepreneurs, displayed hatred and contempt for the black churchgoers, while the abolitionist white elite—through the *Courant* article—expressed sympathy for the black victims to the extent of regret over their property losses.

The specific trigger for the Hartford disturbance remains unknown, but the meetings in the Talcott Street Church and elsewhere were almost certainly connected to the antislavery question. In 1835, white abolitionists loosed a flood of printed matter attacking slavery, and this in turn set off the "violent anti-abolitionist backlash"—the riots.[16] The immediate purpose was to intimidate blacks into giving up their quest for equality and thus stave off the ultimate threat to white supremacy—amalgamation of races.[17] Historian Winthrop Jordan, analyzing "American attitudes towards the Negro," writes: "One of the most interesting and revealing aspects . . . was the nearly universal belief that emancipation of Negroes from slavery would inevitably lead to increased racial mixture."[18] Class resentment also played a part in the riots. White workers, empowered by the Jacksonian democratization underway in the 1830s, sought equality with privileged whites; the riots expressed their unwillingness to share class status with African Americans.

Predictably, Holdridge Primus was not among the blacks named in accounts of the Hartford riot. Whatever his views on black/white tensions, he kept them to himself. He had come to Hartford expecting to work hard and hoping to make himself a part of black community life, and Mehitable shared his belief in the importance of family and security. The two built useful contacts with powerful white elites and avoided association with any form of racial protest, even when such avoidance put them at odds with family members and friends. Was it a difficult choice? They left us no word on this, but their actions show an unwavering adherence to their particular approach. The public face of that choice, particularly for Holdridge, entailed a willingness to accept—or appear to accept—the status quo on race: white elites at the top, African Americans and Native Americans on the lowest rung. And yet two of the Primus children, Rebecca and Nelson, in their letters home recounted and deplored the acts of discrimination and oppression they encountered. Stating their resentment, they described their own token acts of resistance—clearly assuming the support if not the encouragement of their parents. Thus we might speculate that family members and other

Hartford blacks knew a Holdridge Primus different from the mild-mannered newlywed who may have attended the first meeting on June 9 but avoided any of the confrontations that followed.

The 1835 riot caused some Hartford blacks to question the effectiveness of relying on their own efforts to achieve equality, although the immediate responses ranged from calls for retaliation, to condemnation, to silence. Christopher Cooper rushed home to get his gun. A more complicated but no less angry response was a strong denunciation of white oppression by the Reverend Hosea Easton, an outspoken and controversial figure in African American history. Easton arrived in Hartford at about the same time as Holdridge Primus, but their public lives and political choices represented opposing reactions to white dominance. Easton's rage and his commitment to equal rights have been traced to his father's lifelong efforts. James Easton operated an iron foundry in Massachusetts, where he also conducted a school to teach black youths the trade of ironworking, a skill that would enable them to rise above day labor and domestic service. In the end his efforts failed, as, overwhelmed by debt, he lost both his business and his school. Hosea, inspired by his father's dedication, at first encouraged blacks to improve their skills and live godly lives in order to gain equality. In Hartford, he served as pastor of the African Religious Society on Talcott Street from 1830 to 1831.[19] His leaving that post after a year suggests that he disagreed with the Society's decision to affiliate with the Congregational faith. He stayed in town, however, and represented the black community at the National Colored Convention in 1834.

The dispute with the Talcott Street Church, together with the 1835 riot, appear to have set Easton on a new path.[20] In 1836, having left the Talcott Street Church, he founded Hartford's second black denominational house of worship, the African Methodist Episcopal Zion (AME Zion) Church.[21] It provided a place of worship for those who had voted against the Congregational affiliation and also a forum for Easton's changing views on racial uplift. The new church and its school for black children stood across the street from the rooming house where the Primus family lived at the time, and, although it would have been convenient for them to attend services there, they continued membership in the Talcott Street Church.

The early records of the AME Zion Church have been lost, but its present-day successor, the Metropolitan AME Zion Church, continues as a religious center. Both of Hartford's early black churches have adjusted to changing circumstances, and both retain a viable presence in the city. According to Easton's biographers, within a year of its founding, his new church building was destroyed by fire, and he suspected arson.[22] Angry and disillusioned, in 1837 he published a forceful "Treatise" attacking the idea that by their own efforts blacks could gain equality. He argued that the obligation to reverse the physical and psychological damage inflicted by slavery fell on whites.[23] Easton's dissatisfaction evidently affected his relations with other local leaders, as in 1835 he sued Henry Foster, a Talcott Street Church stalwart, and John A. Smith, whose story is undiscovered, for statements that allegedly attacked his character.[24] Easton's militant views did not gain many adherents at the time, but neither did they disappear.

While the riot and the church fire surely dominated the attention of Hartford blacks at the time, Holdridge and Mehitable were likely more absorbed by family events. In 1836, Jennet Boardman, a white midwife, assisted in the birth of the Primuses' firstborn child, Rebecca, and two years later she returned to help deliver a second daughter, Henrietta.[25] These and two additional children borne by Mehitable survived infancy and grew to adulthood. Given the state of medicine at the time, this points to the good fortune that Holdridge Primus enjoyed through much of his life. Coming to the city as a youth, he was lucky to have relatives who steered him to the household of W. W. Ellsworth. Marrying the competent Mehitable Jacobs connected him to a respected black family and widened his circle of relatives. Securing a job as porter in Nichols's grocery store on Main Street proved fortunate because under successive managements the same business provided him steady employment for forty-seven years.[26] Thus, while Mehitable's income may have fluctuated through the seasons, Holdridge's job provided a reliable base, enabling the couple to plan and save for future needs.

The job of porter required no particular preparation, but among blacks it carried a certain cachet. Primus represented the owners of the store—greeting customers, assembling the goods they required, and in general making sure they were served cheerfully and treated well, assuring their return. In present-day terms, the job had a public relations component, calling for a smiling, obsequious manner and careful attention to the customer's wishes. Primus created a niche for himself at the corner of Main and Gold Streets by making that role his own. An undated photograph shows him standing in front of the store in what may have been his accustomed spot, ready to greet customers, usher them inside, and make sure they were served.[27]

One of the obituaries that marked his death claimed that "[a]ll the old residents of Hartford knew 'Primus' as he was called."[28] The "old residents," we might guess, were upper-class whites. As part of his duties, Primus drove a cart through town, taking orders for groceries, which he

FIGURE 3.2. Holdridge Primus, porter, stands streetside in front of the store he served for more than forty years. *Credit:* The Connecticut Historical Society.

then delivered. "He never was known to use an order book," according to the reporter, "although he could read and write. He would always give the orders at the store and scarcely ever made a mistake."[29] Primus knew how to please the "better sort" of whites who frequented the store. In fact, his genial manner brought him additional work. According to one source, he was "well known to most of the first-class families of the city, often waiting on table and doing similar duties at weddings and parties."[30] The statement hints that the presence of Holdridge Primus as major-domo enhanced the social value of an event or celebration. It is impossible to guess how he reconciled his public stance with Gad Asher's legacy of citizenship or how he viewed the increasing calls by contemporary black activists for assertiveness. In the presence of whites, he remained unfailingly courteous. For him, enduring—or accepting—the condescension of powerful advocates was the best route to a secure future. Historian Darlene Clark Hine writes of the "culture of dissemblance" among Southern black women: clearly Holdridge Primus was a *Northern* black *man* who employed the same strategy in his pursuit of safety and stability.[31]

By the late 1830s, when the two Primus daughters were toddlers, Connecticut was the stage for another racially charged drama. This one involved rebellion at sea. In 1839, a group of Mendi, originally captured in Guinea, West Africa, were being transported in a Spanish ship, the *Amistad*. The slaves managed to arm themselves, break their shackles, and rise up, killing most of the ship's crew. They took over the ship and attempted to return to Africa. Unskilled in navigation, they found themselves towed into the harbor at New London, Connecticut, where they were claimed by Spain as "property."[32] A group of abolitionists, led by the familiar trio, Lewis Tappan, William Lloyd Garrison, and the Reverend Simeon Jocelyn, seized on the incident as an opportunity to highlight the evils of slavery and the universal desire for freedom. The initial trial, held at the United States Circuit Court in Hartford, caused great excitement and brought spectators from New York and Boston.[33] Members of Hartford's black community followed the proceedings as the bold action of the Mendi fixed national attention once again on issues of race and slavery.

The questions before the courts, however, had more to do with jurisdiction and international law than with slavery itself. The mutiny took place outside US territorial waters; it destroyed Spanish property and took Spanish lives—matters for the courts of Spain. The decision in the United States hinged on the status of the Mendi—whether they were slaves or victims of kidnapping. By 1841, the case reached the Supreme Court, with former President John Quincy Adams arguing for the defense. Judge Joseph Story, determining that the Africans had not been legally enslaved, declared them free men and women.[34] The one "legitimate" slave on the *Amistad*, Antonio, had been purchased by the slain ship captain and was not freed but sent back to Cuba, reaffirming US recognition of property rights in slaves legally held. Although the *Amistad* decision of 1841 left the system of slavery in this country intact, it freed the captive Mendi. After a decade of setbacks—the defeat of the proposed black college in New Haven, the closing of Prudence Crandall's school, and the Hartford riot, here was at least one triumph for the abolitionists.

Encouraged by this good news and by the growing focus on the question of slavery, Hartford's African Americans became more active in seeking their rights during the 1840s. Both black churches invited national leaders to visit the city and speak on slavery and its ills. The list includes William Lloyd Garrison; Henry Highland Garnet, a firebrand speaker for black rights; and Frederick Douglass, whose flight from slavery and oratorical skills made him a powerful voice for emancipation.[35] Hartford blacks sent delegates to several of the National Negro Conventions, forums held irregularly between 1830 and 1864 to consider strategies in the struggle for equality. The conventions provided a platform from which black leaders could address both black and white publics, emphasizing the questionable morality of slavery and the injustice of civil rights withheld from native-born Americans.

While few black men in Hartford could afford to leave their work for a week and pay for travel and lodging to attend these convention, the city was represented by Henry Foster, the Rev. Paul Drayton, and Mason Freeman in 1832; by Mason Freeman again in 1833; and as noted earlier by the Reverend Hosea Easton in 1834.[36] These conventions repudiated the Colonization Society's goal of "returning" blacks to Liberia. They continued to insist that blacks born in this country were citizens and to urge that African Americans adopt the reforms associated with respectability to gain citizenship and equality.[37]

During the 1830s, the black community in Hartford used its institutions as centers of unity and cooperation. The connection between the Talcott Street Church and the 1835 riot confirms the importance of the black church as a forum for political discussion, but that was just one of many functions. Both of Hartford's black churches provided religious services and spiritual guidance; hosted fairs and balls to benefit the needy; offered opportunities for members with rhetorical, musical, or literary aspirations to demonstrate their skills; and encouraged temperance and other reform efforts. By 1840, Hartford blacks had founded two temperance societies and a Literary and Religious Institution as well as church-based charitable groups.[38] Such associations encouraged solidarity, built personal connections, and provided experience in organization and leadership skills. The Primus family embraced such efforts. Holdridge, a temperance man, served on the governing Society of the Talcott Street Church for many years and later became its treasurer. Mehitable organized church events and took her turn hosting a church committee to sew for the poor.[39] According to the Primus letters, she occasionally filled in at the piano during Sunday services.

Church work and family responsibilities were important to the Primuses, but financial need demanded that, like most other free African American parents, both work their whole lives. Into his late sixties, Holdridge continued at the store and moonlighted at white social events while Mehitable sewed at home. Both also did various odd jobs for extra money: records show that Mehitable on occasion washed handkerchiefs and Holdridge polished boots for paying customers.[40] Drawing on their separate skills, they cemented ties to Hartford's white elite.

While the couple apparently lived in harmony for fifty years, their attitudes and views were not identical. Mehitable could claim competence in several fields and displayed a high degree of self-confidence. Her multiple roles included the care of the children, running the household, and conducting her own business. She trained young women in cutting, sewing, and clothing construction. Like most women of the time, she was a capable nurse, familiar with herbal remedies. We learn of another of her competencies in a letter Addie Brown wrote to Rebecca Primus. When Addie's employer, the wife of a Trinity College professor, was about to give birth and the doctor was unavailable, the woman sent for Mehitable. Thus we learn of her skill in midwifery, but we also learn of her self-assurance. Mehitable declined the white woman's request, saying that she "had been out of that line of business for sometime."[41] One wonders whether Holdridge ever failed to act on a request from a member of the white elite.

While Mehitable occasionally displayed an independent spirit that her husband either lacked or concealed, she made no known public show of resistance. In her way, she took advantage of a gap created by the combination of patriarchy and racism. As whites grew wary of black men in the wake of Nat Turner's rebellion, they continued to see black women, even those as self-possessed as Mehitable Primus, as doubly inferior—black *and* female—and thus powerless.[42] Black women took advantage of this perception and as a result "played a significant role in the creation of social, cultural, educational, religious, and economic institutions" that not only enriched the lives of blacks, but also raised their self-esteem.[43] Dressing the upper-class white women of the city, Mehitable became known as a skilled, trustworthy, reliable worker. She also maintained her personal dignity and her independence. These qualities may have been part of her legacy as a member of an established and well-regarded black family, and the example of her mother as a widowed householder as well as the radical assertions of the proto-feminist Maria Stewart may have moved Mehitable to push back on occasion against the wall of discrimination.

This failure to recognize women's agency appears again when we examine the public record with information from the Primus Papers. When Holdridge Primus died, an obituary credited him as a reliable source for whites seeking "suitable" domestic workers.[44] This statement omits the role of his wife. Mehitable was known among whites in Hartford and beyond as a source of "good" help. The Primus Papers contain a letter to Mehitable from Mrs. Jacob Newcomb of Waterbury, undoubtedly white, stating that she was "looking for a girl 13 or 14 to take care of a baby and wash dishes" for a dollar a week. "I have had Irish girls," Mrs. Newcomb explained, "but prefer colored if I can get a good one."[45] Whites went to Holdridge when they needed "suitable" servants, but Mehitable was his silent partner and possibly the real source in the informal employment service ascribed to him alone.

The newspaper article mentions the "suitability" of the girls sought but makes no reference to that of the employers. Addie Brown, in one of her early letters, mentions a perennial hazard associated with domestic service. She wrote of an employer whose kisses she "turned away."[46] Addie had no trouble disposing of what would now be defined as sexual harassment, but not all working-class young women were as self-assured and outspoken as she. Because Henrietta, second of the Primus daughters, boarded and worked in white homes from the age of twelve, certainly Mehitable screened white employers, particularly when her own daughter was to be hired. No record tells us whether she made sure that other young women going into white homes were aware of possible advances by privileged males. She was certainly aware of such incidents and knew that the silence of the time protected predatory employers. In the absence of solid information, we might speculate that she did her best to protect the women she helped place.

Black women were not alone in facing the perils of domestic service, but the predations of white males were one more aspect of the racial hierarchy that increasingly drew African Americans into resistance. While Holdridge and Mehitable maintained a firm line between opinion and action, others began to seek new ways to demand their rights.

4

Beyond Uplift

A New Spirit of Resistance

The series of incidents involving race during the 1830s convinced many blacks in Hartford that the time had come to turn their gaze outward from self-improvement and institution building to political protest.[1] New leaders came forward, eager to convert the notion of uplift into active resistance. Several came to Hartford, attracted by the achievements of a small but active black population. Among the first were James Mars and Amos Gerry Beman. Mars arrived before 1840 and immersed himself in community work. One of his early contributions was helping to recruit Beman as the first teacher in Hartford's African School.

Son of the Middletown, CT, clergyman Jehiel Beman, Amos had in common with Holdridge Primus a grandfather who had served in the Revolutionary War.[2] Beman's dedication to racial equality was part of his family heritage but perhaps heightened by the presence of Hosea Easton in Hartford in the 1830s. Easton's bold statements encouraged in Beman, and Mars as well, the notion that blacks should take steps in their own behalf. The three agreed that white power must be addressed directly on the question of black rights, though Easton stood alone in his emphasis on confrontation.[3] Beman taught for four years in the Talcott Street school and tried unsuccessfully along with Easton to promote a high school for blacks in the city. Determined to follow his father into the ministry, Beman left Hartford after four years.[4] Later, as pastor of New Haven's Temple Street African Church and an influential speaker and writer, he maintained his connection with Hartford.

James Mars shared his sister Elizabeth's dedication to religion, a curious legacy of the North Canaan clergyman who had owned James and his parents and siblings. In one of the few slave narratives with a Northern setting, Mars wrote of his family's long struggle to gain their freedom.[5] He finally achieved his goal only through Connecticut's gradual emancipation law. "My time of slavery expired in 1815," he wrote, adding: "Connecticut I love thy name, but not thy restrictions."[6] The peculiar institution lingered in Connecticut until 1849.

After coming to Hartford sometime in the 1830s, Mars made his mark as a community builder by helping found the Talcott Street Congregational Church and subsequently serving as deacon.[7] By 1840, as a member of the

FIGURE 4.1. James Mars, quiet but effective advocate of civil rights. *Credit:* The Connecticut Historical Society.

board of the mostly white Connecticut Anti-Slavery Society, Mars began to take bold steps on behalf of black rights. Along with Amos Beman, he was part of the new activism that took hold in Hartford with the selection of the Reverend James W. C. Pennington as the first settled (ordained) pastor of the Talcott Street Church in 1840. Later known as "the fugitive blacksmith," Pennington rose from illiterate runaway to ordained minister by his thirtieth birthday. He wrote in his narrative that when he was in his late teens, in about 1828, he made the furtive journey from Maryland to freedom not by public conveyance, as Frederick Douglass had, but mostly on foot.[8] Along the way, an Underground Railroad conductor taught him to read and impressed on him the value of education, which became a signature theme in his sermons and lectures. A striking paragraph from his narrative reads as a statement polished with repeated use over time:

> There is one sin that slavery committed against me, which I never can forgive. It robbed me of my education; the injury is irreparable; I feel the embarrassment more seriously now than I ever did before. It cost me two years' hard labour, after I fled, to unshackle my mind; it was three years before I had purged my language of slavery's idioms; it was four years before I had thrown off the crouching aspect of slavery; and now the evil that besets me is a great lack of that general information, the foundation of which is most effectually laid in that part of life which I served as a slave.[9]

Pennington and his first wife, Harriet (Walker), taught in the Talcott Street School in 1842 and 1843, when Rebecca Primus and her sister Henrietta were pupils. It is tempting to guess that the pastor's eloquence on the importance of education may have steered Rebecca Primus toward teaching as her life's work.

Through the 1840s, Pennington's oratorical gifts and his dedication to abolition and equality, religion, and education brought him into the company of nationally known abolitionists, including William Lloyd Garrison, the Rev. Simeon Jocelyn, and Frederick Douglass, at whose marriage he officiated.[10] Pennington's forthright style suited the new determination to speak directly against racial discrimination, and his growing reputation enhanced the image of Hartford as the home of an energetic black community. In 1842 he addressed race prejudice in a widely circulated sermon, "Covenants Involving Moral Wrong Are Not Obligatory Upon Man."[11] Spurred by the

FIGURE 4.2. The Reverend James W. C. Pennington, fugitive slave, ordained minister, educator, first pastor of the Talcott Street Congregational Church. *Credit:* The Connecticut Historical Society.

plight of a fugitive in Boston about to be returned to slavery, Pennington put the power of religion behind an exhortation to civil disobedience.

This more direct approach by Pennington, Mars, and others appealed to many Hartford blacks, but not to Holdridge Primus. Family matters remained his chief concern as, in 1842, Mehitable gave birth to a son, Nelson, named in memory of his father's lost brother. A year later, the couple welcomed a fourth child, Isabella, an addition that possibly reinforced Holdridge's determination to avoid political action that could jeopardize his standing with important whites and thus threaten the security of his family.[12]

No record remains of Holdridge's views on the new pastor's stand, but Pennington proved a popular and effective leader. Within a year of his arrival, he succeeded Henry Foster as president of the State Temperance and Reform Society, presiding at its Hartford convention in 1841 and again in 1845.[13] In the first four years of his pastorate, membership in the Talcott Street Church increased from 47 to 130.[14] As a closet fugitive himself—he hadn't even told his wife—he had personal reasons to become involved with the *Amistad* case. In the mid-1840s, as the Mendi prepared to return to Africa, Pennington proposed sending missionaries along with them. The resulting Union Missionary Society was a forerunner of the American Missionary Association (AMA), a forceful proponent of worldwide Christian outreach that lasted well into the twentieth century.[15]

In keeping with his desire to promote literacy and learning, Pennington ventured into publishing. He arranged to have printed a collection of essays, poems, and short biographies by a member of his church, Ann Plato.[16] She has been difficult to trace, but Ron Welburn, a professor of English, poet, and scholar of Native American life, argues that evidence in her writings suggests that that she herself was of Indian descent and influenced by that heritage.[17] Two known facts of her life, church membership and teaching at the Second African School, connect with two prominent themes in her writing: reliance on religion and proficiency in prose and poetry[18] Pennington, impressed, asked, "As Greece had a Plato, why may we not have a Platoess?'" His purpose in publishing her work was to demonstrate that blacks—and Welburn would include Native Americans—had skills and abilities equal to whites.[19] In the opinion of one historian, "What makes [Plato's] book important is neither its style nor its content. It is important because it was only the second book ever published by an African American woman."[20] The first was that of Phillis Wheatley, published in 1773.

However, beyond its date of publication and the cultural background of the author, Ann Plato's work is remarkable for its Victorian voice, detailing resigned suffering and saintly death in the young. Her work does not appeal to today's taste, but in 1840 it suited the times, much like the work of the renowned (white) Sweet Singer of Hartford, Lydia Huntley Sigourney, poetess, writer, and promoter of the Colonization Society. Now largely forgotten, Sigourney's gloomily rhyming celebrations of death were widely popular, and Ann Plato's writings were tuned to the same themes. Clearly the four doomed but inspiring subjects in her "Exemplary Biographies" were drawn from life, because three of the four surnames appear in the Hartford census.[21] Plato's success may have stirred in young Rebecca Primus a desire to test her own writing skills. As will be discussed later, the Primus papers contain two early attempts by Rebecca to write in the style of Ann Plato and Mrs. Sigourney.

Pennington's challenges to racial discrimination focused on the white assumption of superiority. His acquaintance with national black leaders and his own growing celebrity opened opportunities for him to travel abroad. In 1843 he attended a World Conference in London as a delegate of Connecticut's black and white Anti-Slavery Society. His electrifying sermons brought him a series of invitations to dine, lodge, and preach in various locations in Great Britain. Like other black activists who found acceptance and support abroad, he returned to Hartford with a heightened interest in racial equality. Reporting on his experiences in England to a group of white ministers in Middletown, Connecticut, he confronted them almost as Easton might have done: "You have helped us, to build small schoolhouses and churches, or rather helped us to shoulder a debt, many times. . . . I may as well speak out my convictions—it is done in the spirit of colonization, to get us out of the way."[22] In addition to exposing the motives behind white beneficence, Pennington subtly questioned the effectiveness of blacks maintaining separate institutions as a strategy for achieving inclusion. We can imagine Holdridge Primus either admiring the man's courage or worrying about possible repercussions. Or both. Pennington differed from Easton less in his message than in his manner. He challenged the white ministers forcefully but without Easton's rancor.

Pennington's frank attack resulted in an invitation from the Hartford Central Association of Congregational Clergy to attend its meetings—as a guest, not a member—but, at the same time, ministers of a dozen or so white churches invited him to exchange pulpits on given Sundays. The Reverend Noah Porter of Farmington's Congregational meeting wrote that when Pennington spoke in his church, the members were "astonished, some of them shocked, by seeing one of the blackest of men in their pulpit."[23] Pennington spoke boldly of black objectives, but he maintained a genial, positive stance.

As he widened his horizons through travel to Britain and Europe, Pennington remained grounded in the community he served. He later recorded an incident that illustrated the economic straits some of his parishioners faced. A quick thaw in January 1841 caused an ice breakup on the Connecticut River, and the ensuing flood swamped the area around the docks, predictably occupied by transients and the poor, many of them black. At the time, Pennington lived in the northern sector of the city, but he had stored his books near the church at an address close to the river where the families of three of his church members lived: "brothers [James] Patterson, [Isaac] Cross, and [Charles A.] Johnson."[24] He wrote that the

house, built of brick and three stories high, flooded to within two feet
of the upper windows, but his friends managed to save his books. While
Pennington's purpose in this instance was to thank the men for their effort,
he inadvertently provided a look at black housing options. He explains that
while Patterson and Cross lived in the brick house, Charles Johnson and his
household of six lodged in a "back house" behind it. Johnson's home was
"swept away" in the flood. This structure, perhaps little more than a shed,
may have been built to store the goods of the original owner of the brick
house. Johnson lived there no doubt because it was the best he could afford.
Patterson and Cross, who lived in the substantial brick house, were both
shoemakers and able to afford sturdy if poorly located and shared housing,
while Charles Johnson, who worked as a porter and later as a cook, appears
to have lost everything in the thaw of 1841.

The housing choices of blacks in Hartford make clear the economic
and social reality of black life in the 1830s and 1840s. Many still lodged
with their employers, as Holdridge probably did when he worked for the
Ellsworth family. Confined to the lowest-paid occupations, most found
home ownership out of reach. One alternative was rented rooms, generally
in the less desirable neighborhoods, the route Holdridge and Mehitable
took starting out in the 1830s. Hartford housing was segregated by class
rather than race, and the working poor, including most African Americans,
clustered in substandard housing near the Connecticut riverfront, along the
banks of its tributary, the Little (Park) River, or north of the city center,
where Pennington lived—an area still home to many African Americans.
In 1841, the Primus family, in rented rooms on Elm Street, was near the
Little River as it flowed into the flooding Connecticut River and may have
also experienced the rising waters.

We do know that by 1843, with four youngsters under the age of
nine, Holdridge and Mehitable were looking for a larger place. In 1846,
Holdridge's good luck visited him again in the person of his cousin Edwin
Asher, Jeremiah's younger brother, who by this time had also migrated to
Hartford. Pooling their resources, the two men jointly purchased a lot "and
buildings thereon" on Cooper Lane (now Lafayette Street). The size, condition, and even the number of buildings on the lot is unknown, but a
private house was an improvement over rented rooms, as was the area, away
from both rivers. While Holdridge and Mehitable had clearly saved for this
purchase, they still could afford to buy property only with the help of a
partner. The transaction recalls Gad Asher's earlier partnership with his son
Ruel to buy land in Branford. Cooper Lane, near Hartford's western border

at the time, ran parallel to Washington Street, where W. W. Ellsworth and other wealthy whites had built substantial homes. Fourteen black families lived on Cooper Lane in 1847, suggesting that many served in the nearby mansions. By that time, Holdridge was working at the Main Street grocery store, but Mehitable may have benefited from the location, because some residents of Washington Street were among her clients.

While Pennington's increasing fame took him elsewhere from time to time, he served the Hartford congregation until 1848, when he was called to serve as pastor of the First Colored Presbyterian Church of New York City, a position that offered prestige and undoubtedly a more generous and secure salary.[25] Hartford's relatively small black population could not provide an income that matched the pastor's growing reputation, which continued to attract activists to Hartford. Two of these, Augustus Washington and Selah Africanus, taught for a time in the Talcott Street School, and both joined Pennington in public objections to the continuing exclusion of blacks.[26] Washington, who shared the pastor's views on education, had made up his mind early in life to attend college. He was admitted to the Oneida Institute and later to other schools but dropped out each time because of debt. In 1843 he was accepted at Dartmouth University in Hanover, New Hampshire, but once again was forced to withdraw before completing his course. To pay his creditors, he learned the skill of daguerreotyping, an early form of photography.[27]

Although his studio prospered, in 1844 Washington gave it up and came to Hartford to teach in the Talcott Street School. Thomas Robbins, the city's school inspector, visited Washington's classroom in December of that year and found problems: irregular attendance, poor ventilation, and a scarcity of books. He noted that the teacher had brought in books of his own to supplement what the school could offer, that the students were "judiciously instructed" and had proper religious exercises, and that some were good scholars. He added: "Anti-Colonization is taught earnestly."[28] Rebecca and Henrietta Primus, eight and six, respectively, may have recited for the visiting inspector. In March 1845, Robbins returned to the North African School and found "much improvement."[29] In June, he commended Washington as a "competent good teacher. Well educated," and added, "The scholars do well for their opportunity." Visiting again on December 19, Robbins praised both teacher and pupils, noting improved attendance, good manners, good order "for so large a school," and finally invoking a stereotype: "Sing well of course."[30]

At the time, Augustus Washington agreed with the majority of black leaders in rejecting colonization. In 1845, possibly in need of money again, he left his teaching post to return to the more lucrative work of daguerreotyping. His Main Street studio drew distinguished customers, including William Lloyd Garrison, editor of the antislavery *The Liberator*, and the volatile John Brown.[31] Restless and dissatisfied, Washington was torn between the pursuit of education and his need for money. White oppression, which he blamed for his failure to earn a college degree, continued to rankle, and, as Hosea Easton had done, Washington reversed his stand on racial uplift. In an angry letter to the *New York Tribune*, he charged that "clinging to long-cherished prejudices and fostering hopes that can never be realized, the leaders of the colored people in this country have failed to discharge a great and important duty to their race."[32] Liberia, he wrote, offered an enterprise that would "result in the redemption and enfranchisement of the African race." Acting on this belief in 1853, with his wife and two children, Washington left for Liberia. Five years later, in a long letter to the *Hartford Courant* outlining his experiences, he included this paragraph:

> I think if you inform my Hartford friends who have been so anxious to hear from me, of what I am doing . . . some may decide to come and try their fortune. I can assure them, whatever I can, I will most heartily do to advise, encourage and help them. Such men as Holdridge Primus and Mr. Champion, could not fail to succeed. I am quite certain that they cannot do worse here than they are doing in America.[33]

His assurance that Holdridge Primus and Henry Champion (whose wife was Mehitable's sister Bathsheba) could *not do worse* in Liberia can be read in various ways. Washington chose to address two men of stature in Hartford. But what was he saying? Was he belittling how well Primus and Champion were "doing" in Hartford? Primus owned real estate, held a steady job, served on the board of the Talcott Street Church, and with his wife supported four children, two of whom had been pupils of Washington. Henry Champion also owned his home, worked as a porter for the Samuel Colt family, and managed to support his wife and her five children from a previous marriage. Neither man was wealthy, but both were better off than many of their fellow townsmen. Washington may have been suggesting that,

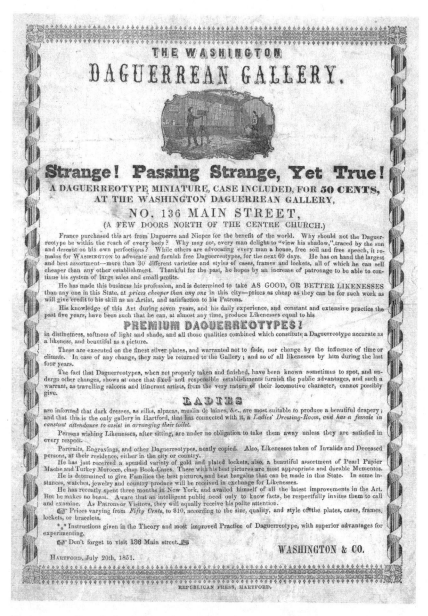

FIGURE 4.3. Broadside announcing Augustus Washington's Daguerrean Gallery. *Credit:* The Connecticut Historical Society.

as American blacks of substance, Primus and Champion would be among the elite in Liberia.

His account of life in Liberia was hardly an unencumbered endorsement of conditions there. He acknowledged initial difficulties in settling and making a living. Economic and social opportunities were less than ideal, and diseases to which Americans lacked immunity threatened newcomers, as Betsy Mars's husband had learned. But Washington had overcome the challenges of Liberia and found life there preferable to the demeaning prejudice he endured in the States. His letter was not only a proud announcement of his success, but also a plea to other men of ambition and capability to join him. It would be interesting to know how the letter was read and interpreted in Hartford, especially by Primus and Champion.

Through the antebellum years, some individuals in Hartford chose to emigrate, and not always out of anger or despair. Elizabeth Mars went as a missionary in 1832, and Henry M. Wilson, a tailor about whom little else is known, set out with his wife in 1843 in response to Pennington's plea for good Christians to accompany the *Amistad* Mendi on their return to Africa.[34] In 1851, not long before Augustus Washington's departure, another Hartford resident, George L. Seymour, left for Liberia. Like Washington, Seymour had lost confidence in the potential of racial uplift, and when he returned to Hartford, it was only to collect his family.[35] Seymour may have spoken to Washington at that time and could have helped persuade him to emigrate.[36] Seymour's brother Lloyd remained in Hartford, as had Elizabeth's brothers, James and John Mars. Washington's decision to leave, and the divided views in the Mars and Seymour families, reinforce the perception of a black population grappling with the question of how to gain equality, or whether it was even possible. Those who left the country were a small minority, but their decisions were undoubtedly examined and discussed.

The teaching position Augustus Washington abandoned at the Talcott Street School was filled in 1847 by Selah Africanus, reportedly a native of New York City.[37] Certainly an activist, in 1849 he helped organize and served as secretary of a State Convention of Colored Men in New Haven. Henry Foster, Henry Nott, Isaac Cross, Perry Davis, Benjamin Randall, and others from Hartford joined him as delegates. According to a published report of the convention, Africanus proved "one of the best speakers of the evening." With evident surprise, the reporter wrote:

> Throughout his remarks we did not observe a single slip in grammar, nor any bad pronunciation. He was a full faced man

of middling height, with a fine shaped head and a remarkably pleasant eye and countenance. His thoughts were connected and logically expressed, without any repetition of language or any waste of words. He said that for the elevation of their characters they must rely upon themselves; and for the exercise of the rights of citizenship, which is the basis of all their rights, they must rely on the justice of their cause.[38]

The reporter's summary unintentionally demonstrates the very injustice the speaker wished to eradicate.

In fact the favorable reception of his speech may have led Africanus to seek a wider arena, because he taught for just two years and then disappeared from local records after 1865. The work of Pennington and others raised the reputation of Hartford's black community, but its small size, relative to those in Boston, Philadelphia, and New York, meant that no black elite developed in the city: Hartford's black leaders were working men and women. The few successful entrepreneurs among them were tailors and shoemakers. There was no class of wealthy blacks who could fund major projects or add significant amounts to the coffers of churches and schools, and consequently the ambitious young go-getters who were attracted to the city tended to leave after establishing themselves as effective leaders.

While Beman and Africanus, as well as Washington and Easton, left Hartford after a few years, the Rev. Pennington and James Mars stayed a little longer, and through the 1840s helped to move local blacks toward an assertiveness that was spreading across the state. Between 1838 and 1850, Connecticut blacks beset the General Assembly with twenty-six petitions seeking the franchise. Hartford blacks filed petitions in 1840, 1841, 1842, 1843, and 1844 requesting the legislature to strike the word "white" from the section on voting rights in the state constitution.[39] Mars introduced three of these requests and signed all five. From a black male population (all ages) of 249 in 1840, petitioners secured, respectively, 73, 97, 93, 43, and 80 signatures.

Clearly a substantial number of blacks agreed that the right to vote was critical. Many of the signers were local leaders and property holders—William Saunders, Henry Nott, Henry and Alfred Plato, Perry Davis, Ishmael Magira, James Williams, and Isaac Cross. Several of Primus's relatives signed: cousin Edwin Asher and brothers-in-law Jeremiah Jacobs and Raphael Sands. Holdridge Primus did not. Was he fearful of antagonizing his white employers or their customers, or was he simply uncomfortable with the act of putting his name on a public petition? There must have been family discussions of the matter, but his reasons remain unknown.

Annoyed by the barrage of requests, the state legislature responded by voting to remove the names of black men from the tax rolls, leaving them with *neither* taxation nor representation in meetings of the school society, the body that determined school budgets.[40] For blacks to be shut out of the chance to argue for much-needed financial help for their schools was a further insult. The "Colored Citizens of Hartford" responded with a petition in which they declared themselves "outraged and oppressed by the unjust distinctions existing respecting them," namely "that enactment which deprives them of participation in the burdens of State Government." They claimed the right to contribute to "the sustenance of the commonwealth in common with our white fellow citizens." Thus did seventy-five black men in Hartford *demand* the right to pay taxes. The signers, many of them property owners and local activists, again did not include Holdridge Primus.[41]

A more satisfying method of undermining white supremacy was the shadowy work of helping runaway slaves, occasionally in the courts but more often through the Underground Railroad. Between 1793 and 1850, a series of laws made such assistance an offense punishable by fine and/or imprisonment, so that few records of the work of "conductors" were made or kept. As early as 1650, according to historian Eric Foner, the colonies of Connecticut and Maryland "encouraged Dutch slaves to escape" from New Netherlands and "refused to return them," raising the ire of Governor Stuyvesant.[42] After the Mendi were freed, the town of Farmington, Connecticut, offered them care, lodging, education, and Christianity, while the Rev. Pennington and other abolitionists raised money to return them to their homes. As a result, Farmington became known as a haven for runaways.[43]

Hartford was not known as a major depot, but, being a river port, it saw its share of runaways. A fugitive himself, Pennington made it part of his mission to help others fleeing bondage. In 1847, he wrote to a friend in England, "I keep here one of the prominent depots of the great Underground R.R."[44] He recalled answering the door one morning at six o'clock to find four men with a letter from the New York Vigilance Committee requesting his assistance, and two days later a whole family— father, mother and five children—came to him. He estimated that he saw on average two fugitives a day.[45]

During his years in Hartford, Pennington was haunted by the fear that his master in Maryland might learn that the valuable runaway had become a Congregational minister in Hartford, Connecticut.[46] Travels in Britain and on the Continent provided respite and eventually a solution. Five years after he left Hartford for New York, Pennington gained his freedom with the help of John Hooker, a lawyer in Farmington, Connecticut. Hooker was the husband of Isabella Beecher and thus related to Harriet and Henry Ward and the whole Beecher clan. The money to free Pennington came from friends and supporters he had met earlier in Scotland, but Hooker contacted James Pembroke's "owner" and made the actual purchase. Hooker later wrote that he kept the bill of sale overnight to experience slave ownership. Satirizing the logic of slavery, which held that anything a slave owned belonged in fact to his owner, Hooker wanted for one night to own the honorary doctorate Pennington had been granted by the University of Heidelberg.[47]

James L. Smith, one of the runaways who passed through Hartford, recorded in his narrative a series of conductors who assisted him on his way from Northern Neck, Virginia, to Canada.[48] When he reached New York, he was directed to take the boat to Hartford and find a Mr. Foster—certainly the tailor Henry Foster. When Smith's boat arrived, an unidentified black man was waiting on the dock and told him how to find Foster's house. Upon reaching it, Smith presented his letter of introduction from the contact in New York, and:

> [Foster] began to congratulate me on my escape. When he had conversed with me awhile, he went out among the friends (Abolitionists), and informed them of my circumstances. . . . Many of them came in to see me, and receive me cordially; I began to realize that I had some friends. I stayed with Mr. Foster till afternoon. He raised three dollars for my benefit and gave it to me, and then took me to the steamboat and started me for Springfield.

There was no fund available: help for fugitives was collected on an ad hoc basis for safety reasons but also because few blacks in Hartford could afford to set money aside even for their own use.

A newspaper article detailed another local incident, the tale of an unnamed fugitive who found work on the *Hero*, a steamboat on the New York–Hartford run.[49] The unnamed fugitive did not know that his former master had traced him and was now in Hartford, expecting to recapture him when he arrived. "On a whim" the fugitive left the ship in East Haddam, a town on the Connecticut River south of Hartford. The article concludes:

When the boat reached Hartford, the hunters could not find
[the runaway]. They sought diligently, but in vain. Four fresh
fugitives reached Hartford, at the same time with this man-
hunter. They and the colored man who saw fit to go ashore at
East Haddam, are now in Canada, where man-stealing is not
lawful. —*Hartford Republican.*[50]

A more public matter involving a slave became a court case in Hartford
that drew the cooperation of white abolitionists, including W. W. Ellsworth.
Nancy, a young black woman, was brought north by her owner, a Mr.
Bullock, in 1840, and after two years in the city Bullock decided to return
with her to Georgia.[51] State law at the time stated that slaves who had
been in the state for two years could not be re-enslaved but did not clarify
the status of those brought to the state on a temporary basis.[52] Hartford's
emboldened blacks decided to take advantage of this loophole and seek a
court ruling.[53] Judge William W. Ellsworth, perennial friend of antislavery
partisans, drew up a petition for a writ of *habeas corpus* to bring Bullock
into court. James Mars was approached as the best man to sign it because of
his prominence as a teacher and community leader and, more importantly,
his willingness to speak out for black rights. Mars writes that he hesitated,
fearing retaliation by proslavery whites, and remembering that only seven
years had elapsed since the riot of 1835. Moved by Nancy's plight, he did
sign and, as he had feared, encountered local hostility:

> During those ten days I had a fair opportunity to see how strong
> a hold slavery had on the feelings of the people in Hartford. I
> was frowned upon; I was blamed; I was told that I had done
> wrong; the house where I lived would be pulled down; I should
> be mobbed; and all kinds of scarecrows were talked about, and
> this by men of wealth and standing."[54]

When Nancy's case advanced to the Supreme Court of Errors, the four
judges split, so that Chief Justice Thomas Williams—brother-in-law of W.
W. Ellsworth and a fellow abolitionist—cast the deciding vote, declaring
Nancy free.[55] Afterward, Mars simply noted: "I could pass along the streets
in quiet."[56]

This increasing activism on the part of Hartford blacks reflected the
national unrest over slavery and related issues. After 1848, when the war

with Mexico ended, gratified cotton planters moved into East Texas, spreading slavery into new territory. In Congress, the diverging interests of North, South, and West gave rise to threats of secession. Attempting to quell if not solve the power struggle, the trio of classic negotiators, Henry Clay, John C. Calhoun, and Daniel Webster, put together a series of measures known as the Compromise of 1850. The provision of immediate concern to African Americans was the Fugitive Slave Act, which penalized those who helped runaway slaves and empowered slaveholders to reclaim fugitives or supposed fugitives on little more than a verbal statement of ownership.

Members of the Talcott Street Church publicly denounced the Fugitive Slave Law, "believing that it violates man's natural rights, the instincts of our nature, the spirit and letter of our Constitution, and the express injunctions of Holy Writ, and is entirely subversive of the ends of government."[57] Printed in the *Hartford Courant*, the statement was signed by Thomas Saunders and Augustus Washington, known activists, and by Timothy Oliver, a fellow parishioner. Assuming that church members voted on the declaration, we might wonder how Holdridge Primus voted on the matter, but in fact he was not in Hartford in 1850. His search for security had taken him across the country to one of the last places where he was likely to find it.

The discovery in 1848 of gold in California provided new enticement to explore the unsettled West. Some two thousand Connecticut men joined thirty joint stock companies—half a dozen in Hartford—and set out for California. Holdridge Primus was among them.[58] According to a newspaper account, "in the early days of the California gold fever, a son of a member of the [Humphrey & Seyms grocery] firm [which employed Holdridge Primus] wanted to go to California and was allowed to go on condition that he should take Primus with him."[59] While this was a tribute to Primus's character, such an opportunity would hardly have appealed to a confirmed family man with four young children and a mortgage. And yet in January 1849, along members of the Warburton Company, he boarded the ship *Pacific* and sailed for San Francisco. The name C. N. Humphrey, age twenty-four, of Hartford, appears on the passenger list. Primus, traveling as a servant, is not named.[60]

The decision to make the voyage was not simply to accommodate his employer and certainly not based on hunger for adventure. The Hartford land records provide an explanation. Shortly before the ship sailed, Primus and his partner and cousin, Edwin Asher, sold their Cooper Lane property for $1,300, presumably netting each $650. Then, a week before he sailed, Primus purchased a two-story frame house on Wadsworth Street for a total price of $1,750.[61] Both the house and the location were an improvement over the Cooper Lane neighborhood. When Primus returned, the owner of the property quitclaimed the land and building, the mortgage "having been fully paid and satisfied."[62] The details of this transaction are nowhere spelled out, but Humphrey had persuaded Primus to go by helping him purchase the house on Wadsworth Street before he left and stipulating that on his return the mortgage would be paid in full.

Still, it must have been with some misgivings that he left his wife and Rebecca, thirteen; Henrietta, eleven; Nelson, seven; and Isabella, six. How would they fare in his absence? How would he fare as a black man traveling to an unsettled part of the country? How long would he be gone? Would he survive the journey? Up until this time, the great adventure of Primus's life had been leaving Branford for an unknown Hartford, but now he took on a dangerous sea voyage and the prospect of primitive conditions in a mining camp in exchange for a two-story frame house on a relatively new block inhabited mostly by whites. It was a risk he and Mehitable must have decided was worthwhile: it was the price of a more secure future for the family, and fully in line with the ideal of racial uplift. Certainly Mehitable would have had no qualms about her ability to manage in his absence. Her mother had provided a blueprint years earlier.

On January 22, 1849, the packet ship *Pacific* sailed out of New York for the 18,000-mile trip around Cape Horn to San Francisco.[63] Primus soon learned that the *Pacific* would not live up to its name. Problems included an arrogant captain, disgruntled passengers, substandard accommodations, lawsuits, and delays.[64] Charles R. Schultz, whose journal provides a description of the voyage, offers this example of Captain Tibbets's temper:

> There were two black men on board the *Pacific* who seem to have agreed to serve as waiter in order to pay their way to California. One was named Charles or Charley. . . . The other was named Primus and was a servant of a Hartford company of which C. N. Humphrey was president. On 15 February Captain Tibbits saw both men apparently relaxing and "took a rope's end to them."[65]

Schultz recalls that the employers of the two black men objected to the captain's action and that Tibbets assured them that "he would flog 'whomever and wherever I damn please. I'll show you that I'm master of this ship.'"[66] Other witnesses remembered the incident in various ways: one said that only Charles was flogged for insolence and deservedly so, because he was a black man.[67] Another passenger, Jacob Stillman, recorded his own disapproval of the flogging and added that others shared his view, although he cited the opinion of one passenger "who had shipped aboard a whaler, [and] felt that the punishment was deserved."[68] Given such varying reports, the incident resists analysis, but if Primus "relaxed" when he should have been working or behaved insolently to the captain, he was displaying traits entirely at odds with his behavior as portrayed in the Primus letters and newspaper accounts. In any case, he was beginning to realize the full price of the house on Wadsworth Street.

The *Pacific* reached San Francisco on August 5, 1849, one hundred and ninety-four days after leaving New York.[69] If Primus wrote home describing the voyage, life in the infamous city where he landed, or conditions in the gold fields, his letters have not survived. Years later, his obituary compressed the events of almost five years into a paragraph:

> Soon after reaching California the company disbanded and Holdridge went into the employ of the Adams express company in Sacramento. He remained with them a considerable time, but finally came east again . . . He made the journey with Mr. Adams, who took a liking to him. He was presented with a gold watch and chain and a gold medal by the company for his faithful services on his departure. . . . When [Primus] was in California he could have made a fortune by leaving the company and setting up a restaurant, but would not leave them. He was a man who always kept his word and could always be depended upon.[70]

The Warburton Company broke up soon after its arrival, and at some point Primus was relieved of his obligation to attend young Humphrey. His common sense intact and his good luck holding, he found a job and began to save his money for the trip home. The Mr. Adams with whom he traveled was Alvin Adams, founder of the highly successful nationwide delivery service that, according to company lore, shipped the fugitive slave Henry "Box" Brown in a wooden crate from Richmond to Philadelphia.[71] Adams may have paid Primus's fare, bringing him along as a valet or servant. A letter in the Primus Papers dated June 28, 1853, signed by seven officers of the Adams Company of Sacramento and addressed to Holdridge Primus, confirms the newspaper report:

Dear Sir,

With this we present you with a gold medal, which we intend as an expression of our good feeling toward you, and of our appreciation of your uniform good conduct, industry, integrity and temperance while you have been with us in this office.

Be pleased to accept our good wishes for your future health and prosperity.

Primus returned to find his wife and children well and the Wadsworth Street house now his property, free and clear. Combining racial uplift with acquiescence to the white hegemony, he and Mehitable had secured their relatively comfortable life within the space allotted to blacks. And yet as encouraging as the outcome of their Gold Rush gamble was, unsettling events on the wider stage continued to draw the nation toward crisis.

5

A Black Middle Class
Takes Shape in Time of War

When Holdridge Primus came home to the two-story frame house on Wadsworth Street, he would have been a celebrity of sorts in the black community. He could have entertained family and friends with stories of the ocean voyage, the wide-open city of San Francisco, characters who peopled the gold fields, and his work for Adams Express. He may have told some few about Captain Tibbets and the flogging incident on the misnamed ship *Pacific*. Mehitable would have brought him up to date on news of friends and relations, and after four years away he might have been surprised by the changes in his children. By 1853, his two older daughters were young ladies. Rebecca, seventeen, had finished school and was presumably helping with household chores and the care of the younger children and doing seamstress work for her mother. Henrietta, sixteen, was living and working in a white home, as she had done from the age of twelve.[1] Nelson, eleven, and Isabella, ten, were still in school, taught at the time by local activist Edwin Freeman. Hartford's whole school system was underfunded and, in a not unfamiliar pattern, underperforming. The African schools reported poor attendance, which may have indicated that black parents had developed "new thoughts about segregated education."[2] It is reasonable to speculate that Rebecca, already set on a teaching career, took on the task of supplementing what her siblings were learning at school. In fact, this may have been when she conceived the idea of conducting her own school in the family home.

Even three thousand miles away, Holdridge Primus would have known in 1850 of the rising ferment over the contents of the Fugitive Slave Law.

He may have read Mrs. Stowe's literary retort, *Uncle Tom's Cabin.* Back in Hartford, he would learn that members of the Talcott Street Church had publicly denounced the law and that William Lloyd Garrison, editor of *The Liberator*, had visited and sat for a daguerreotype in Augustus Washington's Main Street studio.[3]

Primus would have seen in Hartford evidence not only of racial tension, but also of the problems that accompanied industrialization. Factories crowded the residential areas as immigrants overran an inadequate housing stock. By 1860, the Irish in Hartford outnumbered blacks by a ratio of nine to one. With their distinctive dialect, papist belief, and unfamiliar customs, they became a new despised minority. Unskilled for the most part, some found work in the factories, but many competed with blacks for jobs as laborers, waiters, domestics, and laundresses. They posed no threat to Primus: his part in the California adventure secured both his new home and his old place as porter at Humphrey and Seyms's grocery store.

As he resumed his place at the Talcott Street Church, he had much to be thankful for. In spite of or possibly because of the continuing polemics over slavery, many African Americans in Hartford were making measurable progress toward their goals. The Primus family shared in the gains through the 1850s and into the next violent decade. In fact, by 1860, the city's black community reached the peak of its nineteenth-century achievement in economic and social terms. Paradoxically, this high point occurred at the outset of the single most catastrophic national event of the century. By the time General Beauregard's forces fired on Fort Sumter, the number of African Americans in Hartford who owned property reached its peak number and highest percentage. The number was just thirty-five, but it represented over a third of Hartford's 111 black householders. By 1860, some 80 percent of Hartford's African Americans lived in black households, compared with 68 percent in 1830, when Holdridge first came to the city. The rising number of black households means that fewer blacks were isolated in white homes or business establishments.[4] In another measure of improvement, by that time illiteracy among Hartford's African Americans was slightly over 1 percent. In Boston in the same year, the illiteracy rate was 7.6 percent; in Providence it was 6 percent.[5] Still, as historians Lois Horton and James Horton point out:

> It would be misleading to assume that literacy in the mid-nineteenth century meant anything more than a rudimentary knowledge of reading and writing. Many of those judged literate

were, in fact, functional illiterates, able to write little more than their names, and, in some cases, unable to read and comprehend a newspaper.[6]

Nevertheless, the 1860 finding on black literacy attests to the importance blacks placed on education as a stepping-stone to equality. It also reinforces the extent to which Hartford blacks saw themselves as part of the general culture. Indicators of perceived progress in social relations appeared in the 1860s, as black individuals were named to the previously all-white boards of the YMCA and the Hartford Freedmen's Society.

Taken together, these advances were seen as signs that the second of the goals urged by black leadership—efforts to uplift the race—were bearing fruit. A group of Hartford blacks had improved their economic status and made inroads on the prejudice that had separated the races even in charitable and social outreach. By 1860, in fact, a sizable group of African Americans in Hartford had created a recognizable middle class composed of men and women who embodied the goal of racial uplift.

Most of them shared with the rest of the city's black population a common cultural background—a characteristic not found in the larger cities of the North. In 1860, 90 percent of Hartford's black residents had been born in Northern states, and 73 percent had been born in Connecticut. With few exceptions, they were two generations or more removed from Africa and from slavery. They grew up surrounded by New England ways that emphasized religion, education, and personal rectitude—the same qualities that underlay the model of the rising white middle class. The canon of respectability incorporated religious observance, education, temperance, hard work, dependability, and thrift. White middle-class membership had an economic component: a level of income that supported the elements of refinement that characterized the wealthy.

In following this model, Hartford's black middle class valued the impulse toward refinement—externals such as home furnishings, dress, comportment, and lineage. Families with long histories in the city enjoyed stature, just as white descendants of the founding families were viewed as links to the city's origins. African Americans who owned their homes were recognized for an achievement that required middle-class traits—thrift, persistence, and long-range planning. But they did not conform to all of the white criteria.

The most notable variation was an addition: active concern for community welfare. To serve on a church governing board, to represent fellow blacks at a conference devoted to cultural or moral improvement, to participate in programs promoting racial equality and political awareness, to help organize fundraising events to benefit a school or a needy neighbor—such activities were important in the community. What propelled these efforts beyond the benefits of a strong community was the twofold goal outlined by national black leadership: the abolition of slavery and full citizenship—an end of race prejudice. Indeed, many if not most free African Americans emphatically rejected the white assumption of black inferiority in intellect, morals, and general capability. In public statements and personal letters, black leaders and others at the time expressed certitude regarding their inherent equality.

Another difference between the black and white visions of middle-class membership becomes evident in the public records and also in the Primus letters. Hartford blacks did not accept the white ideal of distinct roles for men and women, binding women to homemaking and child rearing and men to the marketplace of work outside the home.[7] In the Primus family, Mehitable filled the female role of homemaker and nurturer, but added a career as an entrepreneurial dressmaker—working at home—along with service to the community. Her contributions ranged from teaching domestic skills to young women and participating with Holdridge in an informal employment service to accompanying the church choir on the piano and membership in a sewing circle to aid the poor. Viewed with due irony from a later century, Mehitable *had it all*, but in fact the range of her activities was typical rather than unique among black women.

Hardly universal among whites, separate spheres depended on a level of income beyond the reach of most Hartford blacks or poor whites. While the white middle class consisted largely of professionals, skilled artisans, and entrepreneurs, African Americans were restricted to the lowest-paid work regardless of skill or education. In the larger populations of Philadelphia, Boston, and New York, an upper class of elite blacks emerged, but in Hartford fewer than half a dozen African Americans could be considered wealthy: there was no black elite.

One more characteristic of Hartford's nineteenth-century black middle class merits notice: its fluidity. The defining features outlined here served more as goals than requirements. Addie Brown, whose letters are examined in a later chapter, came to Hartford as an unattached working-class young woman and breached an indistinct class barrier by forming a close friendship with Rebecca Primus. The Primus family accepted Addie as virtual kin, and other members of the city's black middle class followed suit, including her in social functions and helping her find work and lodging from time to time.

The life of James Williams further underscores the openness of this group. An illiterate fugitive born in New York in the late 1700s, he ran away to sea and spent three years as a sailor. After adventures that included impressment by the British Navy during the War of 1812 and acquaintance with Aaron Burr, he came to Connecticut and worked in the stone quarries in Portland before moving to Hartford. There he found work in the household of Bishop Brownell, founder of Washington (now Trinity) College. As a servant at the college from its founding in 1823, Williams worked as bell

"PROF. JIM."
JANITOR OF TRIN. COLL.

FIGURE 5.1. James Williams, longtime janitor and handyman at Trinity College, known to the students as "Professor Jim, Professor of Dust and Ashes." *Credit:* The Connecticut Historical Society.

ringer, janitor, and eventually head janitor until five years before his death in 1878. He became a fixture in his workplace in much the same way that Primus did in his—through unfailing deference to whites. The students named him "Professor Jim, professor of dust and ashes, and keeper of student secrets."[8] This playful title calls to mind the eighteenth-century practice of naming slaves for gods, rulers, and orators of the ancient world. At the same time, in the black community Williams became a respected elder. In the 1830s, he reportedly participated in the founding of the AME Zion Church, and in 1859, along with Holdridge Primus, he became a charter member of the Hartford lodge of Prince Hall Masons.[9] Like Primus, James Williams came to town a stranger and earned status by participating in church and community matters and by making himself useful to white elites.

The public records reveal the characteristics of Hartford's leading men and women of color, but who exactly were these middle-class blacks? By 1860, many activists of the early years were gone: the Rev. Pennington had moved to New York, James Mars to Massachusetts; Amos Beman was a missionary with the AMA (American Missionary Association). George Seymour and Augustus Washington were in Liberia, along with Betsy Mars; John Blackstone and Joseph Cooke had died, as had the merchant tailor William Saunders, although his wife, Roxanna, inherited his property and his status, and his enterprising sons, Prince and Thomas, took over their father's business as well as his interest in black rights.

An examination of the census and other records reveals the names of forty Hartford individuals who in 1860 embody the criteria set out above. The list of forty is a sampling rather than a full listing, and yet, with spouses and offspring, this arbitrary and incomplete selection accounts for a total of 199 men, women, and children, more than a quarter—28 percent—of the 709 African Americans listed in the 1860 Hartford census. These strivers were not outliers: the middle class encompassed a solid segment of the city's black population.

FORTY BLACK MIDDLE CLASS HOUSEHOLDS
HARTFORD 1860
(asterisks denote property ownership)

Edwin Asher*
Ezekiel Augustus*
Worthy H. E. Brewster*
George Camp*

Henry Champion*
Alfred Cleggett*
Isaac Cross
James Davis*
Perry Davis*
Chauncey Douglas
Betsy Fish
Edwin C. Freeman
Samuel Freeman
Robert Gibbs
Samuel Giles*
John Jackson*
Jeremiah Jacobs
Lorinda Lee*
Nancy Magira*
Edward Mason
Robert B. Mason
William M. Mitchell
Andrew Mitchell*
Ralph Mitchell*
E. D. Nichols*
Henry Nott*
Greensberry W. Offley*
James C. Patterson*
Thomas Paul*
Samuel Pierce*
Deborah Plato*
Holdridge Primus*
John Randall
John T. Rodney
Raphael Sands*
Roxanna Saunders*
Isaac Appleton Scott*
Lloyd Seymour
Harriett Wells*
James A. Williams

Why these forty? Because each meets one or more of the criteria outlined above. Twenty-four owned their homes.[10] All either took part in community-oriented efforts or earned distinction in other ways. They held office in one of the black churches or belonged to one or more of the fraternal or charitable organizations or the temperance society. Jeremiah Jacobs, Mehitabel's brother, did not own property in 1860, but he and his brother-in-law, Raphael Sands, were proprietors of a restaurant. Moreover, Jeremiah was the scion of three generations of local activists.[11] Others who shared his deep roots in Hartford included the Nichols, Nott, and Magira families. Women of the households contributed to the functioning of the churches, including educational, beneficent, and social programs. Betsy Fish and Edwin Freeman had taught school. By 1860, Rebecca Primus opened a school for girls in the family home, a school we know of only because Addie Brown mentioned it in her letters. The Primus letters, newspaper clippings, and Civil War pension applications confirm a web of personal bonds along with associational connections among members of this middle-class network. Many were related by blood or marriage—there were two branches each of the Davis and Mason families, three of the Mitchell family, and five of the Primus-Asher-Jacobs clan.

The path of Holdridge Primus from rural migrant to respected city dweller and his journey with Mehitable from rented rooms to home ownership, from hopeful young couple to recognized community leaders, offers a case study in the emergence of the black middle class. Home ownership and community concern qualify them for the list, and the family home at 210 Wadsworth Street provides clear evidence of refinement. The rooms included a parlor—marker of gentility—and a sitting room downstairs. At the top of the stairs was a "hall," an open space that provided entry to front and back chambers (bedrooms) and a workaday sewing room for Mehitable's trade.[12] In the rooms was the expected assortment of chairs, tables, beds, bedding, and household and kitchen goods—but also rugs, mirrors, books, pictures, silver tableware, a marble-top bureau, and a piano—the quintessential signifier of middle-class status.[13] The single letter written by Mehitable, addressed to Rebecca, contained the news that "Emily has got her piano 160 dollars it looks nice. Round corners. Stands in the sitting room."[14] Emily Sands shared her sister's views on home furnishings and possibly competed with her in acquiring the symbols of refinement.

Beyond announcing the status of its residents, the basic function of 210 Washington Street was as a secure home for family members. The yard around the house had its uses as well: Mehitable kept chickens and cultivated fruits and vegetables—currants, cherries, strawberries, and peaches— bounty she preserved for winter use.[15] The house had social functions as

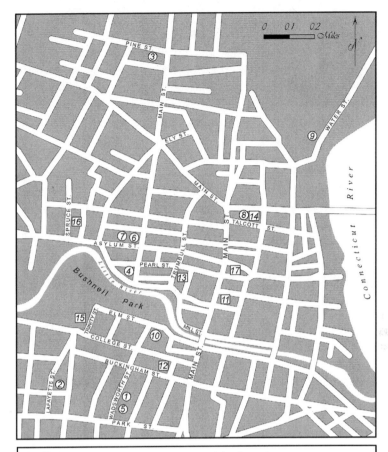

Dwellings:

1 Holdridge Primus
2 Edwin Asher
3 Henry Champion (Bathsheba Jacobs)
4 Jeremiah Jacobs
5 Raphael Sands (Emily Jacobs)
6 Isaac Cross
7 Henry Nott
8 Roxanna Saunders
9 W.W. Daniels (Clara Primus)
10 Deborah Plato

Other Locations:

11 Seyms Grocery Store
12 George Francis Carriage Works
13 AME Zion Church
14 Talcott Street Church
15 Trinity College
16 Railroad Station
17 State House

Map 2. Hartford 1865

Map 5.1. The Primus Family's Hartford. *Credit:* Prepared and created by Map and Geographic Information Center (MAGIC) at the University of Connecticut Libraries, Storrs, CT. University of Connecticut, 2015. Data source: MAGIC at University of Connecticut Libraries, Storrs, CT. University of Connecticut, 2015.

well, occasionally hosting guests as well as boarders. Addie Brown describes evenings when friends and relatives gathered in the parlor to exchange local news and often to make music, accompanied by piano and guitar.[16] The house was a haven for Addie Brown on occasion and for the freed women Mehitable assisted after the war. When Holdridge's father, Ham, could no longer manage on his own in North Branford, he spent his last days in the care of his son's family. The Hartford *Courant* recorded Ham's death on September 10, 1867, noting that the funeral would be held at the Primus home.[17] Holdridge had kept in touch with his father through the years, and, as the only son, inherited Ham's woodlot in North Branford.

One observer of black life in the antebellum North comments that "extraordinary men with very ordinary jobs led the community."[18] What was extraordinary about the Primuses and the other middle-class families was their willingness to move beyond their immediate concerns to build and preserve a sense of community. They were extraordinary locally: similar groups emerged elsewhere. Disenfranchised, demeaned, and insulted on the street, free African Americans spent time and effort working to improve their own lives, but worked as well to strengthen their common welfare.

The public records supply information on some of these individuals and their activities, and from an unexpected source we add one more item. In the Civil War pension application of Lloyd Seymour (brother of George, who chose Liberia), a statement of support from Holdridge Primus attests to long acquaintance with Lloyd, adding that they "belonged to the same band and attended the same church."[19] This quotation, the only known record of a direct statement attributed to Primus, is also the only known reference to his musicality. Regrettably, it does not tell what instrument either man played or name the band they played in, but the entry hints at facets of Holdridge's makeup beyond what other sources reveal and adds to the picture of long-term social, religious, and musical connections among Hartford blacks.

For men, two fraternal lodges fostered social and beneficent work. The Rising Star Lodge of the Grand United Order of Odd Fellows (GUOOF) was founded in 1844 and continued into the twentieth century. The only members so far identified are Isaac Cross, Raphael Sands, and Jeremiah Jacobs—the latter two brothers-in-law of Primus.[20] The second lodge came to Hartford in 1859, when the *Courant* announced the founding of the Excelsior chapter of Prince Hall Masons.[21] Among the founding members were Frederick O. Cross (son of Isaac Cross), John Rodney, Lloyd Seymour, James H. Williams (Trinity College's "Professor Jim"), and Holdridge

Primus.[22] No record of the activities or projects of either group has been found, although in her letters Addie Brown refers to the Masons' annual banquet, no doubt a fundraiser, as an important social event. In other cities, Prince Hall Masons and GUOOF members turned out for parades and other public ceremonies smartly uniformed and marching in military precision—announcing black pride and black dignity. Both lodges were "mutual aid and support organizations . . . [that] produced community leaders and social circles. They gave the black community a sense of unity and independence in a world which challenged both their identity and their sovereignty."[23] In fact, the black lodges grew out of the struggle for equality. When African Americans in the United States sought to form their own chapters, the all-white Odd Fellows and Masons refused to grant charters. Undeterred, blacks secured affiliation through lodges in Britain but were still denied recognition by white chapters at home. This is no longer true, but at the time, black lodges operated under names that distinguished them from their white "brothers"—GUOOF rather than IOOF (International Order of Odd Fellows) and Prince Hall Masons rather than simply Freemasons. "Membership in these [lodges]," according to Nick Salvatore, "by a janitor and handyman . . . suggested a standing within the community that direct economic criteria might never reveal."[24]

Women also took part in organizations dedicated to the common good. As early as 1832, Garrison's *The Liberator* found it newsworthy that the Hartford Colored People's Temperance Society had enrolled seventy-seven members—thirty-two males and, not unexpectedly, forty-five females.[25] During the Civil War, a women's sewing society brought together members of the Talcott Street and AME Zion Churches, strengthening the connection between the two congregations. Mehitable and her sisters, Bathsheba Champion and Emily Sands, along with Clara Mitchell, Clarissa Cleggett, and Addie Brown, were among those who made and collected clothing and bedding for former slaves.[26]

Black women saw to the care of orphans, organized fairs to raise money for needy neighbors, and provided music at church services. Churchwomen took on speaking roles fairly regularly, perhaps taking Maria Stewart as a model. Addie Brown wrote of a debate to be held at the Talcott Street Church at which "Miss A. Cross read [and] Mrs. Mary Randle has composition. . . . I must attend."[27] The young women named were daughters of Isaac Cross and John Randall, both members of the black middle class. In another example, Rebecca Primus, home from Maryland for the 1867 summer break, addressed members of the Talcott Street Church on the progress of her school and her "mission South."[28] Recent scholarship examines the relative independence of women in black communities in the South during the Jim Crow era and notes the importance of their leadership in charitable and community work. In Hartford and certainly elsewhere, they had assumed such roles in earlier years.[29]

In the wider view, the emergence of Hartford's black middle class was a minor event of the decade in comparison with the Civil War, which left few families of any color untouched. For most whites, it was a fight to save the Union, while African Americans understood it from the beginning as a struggle to end slavery. Hartford blacks would have applauded the Reverend Pennington's petition to Congress, sent from his New York pastorate in September 1861:

> The undersigned, Free Colored citizens of these United States, believing that African Slavery as it now exists at the South, is the prime cause of the present Crisis and that permanent peace cannot be restored until said cause be removed, most respectfully petition your honorable body to take such measures, or enact such a law as may, in your wisdom seem best for the immediate abolition of African Slavery.[30]

Frederick Douglass agreed. "The simple way," he wrote, "to put an end to the savage and desolating war now waged by the slaveholders, is to strike down slavery itself, the primal cause of that war."[31] Nelson Primus made or bought bunting to festoon the house on Wadsworth Street as the soldiers paraded through the streets before leaving for active duty. In Boston, after Lincoln's assassination, Nelson wrote to his family: "I am glad to hear that you all took so much interest in our late deceased President, I am pleased to hear that those old flags of mine did something for there [sic] country."[32]

At first, blacks were not accepted in the Union forces, but by 1863 the expectation of a quick and easy victory evaporated, and black recruits were sought as the generals "recognized the grim calculus of military necessity."[33] When Governor Buckingham issued a call for black recruits, the ranks of the Twenty-ninth Regiment of Connecticut Volunteers (Colored) filled quickly. Most of the original nine hundred enlistees were state residents; sixty-one claimed Hartford as their hometown, and thirty-two were reportedly members of the Talcott Street Church.[34] The response was so great that another black regiment was organized to accommodate them. Nelson Primus, by then twenty-one years old, did not volunteer. Neither did his friends Peter and James Nott, Benajah Plato, and Henry Jones, all healthy young men in their twenties. Why not?

Historian James McPherson suggests a number of reasons. First, "the booming war economy had created full employment and prosperity for Negroes in some parts of the North."[35] Secondly, the stated policy of the Confederate Army was to show no quarter to black soldiers, to kill rather than capture them. Thirdly, race prejudice followed black men into the service.[36] A veteran of the Union forces wrote that "African Americans who read black enlistment as a shift of their status in American society quickly learned otherwise as federal administrators formulated policies that confirmed patterns of invidious racial discrimination."[37] Only whites could serve as commissioned officers. Black recruits were paid seven dollars a month, while whites were paid thirteen, with an additional $3.30 clothing allowance. Only after a number of North Carolina black troops "stacked their guns"—refused all duty—and white abolitionists protested did Congress authorize equal pay.[38] African American troops received substandard medical care, drew fatigue duty not imposed on white soldiers, and were issued inferior weapons, insufficient ammunition, and inadequate gear.[39] Nelson and his friends had numerous reasons not to join the military.

What about those who did? A number of Hartford's middle-class blacks enlisted in the Twenty-ninth and later in the Thirtieth Regiment, which was eventually folded into the Thirty-first. Whether they volunteered in order to help end slavery, in search of adventure, or for the promised cash bounty, in putting on the uniform colored troops carried the goal of racial uplift into a life-or-death setting. As in previous and later wars, African Americans enlisted at least in part to demonstrate the courage, stamina, and patriotism of the black man.

Among the Primus correspondents, only Addie Brown wrote letters during the war years, and for much of that time she was in New York City. She wrote directly about the war only once, on July 22, 1861—just after the Battle of Bull Run: "I see by the papers that they have commence to fighting."[40] She makes no mention of the Union's poor showing. Some months later, she wrote that Fred Cross, twenty-three-year-old son of shoemaker Isaac Cross, had written to inform her that he and "Mr. [Lloyd] Seymour were going to war."[41] The two men did join the Union forces but not until 1863, when the Twenty-Ninth Regiment was organized.

Along with Isaac Cross and Lloyd Seymour, Hartford black middle-class enlistees included Worthy Brewster, Chauncey Douglas, John Jackson, and Thomas Paul. Connecticut troops saw action notably in the battle of

FIGURE 5.2. Soldiers of the Twenty-Ninth (Colored) Regiment Connecticut Volunteer Infantry. In Beaufort, South Carolina, 1864, before seeing action in Virginia. *Credit:* Library of Congress Prints and Photographs. LC-DIG-cwpbh-03374.

the Crater and at Petersburg.[42] When Richmond fell, men of the C and G Companies of the Twenty-ninth, Isaac Scott, Chauncey Douglas, and Justin Francis among them, helped lead the march into the city.[43] After Appomattox, most Union troops were mustered out and sent home, but the Connecticut Colored Regiments were sent to Texas, where they complained of inadequate housing, hard labor, and excessive heat. Finally, in November 1865 the surviving members of the Twenty-ninth returned home on the steamboat *Hero*. As they sailed up the Connecticut River to Hartford, they were heartened to see that "the villages were illuminated" in celebration of their return.[44] Addie Brown's firsthand description of the welcome they received is in Chapter 8.

Many came home unable to take up their former occupations, some unable to earn a living even with the government's "invalid pensions." To obtain the monthly payments, the veteran or his family filled out a questionnaire that required not only his military history, but also information about his personal and family life. Such data, available nowhere else, throw light on lives and events otherwise unrecoverable. The candidate was also required to supply statements from friends testifying that his war injuries had affected his ability to function normally. Lloyd Seymour, who served as first sergeant, Company E of the Twenty-ninth Regiment, returned home with malaria, inguinal hernia, and heart disease.[45] His application provided the statement from Holdridge Primus noted previously and others from Ralph Mitchell and Isaac Cross. All attested to Seymour's upright habits and good health before the war and incidentally illuminated connections among members of the middle class. Seymour's discharge stated that with only two remaining teeth he was unable to chew and thus unfit for duty. Before the war he had farmed and worked with horses; after his return he worked as a driver for the Weed Sewing Machine Company but was "often absent for chills and fever."[46]

While Seymour at thirty-eight was not a young man when he enlisted, others even older were accepted by a needy military. Worthy Brewster, forty-one, and Isaac Scott, forty-five, were at a disadvantage in adapting to the physical demands of army life, particularly in view of the primitive conditions black troops encountered and the inadequacy of their equipment. In November 1863, within months of his enlistment, Brewster suffered frostbite while on guard duty near New Haven, so that toes on both his feet were amputated. A month later, he contracted rheumatism, which would, as his Certificate of Disability put it, "trouble him the rest of his life." Able to walk only with a crutch or cane, he was given a disability discharge in February 1865, never having encountered the enemy, never having even left the state.[47]

Isaac Scott, on the other hand, forty-five when he enlisted, saw action in Annapolis, Beaufort, Petersburg, Richmond, and Fair Oaks. After Lee's surrender, he was sent to Brownsville, Texas, where he was discharged with a fractured leg, inflammatory rheumatism, fever, ague, and "general disability." His health problems lingered, and in later years he was wholly dependent on the care of his son and daughter-in-law.[48]

After the war, when Addie Brown was in Hartford, she offered a scrap of information about another Hartford-based veteran. She wrote to Rebecca that Raphael Sands's son Thomas returned from the war with a condition that required daily treatment, but she was not told the nature of the injury.[49] Thomas Sands had been adopted at the age of four by the Reverend Pennington and was living with the minister's family in New York when he joined the Union Army. After the war, he returned to the Sands's home in Hartford. Raphael Sands was his birth father; his birth mother was Sands's first wife.[50] The nature of his injury remains unexplained, as does his adoption by Pennington and his return to the Sands home after the war. As historians dig deeper into the past and technology expands the limits of research, such questions may eventually be answered.

As was true of earlier and later wars, black veterans returned with grim memories of battle and stories of the people and places they had seen. And, like black veterans of earlier and later wars, they came home to find that the color line remained firmly in place. Those who were able took up their former lives and occupations. Members of the middle class resumed their community interests. Lloyd Seymour and Thomas Paul rejoined the Excelsior Lodge of Prince Hall Masons. Chauncey Douglas served the AME Zion Church as trustee.

Through the decades of a tumultuous century, the quest for equality adjusted its focus from time to time. Early efforts to gain equality were directed within the black community—in the formation of temperance societies and other reform groups. By the 1840s, seeing little progress toward their goals, African Americans in Hartford and elsewhere began to address the sources of power directly, for example, in seeking the right to vote. When the war came, they enlisted less to defend the Union than to end slavery. The formation of the black middle class was a by-product of the same quest, and its emergence brought unintended consequences in the form of a new paradox. The middle-class embrace of education, religion, industry, and thrift engendered class consciousness even as it maintained the importance of black unity. Discussing this conundrum, historian Patrick Rael upends the notion that the one necessarily undercut the other:

> African Americans, perhaps more than any other group of Americans at the time, successfully crafted alliances and affinities among themselves across lines of class and culture. . . . Tension thus often appeared as a by-product of success rather than as a herald of failure.[51]

Two black churches and two fraternal lodges coexisted in Hartford as symbols of black unity, a goal that did not require agreement on every issue.

At the end of the war, Hartford's black community joined in celebrating the victory of the Union troops and, in spite of the loss of a revered president, looked forward to fulfillment of the promises of the Civil Rights Act of 1866 and the constitutional amendments guaranteeing freedom, citizenship and the right to vote.

❧

Subsequent chapters examine the effects of Reconstruction on African Americans in Hartford and particularly on members of the middle class, but first we look at the lives and letters of the three writers, all of whom wrote and acted in the belief that the gains they had witnessed in their lifetime would continue—that the Union victory and the end of slavery also signaled the beginning of the end of race prejudice.

First we follow Nelson to Boston in the spring of 1865 with his wife and newborn daughter as he launched his career as an artist. In his letters to the family in Hartford, he reveals dependence on family and strong ties to Hartford friends alongside mixed feelings about his home city. Though few in number, Nelson's letters are rich in detail and provide the one male viewpoint in the letters. Next we accompany his older sister Rebecca to Royal Oak, Maryland, where she founded a school for former slaves. She was somewhat dismayed to discover there the distance between her New England middle-class identity and the customs and ways of the mid-South. Her constant references to friends and events in Hartford emphasize the importance to her of the family and community she had left behind. Finally, we turn to what one historian called "Addie Brown's Hartford," as she describes her duties in a variety of homes and establishments, most but not all of them owned by whites.[52] Her candid opinions and pithy vignettes produce an original look at a long-forgotten community. In addition, she reveals an intimate relationship she shared with Rebecca Primus. As an ardent admirer of Rebecca and her family, Addie has hopes of achieving for herself the level of comfort and security she sees in the Primuses.

None of the three young people realized that as they wrote they stood at the peak of the trajectory of black fortunes in Hartford.

Note: the excerpts quote the letters as originally written.

EXPECTATIONS AT WORK

6

Nelson Primus

The Artist in Boston

I heard one of the finest things that you ever heard, last sunday after noon as i was crossing common through the flour garden all of [the] church bells commenced to ring for church, one fine large magnifficint church stood on the west side of the common. . . . this church commenced to charme [chime] hym's i had to stop still and look. it charmed several familliar airs which i have often heard sung, it was beautifull, i never heard its equal and rearly [really] it also charmed me.[1]

Indifferent to the niceties of spelling, punctuation, and grammar, on April 25, 1865, Nelson Primus recollected in the manner of Wordsworth an emotion he had experienced on Boston Common a few days earlier. Twenty-three years old and newly settled in the city with his wife, Amoretta, and infant daughter, Leila, Nelson had taken on a much larger, more cosmopolitan city than the Hartford he had just left. Caught on that spring afternoon like many of his countrymen between thankfulness that the Civil War was ended and sorrow over the death of President Lincoln, Nelson had an epiphany of sorts as he stood among the flowers with the old hymns reverberating around him.[2] The moment may have been sharpened by a sudden recognition of the magnitude of the goal he sought: "I am bound to be an Artist, if there is any such thing."[3]

What did it mean to be an artist? According to James A. Porter, pioneer historian of black art, in the eighteenth and early nineteenth centuries

85

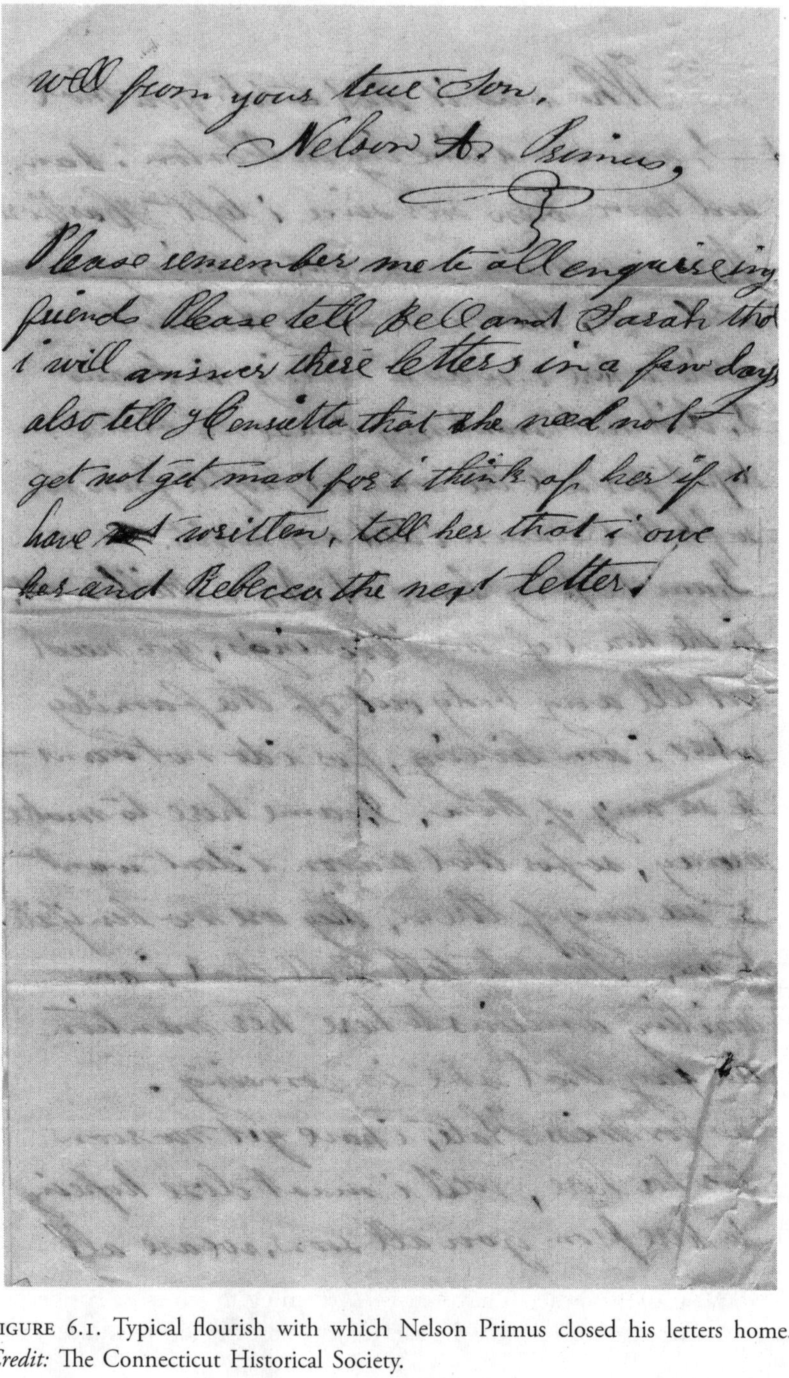

well from your true Son.
Nelson A. Primus.

Please remember me to all enquireing friend Please tell Bell and Sarah tha i will answer there letters in a few days also tell Jennetta that she need not get not get mad for i think of her if i have not written, tell her that i owe her and Rebecca the next letter.

FIGURE 6.1. Typical flourish with which Nelson Primus closed his letters home. *Credit:* The Connecticut Historical Society.

an artist was one who learned "steel engraving, lithography, sign and coach painting, portrait painting, and clay modeling."[4] As Porter explained, "The American middle-class point of view at this time was to regard painting as a 'manual art.'"[5] That view, however, was being challenged. Alexis de Tocqueville had fixed a European eye on the young country's fascination with invention and technology: "Democratic nations," he declared, "cultivate the arts that serve to render life easy in preference to those whose object is to adorn it. They will habitually prefer the useful to the beautiful."[6] A stinging criticism, according to present-day art historian Sharon Patton, who describes American artists of the mid- and late nineteenth century "struggling against the European view that Americans lacked any significant achievement in the arts."[7] To counteract European disdain, American artists sought academy training, preferably in Europe, to master traditional subject matter, styles, and techniques. By the 1860s, major American cities boasted their own art academies, although African Americans had access to classical training only in Europe. Nelson wrote several times that he thought of going abroad to study and later complained: "if my pictures sold fast i'd soon make money enough to go to Europe and spend two years."[8] His final statement on the subject was, "Oh i wish that i had money so I could go to Europe to study . . . I do not suppose that I ever shall be able to go."[9] He lacked training, money, and patronage, but the incalculable hurdle was his color, which reduced his chances even as it imposed on him the burden of disproving black inferiority. Amos Gerry Beman, former teacher in the Talcott Street School, noted that charge as he praised Nelson's early work:

> If my friend, E. M. Thomas, of Washington, who takes such an enthusiastic interest in works of arts and artists, could see the manifestations of skill and genius which Nelson Augustus Primus shows, his heart would rejoice, and his tongue, if possible, grow more eloquent and enthusiastic in relation to artists among us as a people.[10]

Few African Americans at the time set out to become artists, and fewer still gained wide recognition. One who did was Nelson's first Boston mentor, the landscape artist Edward Mitchell Bannister (1826/7–1901), whose crowning achievement years later would bring him face to face with the burden of color. At the 1876 Centennial Exposition in Philadelphia, competing against works by Albert Bierstadt, J. F. Kensett, and Hartford's Frederic Church, Bannister's *Under the Oaks* won a bronze medal. When he appeared in the hall to claim his prize, the white officials demanded to know what he was doing in the building:

> I was not an artist to them, simply an inquisitive colored man; controlling myself, I said deliberately, I am interested in the report that *Under the Oaks* has received a prize; I painted the picture. An explosion could not have made a more marked impression. Without hesitation he apologized, and soon every one in the room was bowing and scraping to me.[11]

Bannister's bronze medal buoyed the spirits of struggling black artists who felt obliged to compete with white artists on their own ground— producing sentimental genre pictures, picturesque landscapes, and religious scenes. Later generations would explicitly depict the African American experience, and some critics theorize now that nineteenth-century artists "subtly manipulated subject-matter to create works whose narratives . . . contained allegory which could be interpreted differently according to whether the onlooker took a black or a white viewpoint."[12] Such subtlety has been ascribed to some of Nelson's later paintings. While his was not a major gift, the dozen or so works that have been discovered show talent and skill.

Nelson's letters, conversational, disjointed, good-natured, and frank, produce a self-portrait of an artist who as a young man read a temporary rise in local black fortunes as a trend that would continue, encouraging him to embark on a career outside the experience of those around him. "If I study hard and tend strict to my profession," he wrote, "I hope to reach the height of my ambition."[13] That unshakeable ambition sustained him through his long life.

The letters show that he was aware of his special status in the family as the only son. While Rebecca chided her mother for buying the package of gumdrops she found in her trunk when she arrived in Royal Oak, Nelson repeatedly asked for and accepted his parents' substantial contributions to his welfare. The generally buoyant tone of his letters mixed bravado with impatience: he expected to succeed. His signature was nearly always embellished with a looping flourish, an artistic touch not found in the letters of Rebecca and Addie Brown, nor of most letter writers of the time.

The outlines of his life emerge from newspaper clippings and the public records, but in the twenty-four letters he wrote between April 25, 1865, and March 7, 1868, we hear his story in his own voice. Two of the letters were addressed to his father, ten to his mother, and twelve to his sister

Isabella. They reveal a young man anxious to get ahead and increasingly dependent on his family as he discovers how hard a road he has chosen.

Jennet Boardman, the white midwife who delivered all four of the Primus children, recorded the birth of their third child, a son, to Holdridge and Mehitable on March 25, 1842.[14] Holdridge named the baby for the brother and childhood companion who had died at the age of seven. Raised in a close-knit but disciplined family, the latter-day Nelson enjoyed his role. His older sisters, Rebecca and Henrietta, showed a motherly interest in his progress, and his younger sister, Isabella, was a confidant. When he reminded his mother that she had hidden "many a piece" of pie from him, he offered a glimpse of a mischievous youth.[15] Mischievous perhaps, but hardly rebellious. Along with his older sisters, he dutifully attended the Talcott Street School, taught by Selah Africanus, a commanding physical presence and an effective speaker on behalf of black rights. The school curriculum included standard works of English literature, evidenced by Nelson's quoting, with his usual imaginative spelling, lines from Gray's *Elegy in a Country Churchyard*:

> Fool many a gem of purest rays serene
> The dark unfathomed cave of ocean bear
> Full many a flower has born to blush unseen
> & waist its sweetness on the desert air.[16]

It is tempting to imagine Nelson's schoolteacher sister, Rebecca, reacting to this rendition of a standard classic.

As was customary, Nelson finished his schooling at the age of fifteen and then began an apprenticeship as a decorative painter in a white-owned carriage shop. He must have shown an early affinity for art, perhaps sketching his classmates or drawing animals or steam locomotives in the margins of his school notebooks. The carriage shop, located on Buckingham Street, was a short walk from the Primus home on Wadsworth Street (Hartford was still a walking city). The shop owner, George Francis, had academic training, and planned to follow art as a career, but his father's death pulled him into the family business. According to later accounts, Francis gave Nelson his first drawing lessons.[17] He may have introduced his gifted apprentice to Mrs. Elizabeth Gilbert Jerome, a local art teacher trained at the Springley Institute in New York and the National Academy of Design. Mrs. Jerome advertised as a portrait painter and offered art lessons to white girls, but she made an exception for Nelson, accepting him as one of her students for an unknown period.[18] One or both of these mentors may have encouraged him to begin to show his work, and by the time he was seventeen his oil painting on wood of dogs and birds was exhibited at the Hartford County Fair. Soon afterward, a group of his sketches was singled out for notice in the local newspaper.[19] The scholars of the Talcott Street Sunday School purchased his painting of a trout and presented it to the superintendent.[20] It is safe to assume that Nelson's parents encouraged or perhaps arranged his apprenticeship in George Francis's shop as the best use of his talent. They would have seen the training with George Francis as a pathway to a secure and comfortable future for their son.

Years later, viewers at exhibitions of a mural-size painting by Nelson Primus were given printed programs describing the scene depicted and outlining the artist's life. The brief biography features a defining moment during his apprenticeship: "While grinding colors he saw the foreman ornament a carriage and was filled with longing to be an artist. That night he bought a few colors and painted his first picture on a bit of sand-paper."[21] The narrative continues:

> After serving his apprenticeship, he came to Boston and secured work at the South End. On account of his color, his fellow-workmen would not at first speak to him, but one noon he made a sketch on the wall which so delighted them that he at once became one of the most popular men in the shop.

While it is difficult to evaluate this material, either Nelson or his wife supplied the information it contained, lending a measure of authenticity to the story. The reference to "grinding colors" reveals something of his training, and the incident purports to show how and when his ambition to become an artist took shape. George Francis and Elizabeth Jerome would have opened his eyes to the distinction of the profession they both originally sought, and they may also have warned him of the struggle it entailed. The tale of Nelson's acceptance by the workers in the Boston shop—probably a carriage factory—remains unconfirmed but suggests that his talent set him apart from his fellow workers even in his early days.

In 1863, when the all-black Twenty-ninth Connecticut volunteer regiment was formed, Nelson was twenty-one years old. As noted earlier, he did not sign on. In addition to the known risks of a war that was proving bloodier, longer, and more costly than expected, it is more than likely that Holdridge and Mehitable would have been reluctant to see their only son go off to war. Clearly Nelson's own choice was to complete his apprentice-ship and start his career. In view of this already fixed ambition, it comes as something of a surprise that on June 18, 1864, at the age of twenty-two, Nelson married. His bride, Amoretta Prime, was the daughter of James and Wealthy Prime of Norfolk, Connecticut.[22] She had come to Hartford to find work and was placed as a domestic in the home of a local white fam-ily—we might guess with the help of Holdridge and Mehitable. Other than her rural background, little has been discovered about Amoretta, although her mother and younger sister Mary were in Hartford for a time. She and Nelson were married in St. Paul's Episcopal Church, perhaps her preference and possibly because the Talcott Street Church was without a settled pas-tor at the time.[23] Their daughter, Leila, was born twenty-seven weeks later on December 22, 1864. Either the birth was premature or Amoretta was pregnant at the time of the marriage, a circumstance that would explain Nelson's adding family responsibility to the other obstacles he faced in his quest for recognition as an artist.

If Leila's birth was premature, she would have weighed about two pounds and in the mid-nineteenth century would have had a fifty-fifty chance of survival.[24] Whatever the circumstances, the Primus family wel-comed their new daughter-in-law and their first grandchild. As for Nelson, marriage and fatherhood did not turn him from pursuing his chosen career.

In the spring of 1865, when he wrote his first letter home, he had settled his family in a boarding house, replicating the way his parents began married life. The letter was full of household news, projecting the image of a conscientious husband and father. He reported the width and the cost of the muslin he and Amoretta had bought and described her making sheets and pillowcases. "The baby has got quite used to the children now," he wrote, complaining that "one of the boy's is trying to spoil her by rocking her all the time so that she wakes up in the night and cries and will not stop untill she is rocked to sleep."[25] Along with depicting the interactions of boarders in a multifamily dwelling, Nelson shows himself a doting if inexperienced father.

In the same letter, he wrote: "I am a getting along finely with Banester." Edward Mitchell Bannister, whose later experience at the Philadelphia Exposition was described above, had moved to Boston from New Brunswick, Canada, around 1850. By 1865, when Nelson Primus met him, Bannister was widely recognized as a portraitist and landscape artist.[26] At first the arrangement went well, but three months later Nelson had changed his mind:

> Mr. Banister i think is a little Jealous of me he says that i have got good tast in art. But does not try very hard to get me any work. The Colored people here think he could get me wirk if he was a mind to. . . . Mr. Banister has got in with the white people here and they think a great deal of him. he is afraid that i would be liked as much as himself.[27]

Perhaps misled by the ease with which he had gained notice in Hartford and certainly eager to advance in his career, Nelson ended his association with Bannister. In the comment on his mentor's winning the support of influential whites, Nelson implied that he wished to do the same. It was the method his parents had followed. At the same time, Bannister was known as a "race man" with a record of political activism on behalf of abolition and black equality. This may have collided with Nelson's apolitical stance, another characteristic easily traced to his father.[28]

Like Nelson, Bannister lacked academy training, but the older artist had, along with unmistakable talent, a patron—his wife. He had married a well-to-do businesswoman, Madame Christiana Carteaux, in whose enterprise he had been a hairdresser and barber. She subsequently supported him as he pursued his career, which included photography—a process that came into use during the Civil War. Because it posed a threat to traditional portrait painting, many artists incorporated it into their services.

Nelson found a new mentor, Charles E. Stetfield, who maintained a studio in the same building with Bannister and several other painters. Stetfield was known chiefly as a lithographer, although he would most likely have had training as an artist.[29] The only work of his that has been located is a small lithograph of Ulysses S. Grant, possibly from a photograph.[30] Comparing this dearth of data with the acclaim Bannister enjoyed in his lifetime, it appears that Stetfield was the lesser artist but a more attentive teacher. At one point Nelson wrote: "Mr. Stetfield says that i improve in every picture i paint."[31]

Arriving in Boston in 1865, Nelson Primus found in the city a small group of African American artists. According to art historian Juanita Marie Holland, the group included Edward Bannister, sculptress Edmonia Lewis, portraitist William Simpson, and gilder Jacob Andrews—an artist in the old sense of skilled craftsman. These artists, and Bannister especially, made themselves part of the African American community by working with anti-slavery groups, joining a local glee club, or taking part in amateur theater productions.[32] Younger, just starting out as an artist, and subsisting on what he and Amoretta could earn hiring out by the day, Nelson Primus did not, or could not, follow this pattern. In his letters he mentioned, but evidently did not meet, either William Simpson or Edmonia Lewis, both of whom left the city shortly after he arrived. Lewis in particular found both fame and fortune, at least for a time. Her sculptures depicted figures from the bible and from Greek mythology as well as idealized, newly freed slaves. Lewis enjoyed recognition and support until after the Civil War, when abolitionists evidently lost interest in black artists.[33]

Nelson started out as art students customarily do, copying the works of recognized artists. In his early letters he describes subjects he is working on, noting the source and the size of his copy. He placed some of these in Boston stores and sent others to Hartford for sale. He mentioned such titles as "His Only Pair," "Sunset Italian Scene," "Boston Boot Blacks," and "The Plough." None of these has been found. In a letter to his father, he wrote of a scene he was copying, "Alone in the World," depicting a barefoot woman sitting on a tree stump with a small dog at her feet. She was "apparently feeling very sorry as if she had lost all of her friends."[34] He planned to have it framed and "put it in one of the gallery's of art to sell for what it will bring." This fairly detailed description, and his plan to market the work, may have been meant to reassure Holdridge that his ambitious son knew how to go about selling his works.

Along with other artists of the time, Nelson developed sidelines: one was tinting *cartes de visite*, the printed "calling cards" popular in the nineteenth century. These generally featured photographs of the subject, colored by hand and otherwise embellished to simulate original artworks. There is no evidence that Nelson took up photography himself, but it is possible that Stetfield, his new mentor, supplied the original *cartes* and Nelson colored them. In February 1867, he wrote that the next time he came to Hartford he would "take the four Seymses card photographs [back to Boston] & paint them & send them to H[artford] to be exhibited in one of the gallerys there where they [members of the Seyms family] can see it. i am pretty shure that they will buy them.[35] Nelson was making use of his father's connections at Humphrey and Seyms, the grocery store where he worked. Neighbors of the Primuses were also sought as customers: "Next week," Nelson wrote to his mother, "i am going to start Mrs. Fairwell's picture. . . . i will paint the one that she ordered first & then if i have time i will paint the other."[36] Mrs. Fairwell, a white neighbor of the Primuses', had commissioned portraits of members of her family.

With income from his art slow and intermittent, making a living was a constant theme in Nelson's letters. Among other day jobs, he mentioned

waiting tables. On the Fourth of July, 1865, three months after he arrived
in the city, he took part in a Boston tradition:

> The city Council gave a dinner at Faneuil Hall, for the Bostonians,
> there were more than a thousand that eat. . . . There were fifty
> colored men employed to wait upon them. I was one to help
> make the number, it was the largest dinner I ever witnessed, every
> thing was served up in the best of stile and a plenty (so you
> may cacculate that I, lived well that day, if I never do agane.)[37]

If his numbers are correct, each waiter served more than twenty guests.
Impressed by the event, Nelson copied the whole staggering menu as printed
on the program.

Some of the jobs he found were related to his own calling. One
was painting a skeleton on a sign for "the good semeriton's for $10.00."[38]
Painting in the workaday sense of the word, he "striped and gilded" poles for
a barbershop and painted the interior of the barbershop of Henry Jones, a
Hartford friend who had moved to Boston.[39] In the spring of 1866, Nelson
wrote that he had been hired to paint a large sign, nine feet by five feet,
for Steamburg and Tredwell, another black-owned barbershop. He saw it
as an opportunity:

> if i succeed in makeing a good job of it, it will be the means
> of giveing me a great deal of wirk, for it is on one of the most
> principle st[reets]. in B[oston]. I do them at my house, by next
> year i shall be able to have a shop of my own, every body that
> sees my wirk are much pleased.[40]

Although Tredwell became one of Nelson's few new friends in Boston, sign
painting did not produce a great deal of work. He took whatever he could
find. Offered three dollars and carfare, he went to Worcester, Massachusetts,
for a day's work, and on another occasion wrote that he had been to Lowell,
Massachusetts, "on business."[41] He continued painting signs, houses, shops,
and carriages—but occasionally also portraits. At times, things went well,
but by the end of 1866 he was asking his mother to advance him the price
of paintings he had sent home for sale. Disappointed and obviously worried,
he wrote, "i am sorry that my pictures do not sell any faster, those who
pretend to think so much of me & and my greatest friends are not willing
to spend a dollar to help me. . . . i am depending wholly on them i have

no other means to support my family."[42] Nelson counted on Hartford supporters, black and white, to buy as many works as he could send home.

The following year was worse. In January 1867 he wrote: "Boston has been very dull for this season of the year. The truble is business is flat & money scarce, therefore people do not spend it [un]necessarily."[43] Boston was experiencing one of a series of recessions that followed the Civil War off and on almost to the end of the century. Holdridge and Mehitable decided to do more than send produce and baked goods to Boston. Holdridge sent fifty dollars, an enormous sum for the time.[44] Nelson wrote to Isabella: "I hope that I shall be able to repay [father] for his kindness to me . . . at no far distant day. he has been a good father to us all, I did not apretiate it until I went out into the world. . . . I am willing to spend a life time to please him, if it will only repay him for his kindness."[45] If Nelson had taken a full-time job as a carriage painter in Boston, his weekly wage would have been just under fifteen dollars, but, focused on his career, he took only day jobs. If he had found work as a house painter, he would have earned $2.40 a day, or $14.40 for a six-day week. Obviously, he did not seek such a schedule. At times, like Amoretta, he worked as a domestic, earning $1.53 per day.[46] His priority was his art; he worked for money only when pressed. Amoretta worked intermittently, and when she did, Nelson, at home producing his artworks, cared for Leila.

In March of that difficult year, Nelson undertook a new kind of work. Because his other sources of income had dried up, his mother suggested that he try selling Frank Moore's *Women of the War: Their Heroism and Self-Sacrifice*, a book published in Hartford the previous year.[47] Before bookstores, well before Amazon, publishers distributed books by hiring "agents" who sold them door-to-door. Close to desperation, Nelson agreed and asked that Mehitable send a copy of the book and the canvassing instructions.[48] She complied of course, and Nelson, his optimism restored, envisioned quick success. "I will go all over Boston," he promised, "& after I finish that I will go to all its ajoining towns, such as Cambridge, Roxbury, Chelsea, Charlestown, Dover, South Boston and East Boston. There will not be a house of importance that I shall miss."[49]

Unfortunately, a group of women got to area readers ahead of him.[50] He sold very few books but learned that opportunities existed in that line of work. During his brief stint as a salesman, he met William Wells Brown, a nationally known abolitionist speaker and author who had just published *The Negro in the Rebellion*, an account of the heroism and courage of African Americans during the war. It may have been with some chagrin that Nelson wrote, "[Brown} wants me to take the agency of that."[51] He confessed to his mother: "I do not like this kind of wirk it is to dry."[52] By April he was back doing the work for which he had trained. "I am wirking at my old traid again carriage painting. . . . I have given portrait painting up for a while."[53] His old trade was a reliable fallback, but he chose not to pursue it. He was determined to work as an artist and achieve success through. persistence—persistence and right living:

> Since I have been in the city of Boston i have met with misfor-tune, bad luck, every thing seams to go against me, but i have kept father's last words of advice to me when i left Hartford to keep out of bad company, not to have many associates, & not take to drinking. i mean to stick to it through life.[54]

Evidence shows that he did. Still, he spent Thanksgiving of that year work-ing in a white man's home, "helping Ret [Amoretta]. They sent for me to come up & do the carving they had twelve to dinner."[55]

To make a life in art and provide for his family proved a testing combination. Nelson's letters chronicle his attempt to straddle the fault line between the two goals. He managed only with the help of his parents and Amoretta's willingness to accept an erratic schedule cleaning the homes, washing the clothes, and serving the meals of white Bostonians. Nelson's frequent references to food reflect his own hearty appetite but also hint at hard times and an occasionally bare cupboard, as in this letter to his sister:

> I received the box of fruit that Father & mother sent, i tell you Bell it was the first time since i have been in B[oston] that i enjoyed any thing as much as i did the cake & cherries. . . . we eat them all up the day that i received them . . . Leila enjoyed the strawberry's very much and eat them all.[56]

In a letter the following year, he wrote again in praise of food from home:

> . the basket came filled with so many nice things. . . . the corn was very nice & tender. . . . We had it sunday for breakfast, dinner, & supper, and monday also until it was gone. Leila eat it like a pig. We made pies of the apples. We all thank you all very much for your kindness, until you are better paid."[57]

Presumably Amoretta made the pies. In his letters Nelson often mentioned his wife, and through his eyes we see her sewing, going out to work, making pies and dumplings, and grieving when she learned that her younger sister Mary died. In one letter he wrote of a visit that offers additional insight into family dynamics. In July 1866, Nelson's sisters Rebecca and Isabella traveled to Boston, and while their visit was familial and social, they had another purpose as well. They brought dress patterns and fabric and during their stay instructed Amoretta and one of her friends in the skill of dressmaking. Later, Nelson wrote, "Ret & Sylvie have got their dresses done Ret had hers on Sunday."[58] Sylvie was the wife of Henry Jones, Nelson's friend from Hartford. The Primus women had come to encourage Amoretta to increase her earning power by going into business as a dressmaker—a trade Mehitable had found rewarding.

In Nelson's last surviving letter, we learn the outcome of this effort. He described his wife as he might have outlined the subject of a typical melancholy nineteenth-century genre painting: "Ret sets playing on the guitar, she sends her love to all. She has worn that dress you made just twice. She has lost her courage in dressmaking, & daires not to make the attempt & put out her sign."[59] Ret could have been the woman in the scene Nelson had painted earlier, "Alone in the World." She remains a tentative, retiring presence in the letters. Her general health may have been poor: she could have been chronically weary or underfed or naturally diffident. If she felt a class difference in relation to the Primuses, there is nothing in the letters to show that the feeling was reciprocal. What is clear is that, in comparison with the more confident Primus women, Amoretta was agreeable but shy, perhaps saintly in the mode of the young women Ann Plato depicted in her writings. Beyond that, in Nelson's letters she remains indistinct.

In contrast, he wrote in detail about Leila. Working on his canvases at home, he often took care of his daughter when Amoretta was out working. He described in nearly every letter what the child was doing: building a house out of kindling, "sitting in her little chair eating an orange," refusing to take off her new sash at bedtime. Leila's scribbles appear on the overleaf of one letter, and in another he happily complained that he had to close because she kept sticking pieces of paper in his ear. When she failed to walk by the age of eighteen months, Nelson was anxious but hopeful, writing to Isabella:

[S]he stands up by my side holding on my knee & her mother
sits next to me Leila will reach out & take hold of her dress

& go backward & forwards from Ret to me. all alone this is
some thing that she never did before. she will walk by the time
you get here.[60]

But she didn't, and when she passed her second birthday still unable to
walk, the Hartford Primuses decided she would benefit by spending time
with them. A warm house, improved diet, and Isabella as nanny argued
for the arrangement.

By March of that lean year, 1867, Nelson acquiesced and sent Leila to
Hartford. Afterward, he wrote, "Ret & i went last night to meeting for it was
to[o] lonesome to stay in the house," adding, "Please learn her to walk."[61]
Leila initially spent seven months in Hartford and was brought home to
Boston in September 1867. She was taken back to Hartford a month later
and stayed with her grandparents and Isabella for more than a year.

Nelson was willing to part with his daughter rather than abandon his
career. His parents' chief concern was the welfare of the family. They had
most likely considered his apprenticeship a sensible preparation for life as an
artist in the old style—a tradesman with a useful skill. When he announced
that he had another future in mind, they may have been surprised, but they
were willing to help. They could not send him to Europe for training, but
they could and did send bedding, garden produce, baked goods, and money.
Now they offered to provide Leila the diet and care that might improve her
health. With his parents' help and Amoretta's compliance, Nelson continued
to travel two diverging paths. He even found ways to socialize in Boston.

He and Ret attended free lectures and concerts and managed to meet
a number of prominent local blacks, including the popular caterer Joshua
B. Smith. Nelson was interested in the life of the city but lacked the funds
to pursue wide social connections. His relationship to Boston's black community is unclear. He mentions only one new friend there, Tredwell, the
barber for whom he had painted a large sign. Their shared interest in music
afforded Nelson a source of free entertainment. "Last night I set up until
twelve o'clock accompanied Mr. Tredwell with the gatarrh he plays the flute
he also has a friend that plays the flute . . . we produce some sweet and
harmonius music, we are a going to practice regular."[62]

Perhaps mindful of his father's advice not to have many associates,
Nelson mostly sought the company of friends from Hartford: Henry Jones,
Benajah Plato, and Peter Nott. Like Nelson, all three were members of
the black middle class in Hartford and had moved to Boston believing it
offered wider opportunities. Nelson trusted these longtime friends to take his

artworks and even his daughter to Hartford. On occasion, one or another would return to Boston with food and other gifts from the family.

Reliance on family and friends is not exclusive to African Americans, but it has been critical to their survival; certainly for Nelson it was. Sociologists trace the "Helping Tradition" among blacks to origins in Africa.[63] Nelson provided an example of that quality when he commented on the death of a woman in Hartford: "I suppose Mr. Ed. Freeman he feels very badly & i really pitty him & his three little children. . . . i presume her mother will take charge of his house & children for him now.[64] Freeman, a schoolteacher turned porter, served along with Holdridge Primus on the governing board of the Talcott Street Church. Nelson took it for granted that Freeman's mother-in-law would move in and assume the household duties after her daughter died.

One of Nelson's trusted friends in Boston, Henry Jones, was the son of an early Hartford activist, Noble Jones. Henry moved to the city with his wife, Sylvie, and their daughter, Pinkie, who was Leila's age, at about the time Nelson and Amoretta arrived. With money inherited from his father, Jones opened a barbershop in the city's North End and hired Nelson to paint the interior. Living in the same neighborhood, the two families visited one another regularly. The two youngsters, Leila and Pinkie, played together, and the wives, Amoretta and Sylvie, became friends. Sylvie, as noted, joined Amoretta for dressmaking instructions when Rebecca and Isabella visited Boston in the summer of 1866. Another Hartford friend, Peter Nott, had also recently inherited money. Nelson saw Peter fairly often and in one letter described him as "Gay as a lark" over his inheritance.[65] Nelson's best friend in Boston was Benajah Plato, son of another middle-class black Hartford family. In 1867, Benajah was a student in Boston and visited Nelson on a daily basis. When Benajah left for medical school in Philadelphia, Nelson missed their daily visits and considered moving there.[66]

As newcomers, Nelson and Amoretta would have explored some of the established black neighborhoods. On Joy Street, for example, among other landmarks they would have looked for the house where Maria Stewart, the Hartford-born proto-feminist public speaker, had lived, and, before her, David Walker, author of the controversial *Appeal to the Coloured Citizens of the World*. A short distance away was the African Meeting House, Boston's first black house of worship. Nelson wrote that he and Amoretta visited various houses of worship in search of a comfortable church "home." For a time they attended the Twelfth Street Baptist Church, perhaps because Nelson's first mentor, Edward Bannister, was a member. The principal

FIGURE 6.2. Boston's first African American meetinghouse, and the former homes of David Walker and Maria Stewart would have drawn Nelson Primus to explore Joy Street, shown here from Beacon Street. *Credit:* Collection of the Massachusetts Historical Society.

attraction there was the popular pastor, Leonard A. Grimes, who before the war had been an outspoken and freewheeling abolitionist and his church an important station on the Underground Railroad. In later years, Grimes continued to advocate black rights.[67] At the Twelfth Baptist Church, Nelson and Amoretta attended lectures by a number of black activists, including Robert Hamilton, former editor of the abolitionist *Anglo-African Magazine*; and William Wells Brown, who later offered Nelson a chance to sell his book.[68] In spite of the popularity of the church, Nelson grew disillusioned with the Reverend Grimes: "when i see so many hypocritical people that profess to be followers of crist & are not it makes me mad. all that Mr. Grimes is for [is] money i see so much of it [hypocrisy] that i get provoked." He added, "Ret & i attend the white episcople church, i like there way of worshoping god. if i could understand them i think that i would like to join them."[69] Because an Episcopal clergyman had officiated at their wed-

ding, that may have been Amoretta's preference, and because Nelson had
been raised in the Congregational church, the two may have preferred more
formal services over the evangelical gusto for which Grimes was famous.
The prominent Phillips Brooks, rector of Boston's Trinity Episcopal Church
in Copley Square, was reportedly the subject of one of Nelson's portraits,
pointing to the possibility that he and Amoretta attended services there.[70]

Nelson's preference for the Episcopal rite reflects the class identity that
shaped many of his opinions. Even his views on race carry overtones of class
bias, as in his description of the reunion of the Anti-Slavery Society in 1866:

> I see Miss Clara Mitchell last Wednesday eve at the music Hall,
> Winters St. at the Anti-Slavery Anniversary . . . bothe colored
> and white meet there as if they were all of one color, & walk
> about and chat one to the other . . . I never see so fine a set
> of colored people in all my life they acted very sociable & lady
> and gentleman-like.[71]

Nelson may have found a more affluent society at the reunion than he
would have seen in Hartford, for Boston had a class of elite blacks, some of
whom were certainly present that night. For him, the meeting confirmed the
soundness of the theory of racial uplift: he saw educated and well-turned-
out blacks socializing easily with whites. Clara Mitchell, whom he singled
out for notice, was the seventeen-year-old daughter of William Mitchell,
one of Hartford's middle-class blacks. Clara was in Boston visiting her older
brother, Charles L. Mitchell, himself an exemplar of black achievement.[72]
Originally trained as a printer, he moved from Hartford to Boston shortly
before the Civil War and set type for Garrison's *The Liberator*. Later he
served as a second lieutenant in the Fifty-fifth Massachusetts Regiment and
lost his right foot in combat. He returned to Boston and was elected to the
state legislature in 1866. Appointed an inspector in the Custom House in
1869, Mitchell served in that post for forty years.[73] Hartford blacks proudly
pointed to him as one of their own, a man whose achievements lent cred-
ibility to the vision of racial harmony that Nelson saw at the antislavery
reunion—the promise of uplift fulfilled.

In another letter, Nelson reported a different kind of interracial
encounter. "[T]he man that I was painting the house for," he wrote, "did
not amount to much, he thought I was going to wirk for nothing be cause
I were colored we could not come to terms, in consiquence we parted."[74]
For Nelson, the man's race prejudice defined his class ranking. In addition

to informing his family of the incident, Nelson explained how he handled it. As we will see, Rebecca also reported racial insults and told how she responded. While his sister generally masked her anger with what might be described as dignified restraint, Nelson tended to be blunt. His view of an 1867 incident in Brooklyn, New York, is a case in point:

> I see by the papers that we have had quite a riot in New York, Sa[i]nt Pat day, i would like to take those mick's & have my way with them, i would soon show them what it was to fite, the New York people are eat up with them, & now they can see how they treat them in return, i donot care if they only let the colored people alone.[75]

According to the *New York Times*, members of a "Hibernian temperance society" gathering for a St. Patrick's Day parade attacked a black driver whose offense had been to stop his rig in the street to make a delivery.[76] When the police came to the deliveryman's aid, the Irish fought them as well. Sharing nativist disdain for the Irish immigrants, Nelson identified with the New York (white) police as well as with the black deliveryman.

The most striking example of class bias in Nelson's correspondence came when he learned that his mother was working with freed women sent North from Virginia, training them for domestic work. Between 1864 and 1868, the Freedman's Bureau transported a number of former slaves North to "remove the 'press of population' in the Tidewater region of Virginia."[77] This project resulted in what was called the first large-scale Northern migration of former slaves, although it was dwarfed by those that came later. The cities of Boston and Hartford both took part.[78] Nelson observed some of the freedwomen either on the streets or possibly in a Boston workplace, and in his judgment:

> [I]t is turning out with those freed girles just as i said. the only way to get along with them is, when you tell them any thing is to have a big club, & every word you say knock them on the head, that is the only way i find to keep them in there place."[79]

His angry statement, reminiscent of folk advice on training a mule or a wife, highlights the importance of class—and gender as well—to Nelson. His dismissal of the freed women is fiercely classist. On another occasion, he widened the target to include many Northern blacks, writing, "I often feel greatful to see how I have been traned up, different from most of our poor low colored people."[80] His phrasing in this instance conveys a note of sympathy. Class provided identity among blacks as well as whites and played a part in Nelson's sense of his own worth.

The episode concerning the freedwomen who came North after the war points up one of the great advantages of the Primus letters, as each of the three correspondents supplied a different response to it. When Rebecca, with two years' experience teaching in the South, learned of her mother's work with the freedwomen in Hartford, she wrote, "I'm surprised to hear you've cleaned the whole house. I think you've been very expeditious . . . I hope that girl will try to do well at whatever place you get for her; she's a fair specimen of these southern blacks."[81] Rebecca discovered her own class identity as she became acquainted with the blacks of Royal Oak, Maryland, and she applauded her mother's readiness to help the freedwomen through a difficult transition. Mehitable, for her part, chose compassion over class bias, taking some of the women into her home. The final opinion comes from Addie Brown, whose comment only seems innocuous: "There was a freed girl at your Mother on Saturday. Look and act like Bell Sands."[82] The wife of Thomas Sands, Bell was staying temporarily in the home of her father-in-law, Raphael Sands, and his second wife, Emily Jacobs. Because Addie was rooming with the Sands family, she often spent time in Bell's company and wrote about her to Rebecca. "I think she is very fond of the Gents society," Addie sniffed, "they all make nothing in kissing her. I dont think Aunt Em [Mehitable's sister, Emily Sands] has much opinion of her daughter in law."[84] Class bias existed within Hartford's black community in varying degrees. Regarding the project to help former slaves find their way in a free society, we discover a continuum from acceptance (Mehitabel) to rejection (Nelson), and in between were Rebecca, who was somewhat sympathetic, and Addie Brown, who was less so.

Class was not a preoccupation for Nelson; it was an unexamined set of opinions. On matters involving race and politics, he followed his father's example by avoiding overt public protest, although he aired strong views in his letters. He had little use for President Andrew Johnson, whose daunting task was to follow a martyred president. By granting pardons to many former Confederates, and thus restoring their political power, Johnson managed to alienate a wide spectrum of Northerners. He earned the enmity of African Americans by vetoing two important bills, one to extend the life of the Freedmen's Bureau and the other a civil rights bill guaranteeing blacks the rights of citizenship. In April 1866, after Johnson vetoed the Civil Rights

Act, Nelson wrote: "The loyal papers of this state continue to comment on Prest Andy Johnson's reconstruction; they call him the meanest man on record of which he deserves, and to impeach him would be doing justice."[85] This was another case in which all three letter writers commented. Rebecca had stated her opinion earlier: "I have had real benefit all this week in perusing the '*Independent*' it goes down on Johnson pretty hard, & gives him his just dues."[86] Congress overrode the veto, but later, when Johnson announced a visit to Hartford Addie Brown wrote, "I wish someone would present him with a ball through his head."[87] On this subject the three letter writers were in agreement.

Along with providing various points of view on issues and individuals, the Primus letters reveal family and community dynamics, although some references resist explanation. The easy style in Nelson's letters to Isabella contrasts with the more serious way he addresses his mother and especially his father. Even so, on one occasion he departed from that tone with a burst of whimsy. Complaining about the lack of letters from home, he opened with: "Dear Father, Are you all dead at home, or lost the use of your hands for writing. For I have not heard from home since Henry Jones first came to Boston."[88] Henry Jones moved to Boston around the first of that year. Nelson needed close contact with his family. Another glimpse of his humor came after a blizzard dumped three feet of snow on Boston. Just after the worst of it, Nelson wrote, "We are having fine weather overhed but under foot do not say a word."[89]

As revealing and candid as the letters are, inevitably they contain references to events, relationships, incidents, and "conditions" that mystify today's reader. In the spring of 1867, when Leila was in Hartford, Nelson wrote about an unnamed problem—illness or disappointment or disgrace—concerning Isabella:

> I am willing for [Leila] to remain on Bell's account, i thought if she were there she would devote Bell's leasure time & make her think less of the beau's . . . hope that she will be restored back to her former he[a]l[t]h again . . . I hope that she will take my advice & let the young men slide, & never get married her condition <u>cannot never</u> be bettered.[90]

In spite of Nelson's dire prediction, Isabella married in 1873 and had the first of her three children in 1874. Even so, according to Addie Brown, Bell Primus was something of a renegade in her younger years.

Nelson wrote of another or perhaps a related problem after a trip to Hartford in the fall of 1867, just before Rebecca returned to her school in Maryland:

> I was pleased the last sunday eve that Rebecca was there to see all the family united in one band again around the table at tea, i hope that it will always continue to be so . . . it has been a pest to the hartford people to see us trying to get along & they have done all they could to brake us up. let them do what they are a mind to but let us stick together & help each other & let outsiders go.[91]

What was the incident that threatened family unity? How and why would the people of Hartford—white or black—try to divide the family? Rebecca certainly knew of this matter. She may have had her say on it before she returned to Royal Oak, for nothing in her letters or Addie's refers to family difficulties at this time. This problem troubled Nelson, but, like his worry over Isabella, it appears to have been resolved.

Although he raised questions that remain unanswered, Nelson made quite clear his own goals and priorities. Increasingly torn between his ambition and the cost to his wife and child, without proper formal training or a patron, he nevertheless persisted in his pursuit of a career as an artist. By the late 1860s, he began to gain notice as a portraitist and was able to rent a studio—the mark of a professional. Nelson's affection for his daughter and his appreciation of his parents as well as his loyalty to Amoretta soften the edges of his driving ambition. His occasional flashes of anger remind us of his youth; his own problems and the unexplained family troubles remind us of the real world the Primus family inhabited.

7

Rebecca Primus

The Teacher in Royal Oak

Whites are mostly secesh here they give colored men employment; the greatest difficulty is they do not pay sufficient wages
& if the people will not accept their terms they send off and get
"contrabands" as they are here denominated, to work for them
so that it takes the labor right out of these people's hands &
they are obliged to submit. I hope there will be justice, impartial
justice, given to the colored people one of these days.[1]

Indignation over the everyday unconcealed oppression of blacks in the mid-
South was a recurring theme in the letters of Rebecca Primus. She knew the
Northern ways of insult and abuse, but the openness of the racial divide
in the South seemed worse to her. It redoubled her dedication to her role
as teacher. Her brother Nelson and her friend Addie Brown occasionally
wrote about race, but their major concerns were their daily lives and their
personal goals. Rebecca had chosen to become a teacher confident that
education was the key to racial uplift and eventually "racial justice." In 1865
she was handed the opportunity of a lifetime: a chance to offer literacy to
those most in need of it.

Between December 1865 and July 1869, in letters to her family
she chronicled her life as a teacher of freed people on Maryland's Eastern
Shore.[2] Her "home weeklies" give evidence of close family ties and show
her deep interest in Hartford's black community. Rebecca's carefully correct writing style reveals a self-made model of the educated woman and a

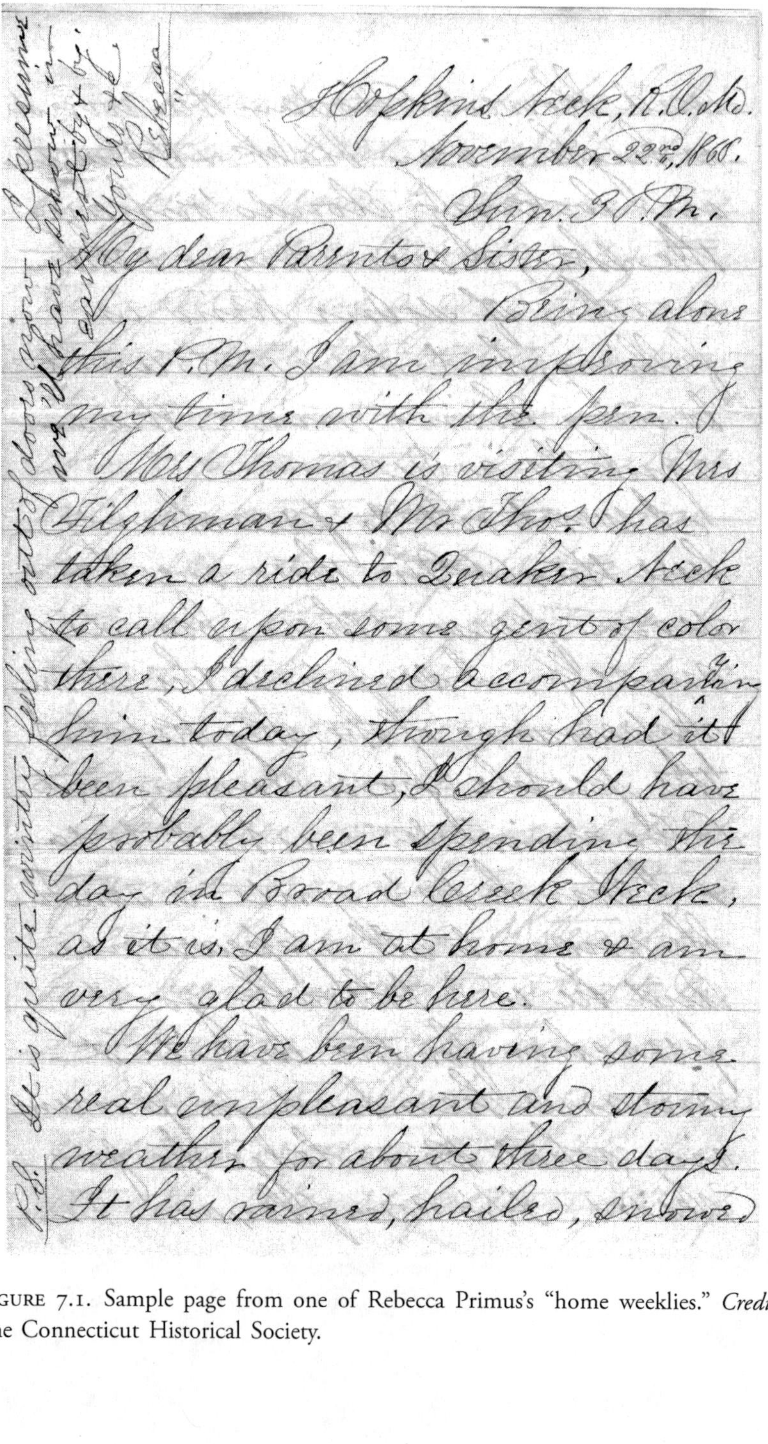
Hopkins Neck, T.C. Md.
November 22nd 1868.
Sun. 3 P.M.

My dear Parents & Sister,

Being alone this P.M. I am improving my time with the pen.

Mrs Thomas is visiting Mrs Tilghman & Mr Thos. has taken a ride to Quaker Neck to call upon some gent of color there, I declined accompanying him today, though had it been pleasant, I should have probably been spending the day in Broad Creek Neck, as it is, I am at home & am very glad to be here.

We have been having some real unpleasant and stormy weather for about three days. It has rained, hailed, snowed

P.S. It is quite wintry feeling out of doors now.

FIGURE 7.1. Sample page from one of Rebecca Primus's "home weeklies." *Credit:* The Connecticut Historical Society.

staunch defender of middle-class propriety. She comments on race, certainly, but also on gender, religion, politics, food, fashions, and herbal remedies. Discovering that doughnuts were unknown in the South, appalled by the unmarried servant girl who bore two infants in fewer than two years, and lamenting poor school attendance during "the great hog sacrifice," as she called hog-killing week, she showed her family, and all who read her letters now, her dedication to her mission. Her letters also show how her cultural and class affinities affected her ability to understand those she had come to help.

The firstborn child of Holdridge and Mehitable Primus, Rebecca arrived on July 10, 1836, in the rented rooms on Elm Street with the assistance of the white midwife who attended all the Primus births.[3] At the age of five, she would have entered the First African School held in the basement of the Talcott Street Congregational Church. Her first teachers were the Reverend J. W. C. Pennington and his wife, Harriet, and later Augustus Washington and Selah Africanus. As is the case with Nelson, we have no information about Rebecca's childhood, but her later life argues that she was a bright, purposeful child who noted the dedication of her teachers and admired their elevated language. They impressed on her the importance of their work and the value of education.

Among the few clues to her early life are two short essays, "I've Lost a Day" and "History of My Poodle Dog," written when she was eighteen and twenty years old, respectively.[4] In the first, she regrets time wasted and resolves to do better in the future; in the second, she chronicles the short life of a much-loved dog. The fact that the essays were saved hints at an ambition to follow the lead of Ann Plato, whose writings the Reverend Pennington had published in 1841. Rebecca's themes, like Plato's, involve the Puritan charge to make the best use of one's time, and the ubiquity of death and mourning. Although the two pieces contain no hint of the interest in racial justice that runs through her letters, they display an interest in creative writing and a desire to instruct.

In 1860, when she was twenty-four years old, the census lists Rebecca Primus as a teacher. Her friend Addie Brown later confirms this occupation, writing: "You remember Julia Woodbridge that attended the Young Ladies night school Miss Primus was the teacher of it several winters ago."[5] The city directory lists no such school and we find no newspaper notices announcing its existence. Rebecca, as an education entrepreneur, likely recruited students by word of mouth and held classes in the family home. That she taught is certain, but how she became a teacher is unknown. The association that later supervised her work in Maryland stipulated that its teachers must be "trained for the special work of teaching, employing all the most approved Normal School methods, and subject to the most rigorous examination before we send them to take charge of a school."[6] That she was accepted shows that Rebecca met those requirements. Certainly she was a dedicated reader: she mentions Hartford newspapers and several periodicals that addressed African American interests: the *Communicator*, the *Independent*, the *National Anti-Slavery Standard*, and *Freedmen's Record*. She reports reading *Pilgrim's Progress*, the *Life of Bunyan*, Harriet Beecher Stowe's *Men of Our Time*, Lydia Maria Child's *Freedmen's Book*, poems of Lydia Huntley Sigourney, a life of Lincoln, and the Bible.

Her familiarity with political issues along with her emphasis on correct speech and manners may have intimidated the young men of Hartford, so that at twenty-six, unmarried and somewhat restless, she considered moving elsewhere.[7] Alarmed, her friend Addie Brown wrote: "You say you are bent and bond to leave your home don't my Dear Dear friend do anything that you will repent," she cautioned. "You have never had to go out in the world do for yourself.[8] Addie had had that experience, but, more importantly, she feared that separation would end their close relationship. Rebecca did not act on her restlessness at that time, but before long, opportunity sought her out.

In the wake of Emancipation, the needs of the freed people led to the formation in the North of numerous groups dedicated to their needs. Hartford's white elites established a Freedmen's Aid Society and elected the Reverend Calvin Stowe, husband of Harriet Beecher, as president.[9] Members, mostly women, sent bedding and clothing South for the needy, but their most ambitious undertaking was to supply teachers to schools for former slaves, a project of the United States Bureau of Refugees, Freedmen, and Abandoned Lands (hereafter called the Freedmen's Bureau). A third partner in the arrangement, the Baltimore Association for the Moral and Educational Advancement of Colored People (hereafter called the Baltimore Association), set up and supervised such schools in Maryland.[10]

During the four and a half years of its existence, the Hartford Freedmen's Aid Society sent five teachers South, but in its first year just two were chosen, one white and one black: Harriet Hamilton and Rebecca Primus.[11] Rebecca would have seen her selection as additional evidence of waning racial prejudice. It answered her earlier wish to explore a part of the country she had never seen, and better yet, it sent her to those most in need of education. Surely it was a heady experience to board the train in November 1865 for her journey South: by rail to New York City, by ferry to Jersey City, by carriage to Philadelphia, and finally by train to Baltimore. The cost of the trip was ten dollars and forty cents, including seventy-five cents for baggage.[12]

Arriving in Baltimore, Rebecca was directed to the "rendezvous for the coloured teachers."[13] Black and white teachers were housed separately, as they would have been in the North. She was one of forty-seven black and thirty-one white educators whose combined efforts would reach an average daily attendance of 5,645 students in Maryland during the 1865–1866 school year.[14] She found in her new coworkers instant camaraderie. Her network of friends and trusted acquaintances, hitherto acquired mostly through connections in Hartford, expanded to include many black and white teachers whose names would appear in her letters over the next four years. They became a community of sorts, meeting when they could to share experiences, advice, cautions, and classroom supplies. One study of antebellum urban African Americans found that "Black communities were networks of

FIGURE 7.2. Hartford's Railroad Station, where Rebecca Primus boarded the train for her trip to Baltimore and ultimately Royal Oak, Maryland. *Credit:* Hartford History Center, Hartford Public Library.

family, friends, and coworkers cemented by bonds of obligation and shared disadvantage and were both based in and transcended geography."[15] For Rebecca, at least for a time, shared interest in racial uplift through education transcended race as well.

The teachers she met in Baltimore were part of a public-private venture meant to fill an educational void. The Emancipation Proclamation in 1863 freed only the slaves in states of the Confederacy. Maryland, a border state, freed its slaves in 1864 but provided no schools for them.[16] As a remedy, Freedmen's Societies in the North supplied teachers and contributed to their salaries; the Baltimore Association assigned the teachers to their posts, provided the texts to be sold to the students, and oversaw the conduct of the schools.[17] The Freedmen's Bureau provided government oversight and supplies for building schoolhouses. In an age before copy machines, typewriters, or carbon paper, each of the three agencies required monthly reports. The amount of paperwork, added to the hostility of whites in the region, helps to explain the average tenure of teachers in the new Southern schools: about two years. Many moved from one school to another, sometimes from one sponsoring agency to another. Rebecca served in the same Royal Oak community for four school years. She was one of the 3,000 teachers who taught some 150,000 pupils in Freedmen's Bureau schools throughout the South.[18]

Maryland held surprises that began with her arrival in Baltimore. Walking around the city the first morning, she was struck by the number of blacks: "I have already seen as many coloured people as there are in the whole of Hartford." An accurate observation: the black population of Baltimore in 1860 was more than 29,000—equal to the total population of Hartford, black and white. Hartford's black population at the time was 706. When she reported to the Association offices that first morning, Rebecca was sent without preparation or introduction to a local school as a substitute—evidence of the Association's confidence in its hires but also of the great need for teachers. At the end of the school day, Rebecca visited a Mrs. Hall, resident of the city, who had been alerted by Mehitable to expect Rebecca to call on her. "She wished me to tell you [Mother] that she had been quite anxious about me for fear I had got lost or met with some difficulty enroute. If I remain here in the city she wants me to call & see her often and she will look out for me. I think I shall like her much."[19] Mrs. Hall's connection to Mehitable is not explained, although Nelson mentions a Justin Hall as one of his Hartford friends. The visit illustrates the reach and effectiveness of the networking system—an extension of the "helping tradition" vital to African Americans.

As it happened, Rebecca did not have a chance to get better acquainted with Mrs. Hall. Within a week she was on her way to a small village on the Eastern Shore best reached by boat. Royal Oak is perched on a finger of land on the Miles River, which empties into Chesapeake Bay. In accordance with Baltimore Association requirements, black residents there had formed a school society, elected five of their "best men" to a board of managers, and requested a teacher.[20] They agreed to "provide room and board and to contribute from \$5.00 to \$10.00 a month to the Association."[21] While few of the blacks in Royal Oak had any experience of schooling, they understood its importance.

We can only guess at Rebecca's first reaction upon reaching the village. While Baltimore was much larger than Hartford, Royal Oak was a good deal smaller and isolated by the convoluted geography of the Eastern Shore.[22] Water nearly surrounded the community, which stood just seven feet above sea level. The distance from Royal Oak to nearby Oxford, Maryland, was three miles by water, sixteen by land. Royal Oak's total population in 1860 was 849, compared to Hartford's 29,000. Hartford's 709 blacks were 2 percent of the total population; Royal Oak's 290 blacks were 34 percent of the total there.[23]

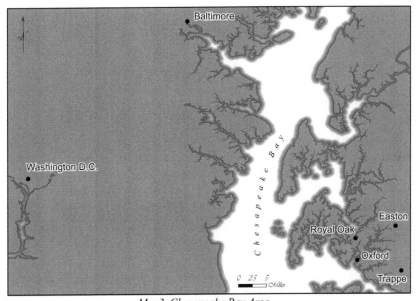

Map3. Chesapeake Bay Area

MAP 7.1. Royal Oak and other destinations Rebecca mentions in her letters.

All or nearly all had been slaves in their lifetime; most if not all were illiterate and poor. As was true for Hartford blacks, most worked in menial occupations: the women as domestic servants, the men as farmhands or laborers.[24]

Probably the first residents Rebecca met were Charles N. Thomas, one of the trustees of her school, and his wife, Sarah. The couple had offered to provide board and room for the teacher.[25] Rebecca found Sarah Thomas amiable but less interested in politics than in household matters. The two women found common ground in domestic concerns—sewing, cooking, and raising chickens. They shared family stories and neighborhood visits, often taking food and clothing to the poor.[26] Later, when they were better acquainted, Sarah Thomas offered Rebecca a tour of her chicken house and pointed out two hens in particular:

> One's name is Rebecca & the other, Bell—they having been named according as they characterize the individual whose names they bear. The latter being more gay than the former wears a crown, & this is the distinguishing feature. But the former produces the largest eggs & is the more independent.[27]

Sarah Thomas correctly read her boarder's "distinguishing features." Judging from Rebecca's letters, their relationship was entirely cordial, but Charles proved her vital link to the community. Born a slave in Maryland in 1834, he "bought his time" at the age of twenty-five and "became a trainer of blooded horses working for Colonel Lloyd whose father owned Fred Douglass."[28] Thomas owned a small parcel of land and kept a few horses. Hardly wealthy, he nevertheless lived in a house with an extra bedroom and owned a basket sleigh. He farmed his land and worked in a sawmill, where eventually he became supervisor.[29] As a trustee of Rebecca's school and an influential member of the black community, Thomas proved invaluable in navigating local customs and politics. Furthermore, she found him colorful and sociable. She enjoyed his sly sense of humor, which surfaced at a Royal Oak wedding:

> Mr. Thos was the only one who saluted the bride with a kiss, & he only did it for mischief—he told me to tell you she was the homeliest woman he believed that lived or ever lived. You should hear him go on about that poor woman, he says if he'd seen how ugly she was before he got so close to her to kiss her, he should never have done it.[30]

Rebecca was not without humor herself. In one letter, she informed the family, tongue in cheek: "I've worn my corsets ever since I left home, they are my chief support."[31] One of her letters is addressed to Jim, her cat, who on occasion wrote to her.

Thomas's sense of fun helped accustom Rebecca to her new surroundings. He accompanied her to social events, sometimes without his wife. He interpreted local customs for her, advised her on reliable workmen, and stepped in to intercede on her behalf when necessary. No less important, he was a political activist. In May 1867, he represented Royal Oak at a convention in Baltimore to debate ratifying the Fourteenth Amendment to the Constitution, which guaranteed the rights of citizenship to all persons born or naturalized in the United States.

> [Charles Thomas] says the convention passed very quietly & pleasantly the Republicans had the majority; the object of it was to add an amendment to the constitution in favor of "Negro Suffrage." . . . All were allowed to speak ten minutes at a time, & he says some of the col'd. delegates spoke well . . . The ambition of the col'd, men in this state is raised high I'll assure you, & they are confident of voting at the next election. It's the general topic of the day now among them.[32]

Rebecca found the Thomas home pleasant and comfortable, and by 1869 she felt sufficiently integrated into the household to write, "We're as a family about the same as usual though we've our little ups & downs with the rest. Yet we're all able to keep at work and to eat our daily allowance."[33] Commenting on this statement, the editor of the Primus letters suggests that it reads as "a letter from the Royal Oak household to the Hartford branch of the family."[34]

Certainly the Thomases helped Rebecca adjust to life in Royal Oak, but it was not an easy fit, for the local ways grated on her notions of propriety. Some years later, a friendly note from a village resident to Rebecca, undated and unsigned, encapsulates the place and its people—how different their ways from hers yet how similar their aspirations:

> This fruit was sent to you by one of your scholars and it growed where the white people's old meeting house stood . . . the meeting house where the col'd woman got her leg down the stove-pipe while shouting the very spot where this house stood

is owned to-day by one of your scholars and she and her family are living on it. The bread is from Aunt Sallie Thomas.[35]

The letter implies that attending Rebecca's school had subsequently led to the writer's success, moving into a house built on the site of the old church where classes were originally held. At the same time, the writer defends the Royal Oak style of life and worship by recalling the woman so carried away "shouting" that the ensuing scene entered into local lore. The bread was edible thanks for the schoolteacher's fruitful mission.

On her arrival there, Rebecca found the behavior and customs of the former slaves embarrassing. She was not the only Freedmen's Bureau teacher who believed that part of the task was to instruct the former slaves in proper conduct and manners.[36] She found much to remake. One Saturday morning when she was writing her letter home, she was interrupted:

> One of the colored women has just been here to get me to write a letter to her daughter in Balto. And she has gone on further intending to call for the letter upon her return. She's not told me a word yet & I've written all that I can think will be suitable, & it now awaits her approval and a few additional words from herself.[37]

Rebecca was expected not only to write the letter but also to supply its contents. This was one of a number of Royal Oak incidents that rattled her middle-class sensibilities. Weddings offered numerous examples:

> The man with whom the bride lived [her employer] was present with two other white men, they all came and went with the minister, 'twas a relief too, to have them gone, immediately following which the entire company . . . relapsed or collapsed I don't know which would be the most applicable term here, into a long and painful silence, I was glad to have some refreshments passed for a relief & a change of scene.[38]

The black celebrants were honored by the presence of the white men but ill at ease until they left. This "double consciousness" later identified by W. E. B. DuBois would not have been new to Rebecca: certainly some blacks in Hartford behaved differently in the presence of whites. What is striking is that she herself proved ill at ease as the evening progressed, pleased to be an honored guest but put off by the nature of the festivities. "After supper and the tables had been removed," she wrote, "play upon play was introduced, which created much amusement. I did not participate in any of them however, but remained a silent and interested spectator." The long evening climaxed with a chivaree—a rite new to Rebecca—as men surrounded the house, "ringing bells, yelling and singing, firing pistols, etc., for about an hour. This is a custom here upon such occasions among both black and white, and is considered very annoying, still it has to be endured."[39] When Mehitable wrote asking why her daughter did not join in the conversation, Rebecca replied: "Simply because I had nothing to say. I went merely as a spectator. I some times think they're almost afraid to talk or move in my presence. I always do what I can to remove their apparent embarrassment."[40] If local customs made her uncomfortable, her own effect on the black celebrants replicated that of the white men, although her difference was tied to class rather than race.

Another example of culture clash came with a sudden spell of warm weather in April 1867:

> The children, having taken advantage of the warm days by taking off their coats, shoes, &c during play hours many of them now have bad colds. It's useless to advise to the contrary, for the adults are no better themselves, like black snakes, as soon as the sun shines & it begins to get warm they come out, one young woman was attired in a black silk basque [a close-fitting bodice or jacket] & a light summer dress last Sunday.[41]

Her objection was related not to color or species but to the reckless response to sunshine. Furthermore, as the daughter of a New England dressmaker, Rebecca had firm views on suitable apparel. She had more to say about Royal Oak fashions a month later when the women came to church in "their new spring hats, bonnets & dresses some in the last styles I judge, & oh! Such looks as some presented! Some of these people do make themselves appear so much more ridiculous than they really are." She added, "I don't know what they think of my always dressing so plainly."[42] Instructing by example as well as by word, Rebecca surely meant for her own plain style to be noticed and copied.

Charlotte Forten [Grimke], another African American teacher, offers an alternate response to the same discoveries. Forten taught freed slaves on the Sea Islands, South Carolina, from 1862 to 1864, and like Rebecca noted cultural differences. As a grandchild of the prosperous Philadelphia sailmaker James Forten, Charlotte was raised in privilege and educated in white schools in Massachusetts. No more free of class bias than Rebecca, she nevertheless understood that she was observing not a lack of culture but a different culture. Describing in her journal the apparel of the brides in a multiple wedding, Forten used the same adjective Rebecca had employed: " 'Twas amusing to see some of the headdresses. One, of tattered flowers and ribbons, was very ridiculous . . . but no matter for that," Forten continued, "I am truly glad that the poor creatures are trying to live right and virtuous lives."[43] At Christmas, she and her fellow teachers abandoned their own notions of proper garb and made bright red dresses as presents for the "babies," the preschool-aged girls. Rebecca Primus didn't—couldn't—see Royal Oak fashions as exuberance over deliverance from slavery's dull garments.[44]

In another example of contrasting perceptions, Charlotte Forten praised the former slaves' church services, writing: "The sermon was quite good. But I enjoyed nothing so much as the singing—the wonderful, beautiful singing." On another occasion, she reported: "All the children had the shouting spirit. . . . "Look upon the Lord," which they sang to-night, seems to me the most beautiful of all their shouting tunes. There is something in it that goes to the depths of one's soul."[45] Rebecca's reaction to the preaching at a revival meeting in Royal Oak reinforces the contrast between the two women:

> His text was, "Let your light so shine before the world, etc." After . . . repeating it over once or twice, . . . he went directly into Genesis where he remained sometime, then he proceeded to John the Revelator repeating & dwelling upon several passages in the Revelations. From thence to Job, repeating the text again, went back to the Gen[esis] & ended with the gospels. 'Twas a great sermon—he got the people to patting & if he'd continued much longer would have them all shouting I presume.[46]

Rebecca had no patience with evangelical preaching, nor did she approve of revivals, noting, "The converted here are like those we have at home—they're only for a season."[47] *Patting* is variously described as a rhythmic tapping of feet on the ground or hands on knees or thighs, often in time to music; *shouting* is responding, also rhythmically, to what is being spoken or sung. These typical characteristics of revival style distressed Rebecca, whose religion was private, and her ideas of worship too formal for "shouting." It puzzled her that the black citizens of Royal Oak sought the advantages of education yet clung to their own notions of dress, movement, speech, and worship. Historian Eric Foner notes that blacks "proved perfectly capable of resisting both interference in their personal lives and efforts to 'reform' their religious worship."[48]

Except for the unsigned letter quoted above, the black citizens of Royal Oak left no written record of their opinion of Rebecca, but clearly they took pride in having created a school of their own and in having secured a bona fide schoolteacher—certainly the first educated black woman many of them had ever seen. They may have considered her standoffish ways and plain dress simply marks of her otherness, her status as teacher. Some probably found her remote or cold, but she was highly respected. When she returned for her second year of teaching, she reported, "After my arrival here yesterday, eleven persons called and . . . since I've been writing this letter five of my old pupils have called upon me."[49] Through the years, local residents came calling, brought her flowers, held fairs to raise money for the school, and each fall the women cleaned and whitewashed her classroom.[50] At times she was overwhelmed by the attentions of the residents of Royal Oak. Her sense of humor came to her rescue on a day when she found it impossible to catch up with her correspondence. Having counted seventeen callers, she wrote: "I've been interrupted again. . . . If any one comes in the Teacher must be seen and hindered at all events, and so it is."[51]

An incident in her second year in Royal Oak caused her to rethink her judgment of its people. She mentioned casually to Charles Thomas that if the weather was pleasant on Thanksgiving she planned to visit some of the neighbors, thinking to drop in for a few minutes as she might have done at home on a holiday.[52] He passed the word around, and when Rebecca did not come calling, she was "sent for" by William Gibson, another of the trustees of her school. She hurried "up in the Neck—every road here is called a neck," to his house. She had noonday dinner with the Gibsons and afterward called on three other families nearby. She had supper with the Williamses and their ten children, and one of the sons drove her home in a carriage. She had called on the four trustees of her school, who, with Charles Thomas were responsible for her presence in the town.

These families were all so delighted to have me visit them, & only wished I had let them know sooner that they could have been better prepared . . . They seem to labor under the false impression that I'm an uncommon personage—that there's no one like me, but what should lead them to think thus is beyond my comprehension. I endeavor to make myself very sociable with them, but I keep them at a certain standpoint . . . I mean to visit more of them too, now I find they are so neatly & comfortably situated & they are so desirous to have me, it will not do to slight any."[53]

Halfway through her second year of teaching, this was the first time Rebecca had visited any of Royal Oak's "better sort" in their homes. Embarrassed by their hospitality, she began to see that the social gap dividing her from the townspeople was of her own making: she had come to address the educational gap but found that her own education was incomplete in ways she had not understood.

She had opened her school immediately after arriving in December 1865, holding classes in the local black church. She soon added a Sabbath School to her weekday duties. In the fall of 1866, returning to Royal Oak after summer vacation, she wrote that many of her scholars were sick and unable to attend, but "those that came," she added, "have lost nothing during the vacation, and I have bright hopes for their future course." At the same time, in schoolteacher mode she scolded, "The Sabbath School has not been attended well this Summer, it will be resumed under my auspices tomorrow A.M. & I requested the children to tell everybody to come."[54]

Rebecca wrote only once of a classroom incident that required disciplinary action: "Yesterday A.M. I suspended two boys from school for the day for fighting, one went home & rec[eived] a severe whipping, and I've not yet learned what has [been] bestowed upon the other."[55] Minimizing the incident, she wrote, "As a general thing my pupils behave very well, but now & then an evil spirit rises among them, and I introduce different methods of punishment to quell it." However foreign she may have seemed to the black citizens of Royal Oak, they welcomed her mission. For her part, she was proud of her school and pleased when its progress was recognized. John T. Graham, secretary of the Baltimore Association, visited Royal Oak in December 1866 and compared it favorably with the older and larger school in nearby Easton. "He said [the Royal Oak school] was ahead of that school, and that there was more interest shown by the people in sending their children etc."[56] She repeated his praise to her students, telling them that "we must keep ahead, & [that they must] encourage their parents to keep ahead too."[57]

The Baltimore Association's standards were reflected in the books and materials its teachers used. Rebecca's students were issued Boston Primary slates and worked through Sheldon's First Readers and Charts; Hilliards Second, Third, and Intermediate Readers; Worcester's Spellers; Davies' Arithmetics; Montieth's Geographies; Mitchell's Outline Maps; Payson, Dunton & Company Copy books; and Walton's Arithmetical Tables.[58] Perhaps the best summary of Rebecca's work in Royal Oak is one she prepared herself midway through her tenure. Just before returning to her school in the fall of 1867, she addressed a meeting of the Talcott Street Sabbath School in Hartford. Concise and factual, her talk includes a nicely phrased request for additional Sunday School materials:

> I began my labors upon the eastern shore of Maryland the 11th of Dec. 1865 by opening a day & night school in the church under the auspices of the Balto. Assn. . . . I began with 10 day and 26 night scholars. The number soon increased to 75, including persons of all ages. The adults attending the [night] session.
>
> But few, very few could read, others only knew the letters or a part of them. Yet, the greater portion knew nothing about them. In a remarkably short time many learned them, & [were] able to read in "Sheldon's First Book" quite well. Now they're using "Hillards Third Reader," can spell well, study Geog. & arith. & are learning to write. The children can make figures rapidly and write upon slates legibly.
>
> The actuary of the Asson. has visited the day school twice & expressed himself well pleased with the proficiency they had made.
>
> We have a flourishing & a very interesting Sabbath School in operation numbering between 50 & 60 members who seem to take great delight in attending it. Two thirds of them read in the Testament & answer questions therefrom with readiness.
>
> They take great delight in perusing the S[abbath] S[chool] papers that have been sent them from this school & by others in the city . . . I have distributed them once a month but having now nearly disposed of my stock, unless I can obtain a fresh supply I shall be unable to gratify them with them very much longer. . . .
>
> We are now building a schoolhouse 34 by 24 ft., which is expected to be completed by the first of Oct. It is of wood &

is being fitted up as comfortably and as nicely as other school-houses. It will probably cost a little [over] $400.00. We've already paid over $300 & $200 of this sum were furnished us by our Hartford friends & sympathizers. The recipients know not how to fully express their gratitude for this munificent gift. They are all just beginning life as it were for many of them were made free by the Emancipation Act—for which they revere the name of "Abraham Lincoln." But they are industrious, & hopeful of the future, their interest in the school is unabated & many of them deny themselves in order to sustain it. . . .

I have now given a sketch of my work South, which I hope may be approved, & for want of time I close.[59]

Not content with the basic curriculum, Rebecca added other subjects to her workload: "Every Friday P.M. the girls bring sewing & some of them sew very neatly."[60] She also added public speaking and music, with an eye to the school's annual exhibition. In May 1867, she had preparations under way:

I've copied off two dialogues for them one in which five will take part & the other for two girls only. There are 30 learning pieces, then I'm also learning them some new pieces to sing. They've got "Auld Lang Syne," "Dare & Do," & "Stars & Stripes" so that they can sing them well, & they've only been practicing them about two weeks. Whatever they like they soon learn & it's just the same with their lessons.[61]

At the end of the following school year, she was again proud of her students:

I presume you would like to know how our exhibition has passed off . . . it is said to have been the best we've yet had. The children all did remarkably well & enjoyed it greatly. The house was filled & the exercises began at 8 [o'clock], closing at about 20 min. to ten. . . . After the speaking was over I gave a general invitation to the refreshment table while I with the assistance of two or three others, distributed some cakes, candies, & [ice] cream among all the children that attend school. I have 42 this month & almost all of them were present. I think about thirty of them spoke."[62]

Two teachers from nearby Baltimore Association schools came to help sell refreshments, adding forty dollars to the school fund.

Along with teaching and writing reports to her sponsoring organizations and keeping in touch with friends and family by letter, Rebecca had another responsibility, which she mentioned in her talk in Hartford: to build a schoolhouse. The Freedmen's Bureau and the Baltimore Association made it clear from the beginning that their assistance was temporary. Participating communities were urged to build dedicated structures so that the schools would become local fixtures, and eventually local blacks were to take over management.[63] It fell to the teacher to raise the necessary funds and expedite construction. In December 1866, her second year in Royal Oak, Rebecca began to plan for the work: "As far as building a school house is concerned, nothing has been done as yet. . . . Mr. Benson [the white carpenter/contractor] has it still under consideration . . . & just as soon as we can have any satisfaction about the matter I'm going to push it ahead."[64] Push she did. In December, she attended a meeting in the Royal Oak black church at which "$23 of the $25 or $30 [necessary] was subscribed towards having the lumber brought here from Baltimore. They seem to be quite active about the matter now, & I think they'll make an effort to go through with it with what aid you [in Hartford] can send us."[65]

The following February, the Hartford Freedmen's Aid Society placed a notice in the *Hartford Courant* announcing to "all who are interested" that "the colored people of this city" would hold a fair on February 11–12 in the hall over Talcott & Post's store, Main Street, "to aid in building a school-house for the use of Miss Rebecca Primus."[66] "The colored people" holding the fair were members of the Talcott Street Church. How did it come about that a white organization was advertising an event sponsored by African Americans? For one thing, the Society had sent Miss Rebecca Primus to her post and paid part of her salary. For another, by 1867 Mehitable Primus was a member of the Society Board along with Lucinda Saunders, wife of the wealthy tailor Prince Saunders. Here, in the view of hopeful blacks, was more evidence that the wall of prejudice was weakening.

The *Hartford Courant* article on the fair quoted Rebecca's announcement that it had raised two hundred dollars toward the cost of building her schoolhouse. The article continued:

> Miss Primus is a native of Hartford, and has during her short stay in Maryland proved herself worthy of the confidence and respect of all classes, and done credit to her race, and to her

native town, in the position which she has gained as a successful and respected teacher of the freedmen.[67]

Addie Brown's account of the fair, examined in the following chapter, emphasized the number of white elites who attended.[68]

The two hundred dollars was a godsend. "We shall have our school-house, built in a substantial and comfortable manner," Rebecca wrote, adding with evident satisfaction, "It will be a little larger than the white schoolhouse here."[69] With the money in hand, the work could go ahead. "I intend to superintend its erection etc. the trustees are very willing that I should."[70] To secure a lot on which to build, she first approached a local white landholder, who refused to sell:

> We could not [get] the piece of land we at first made applica-
> tion for although the owner gave every reason to believe that we
> should have it. He is a hard-headed old Negro-hating secessionist
> and looks like an angry bulldog in the face—which is his most
> pleasant facial appearance.[71]

Rebecca expressed her anger in fairly ladylike terms, but this was a setback. Charles Thomas saved the day by selling a parcel of his own land for the school, although "he would not have disposed of it for any other purpose upon any consideration."[72] Thomas also persuaded his former master to donate trees for the sills, incidentally demonstrating that he had managed to retain amicable relations with his onetime owner.[73] Additional trees for construction of the school were the gift of "southern rights men, which I think shows," Rebecca allowed, "that they have no real hostile feelings towards the col'd school, but are rather in favor of it."[74] Credit where credit is due.

Like most building projects, this one took longer and cost more than projected. Rebecca had intended for the schoolhouse to be completed by the time she went home for the summer in 1867, but that proved impossible. In April, after many delays, a load of lumber stripped from obsolete government buildings reached Royal Oak. "The Carpenter," Rebecca complained, "has been up . . . and finding there's not enough & that much of it has been ruined by rough handling, we have had to send for more & he can not commence work until it comes. It's a disappointment."[75] Her landlord stepped in once again.

Planning his trip to Baltimore as Royal Oak's representative at the state convention, Thomas volunteered to visit the offices of the Baltimore

Association while he was there and request that they send Rebecca money to buy the lumber locally.[76] On his return, he reported success. He and R. M. Janney, a member of the Baltimore Association Executive Committee, had applied to the Freedmen's Bureau on behalf of her school, and as a result by the end of May the builders had enough usable lumber to proceed with the work. The Bureau also agreed to provide desks for the classroom free of charge.[77] During the summer, while Rebecca was in Hartford, Charles Thomas acted as supervisor, once again showing his concern for the school and its teacher. In the fall, when Rebecca returned to Royal Oak, she found the job completed:

> Our schoolhouse is looking finely. I only wish you all could just take a peep into it, the desks are to be forwarded today or tomorrow . . . The Govt. [the Freedmen's Bureau] has taken the balance of our expenses upon itself & it will soon be entirely paid for. It is surrounded with a neat fence which has been whitewashed.[78]

The finished structure measured twenty-four by thirty-four by thirteen feet with two doors, three shuttered windows, and cypress shingle siding.[79] Rebecca organized a dedication ceremony with dignitaries from the Baltimore Association as speakers.[80] The *Hartford Evening Press*, perhaps with information forwarded to Mehitable, reported on the daylong festivities:

> [The school] was filled with the freedmen of Royal Oak and the region about there, and they testified their joy and gratitude over the matter by gifts on the spot, in aid of the school, to the amount of $100—a very large sum for them—and in their appreciation of Miss Primus by a vote that the establishment should be known hereafter as the Primus Institute.[81]

Rebecca passed along to her family a less formal accolade from Charles Thomas's uncle: "[I]f I should get up a dog fight, he said I would do well at it, for whatever I attempt everybody thinks it's all right. I can't vouch for this but I do say, that these people seem to aid me all they can whenever I call upon them."[82]

In the 1970s, historian David White located Rebecca's schoolhouse and learned that it had been in use until 1929.[83] In the 1990s, Farah Griffin, editor of the letters of Rebecca and Addie Brown, found it again.

She described a rectangular structure next to the graveyard with shingles of rotting bare wood. Inside was "an old woodstove and a very big old table on three legs," behind which, she speculated, Rebecca might have stood.[84] But in 1867, the pristine new schoolhouse was a source of satisfaction to the Yankee schoolmarm and the black citizens of Royal Oak. Among the thousands of teachers sharing her mission, Rebecca's success was just one of many, but it was no small thing.

Along with moments of triumph, Rebecca recorded incidents of racial injustice wherever she encountered them. She found particularly unsettling the unthinking cruelty toward blacks and the bitterness among whites over the end of slavery. Royal Oak, as she noted, was not far from the Lloyd plantation, where Frederick Douglass was raised. "[I]t was so bad a place for slaves in those days, that it has been named Georgia & still retains that name."[85] "Georgia" had become a byword for the most brutal manifestations of slavery.

Rebecca found most outrageous the fact that crimes against blacks often went unexamined and unpunished. She wrote of one that occurred in Easton, a nearby town:

> It seems a very respectable colored man who resided with his family there was on his way to church and en-route he was shot by a white rascal so that he fell a dead man immediately. The villain has not yet been caught, he is said to be skulking about in the woods sustained by his secesh sympathizers. He is well known and detectives are after him. . . . There are some very lawless fellows in these towns and there is nothing to bad for them to do to a colored person. I trust something like justice will be given to the black man one of these days, for some are persecuted almost as badly now as in the days of slavery.[86]

The experience of Julia Dickson, a black teacher stationed nearby in Trappe, Maryland, provided another instance of Southern attitudes.

> [Miss Dickson was] stoned by white children and repeatedly subjected to insults from white men. In passing her they have brushed by her so rudely she says "as to almost dislocate her shoulders" she says she tries to bear it patiently. I feel real sorry for her . . . the whites are very mean there I'm told. White children take col'd children's books from them & otherwise misuse and illtreat them.[87]

On her doctor's advice, Miss Dickson left her post for a "change of scenery on account of her nervousness."[88] Later that year she was reassigned to a more congenial location. Commenting on the whole episode, Rebecca uses an exclamation mark, rare in her correspondence: "Poor thing, she has [had] a serious time!"[89]

Whites resented the Freedmen's Bureau and its work, and in 1865 and 1866 they burned a dozen black schools in the vicinity of Royal Oak.[90] When Rebecca's supporters in Hartford expressed concern over the multiple cases of arson, her reply shows a degree of courage and reveals something of her religious views:

> I do not think the people ought to be alarmed for my safety here, it is very quiet all around me, and I feel as safe here as anywhere else. I do not apprehend danger. I hope they'll all lay aside their fears and feel that I am in the hands of the same Supreme Being that has the charge of us all everywhere.[91]

Her God was a loving if somewhat remote arbiter of justice who, we might guess, preferred Congregational hymns to shouts and spirituals; reasoned sermons to exhortation. Her faith was sustained: the Primus Institute was not attacked, although a year later the whites of Royal Oak held a meeting at which "the principal topic under discussion was the 'Nigger' of course and in the midst of one speaker's harangue he cried out, 'put down the Nigger schools.'"[92]

The antagonism toward schooling for blacks drew Rebecca's attention to an unusual housing arrangement for Harriet Hamilton, one of the white teachers from Hartford, who was assigned to a school in Washington, DC:

> I'm quite surprised to hear of Miss Hamilton's boarding with colored people, Mr. Thos. says if it was here the house would be stoned. I'm glad she enjoys her labor, the freed men, women etc. in Washington are [a] different class of people from those in this state I am told.[93]

She may have been surprised that a white woman would board with a black family, but more likely her comment concerned the willingness of blacks to take in a white boarder. She implies that in Washington, DC, at least some blacks were at ease in close contact with whites. Charles Thomas, born and raised on the Eastern Shore, knew how such an arrangement would be treated there. We learn of Rebecca's personal response to a similar case when her mother wrote that she had agreed to house a white woman in the Primus home:

> I hope that queer woman will be gone 'ere I come [home].
> Whose room does she occupy[?] Mrs. Saunders is so desirous
> of white society I don't see why she could not have made some
> arrangement to have accommodated her, instead of framing such
> an excuse and sending her to our house.

Rebecca found common ground with some whites, but when it came to living under the same roof, she recoiled. Her irritation at the thought of a white woman possibly sleeping in her bed was deflected onto Mrs. Saunders, who obviously shared Rebecca's reluctance to house a white person. Mehitable's tolerance exceeded that of her daughter as well as that of Lucinda Saunders.

Rebecca had her own brushes with racism, and her careful descriptions suggest that in sharing accounts of such experiences, blacks not only released some of the anger they could not directly address, but they also helped to inform others within their networks of instances of prejudice they might encounter. Rebecca's first account of such an occurrence was after her initial journey South. She only wrote of it a year later, when her mother and her sister Isabella were to meet her in Baltimore. Within her detailed travel instructions was a warning about seating on the Southern Railroad, the carrier south from Philadelphia to Baltimore:

> The conductor will tell you which cars to take . . . and if you
> find that he puts you in the smoking car and the door of the
> next car is locked, watch the opportunity and as soon as the door
> is unlocked get up and go into that car. For you are not obliged
> to sit in the smoking car. I did not occupy it either time. [94]

Responding to the not-yet-legalized Jim Crow segregation in the "cars," Rebecca chose a position between argument and acquiescence. Later on, a protracted instance of discrimination directed at her personally involved insult but again no physical harm. Her account began offhandedly:

> I had forgotten to tell you about the little difficulty I've had
> with this poor old secesh Postmaster here. It's all on account
> of the papers you've sent me and which he and his old jebusite

wife have taken the liberty to open. The Postmaster says he's had more trouble with the d--m niggers papers than with anyone's else. But I do not intend to trouble with them hereafter. I wrote a note to the Post Master at Easton to take the charge of all my papers and letters hereafter and he sent word that he would.[95]

The Royal Oak postmaster, Richard C. Lane, had invoked a defunct 1850 Maryland law meant to keep abolitionist literature from falling into the hands of slaves.[96] The law instructed postmasters to refuse to deliver a long list of "subversive" publications that included the *New York Tribune* and the *Christian Advocate*. Rebecca did not specify what papers Lane had impounded, but from time to time she mentioned receiving copies of the *Hartford Courant*; the *Independent*, a church journal edited by Henry Ward Beecher; and the *Communicator*, a Baltimore paper advocating equal rights for blacks. Lane was demanding a fine of twenty dollars in addition to the thirty-three cents postage he claimed was due. Martha, his wife, helped run the family store in which the post office was located and evidently played a part in this drama: the Jebusites, as one who read the Bible would know, were a Jerusalem-based tribe that had to be wiped out to make way for the Chosen People.[97]

Rebecca's solution again recalls her father's practice, avoiding confrontation but preserving her dignity. She refused to endanger her mission or herself by challenging white power, but neither would she bow to it by paying the fictitious fine. She instructed her correspondents to address her mail to nearby Easton, where Mr. Thomas, in another instance of his helpfulness, agreed to pick it up. Some months later, she wrote that Postmaster Lane had offered to deliver her mail. She refused. "These white people want all the respect shown them by the col'd people. I give what I receive and no more."[98]

Ever conscious of racial affronts, Rebecca also kept an eye out for advances. On the proposed Civil Rights Act of 1866, she wrote, "The Bill is excellent, only I hope the col'd people will not take the advantage of the privilege it prescribes." The bill overturned the Dred Scott decision by declaring that all persons born in this country were citizens, with rights to "contract, sue, take and dispose of property, bring actions and give evidence."[99] Under the law, agents of the Freedmen's Bureau were *required* to institute proceedings—at government expense—against anyone who violated the guaranteed rights.[100] Rebecca may have suspected that blacks seeking notoriety would institute trivial suits to redress real or imagined wrongs. In any case, President Andrew Johnson vetoed the bill, but Congress overrode in favor, buoying Rebecca's hopes:

> I'm glad there is so much sympathy manifested in behalf of the Col'd. man's Rights, and I hope the subject will continue to be agitated throughout the country by our smart intelligent col'd men as well as white, until these rights which are so unjustly withheld from us now, have been obtained.[101]

Rebecca the teacher specified *intelligent* men, black and white, as the proper spokesmen, but her remarks also contain a glancing reference to gender politics. She advocated equal rights for colored *men*. This could be seen as a generic use of the word if it were not for the complete absence of interest in women's rights in her letters. Anyone who kept abreast of current events as faithfully as Rebecca Primus did certainly knew of the women's rights movement that began in 1848 at Seneca Falls.[102] Her silence on the subject constitutes dismissal. She supported efforts to extend the franchise only to black males because her goal was racial equality. Some blacks, including Frederick Douglass, supported equal rights for women, while others like Rebecca concentrated on the single issue.

As dedicated as she was to racial justice and the importance of her literacy mission, Rebecca was occasionally homesick. Sitting in her room in the Thomas house on Saturday mornings writing to her family, she immersed herself in the society she knew best. She craved news of friends, family, social events, and local news. In spite of her earlier wish to leave Hartford, she missed its streets and parks and the Talcott Street Church. She exchanged letters on a regular basis with Nelson and Henrietta and other relatives and with her dear friend Addie Brown. When Nelson sent Leila to stay with his parents in Hartford, Rebecca wanted to know how the youngster got along and whether she had learned to walk. Learning that Nelson would not be able to come South with Mehitable and Isabella in December 1866, she enclosed money in a letter saying: "I am very sorry for I know he is disappointed, & if I had the money in hand I would defray all of his expenses. Will you please get me a nice little Turkey for him and send it on immediately that they can have it for their Christmas dinner."[103] She also sent money for her mother to order monogrammed silver spoons as gifts for Nelson and for Henrietta, who was newly married.

Another tie to home appears in references to a child about Leila's age, Thronieve (also called Sophronia) Bicinia, or Bicenter, who first appeared in

Rebecca's letter of October 18, 1868. Just returned to Royal Oak for the new school year, Rebecca sent her love to "little Doll." The child's origins and background are nowhere explained in the letters, but Holdridge and Mehitable adopted her, possibly as a companion for Leila. Nelson's daughter was certainly in Hartford for most of the period between March 1867 and spring 1868 and probably again afterward. Rebecca had become particularly fond of Thronieve, calling her "Dolly Dutton" after one of the midgets in P. T. Barnum's "Thumbiana & Lilliputian Opera Company."[104]

A sampling of comments invoking Hartford friends and relatives shows something of Rebecca's circle of relationships in Hartford.

> Remember me to Mr. Mars and Mr. Cross and all the [Sunday School] class . . . I was expecting to hear of Lucy's and Mrs. Snyder's death, they are out of their misery & I trust have gone to that Better land . . . I am glad to hear the Superintendent is endeavoring to make the [Sunday School] present a better appearance . . . Has Charles Mitchell got so that he can walk without his crutches? . . . Did Nelson tell you Henry Johnson expects to come on in May? . . . [I] heard from Gertrude [Plato] and Mr. Tines [Addie Brown's fiancé] . . . So Henrietta and her husband have attended church together once; Gert[rude Plato] alluded to [Henrietta] being out alone one Sabbath and also how very nice she looked . . . Is Benajah [Plato] going to return to Dr. Brown's? I suppose his education is now completed and I've no doubt he feels himself to be somebody of consequence now . . . I am real sorry for Mrs. Ward, Mrs. Cleggett's family have used her very meanly indeed . . . I suppose Aunt Bashy's [Bathsheba Champion] family are all well, the veranda must improve the look of the house much . . . remember me to Mrs. Mitchell and all the friends.[105]

As these examples hint, and as Nelson's letters confirm, not all the relationships among Hartford blacks were positive. When Rebecca's friends in Hartford were raising money to build her school, volunteers solicited "subscriptions" or contributions to the cause. One of the volunteers was Perry Davis, a deacon of the Zion Methodist Church, real estate owner, and certainly a member of the "respectable" class of blacks. Learning that he expected to be paid a portion of the money he raised for her school, Rebecca turned to mild sarcasm: "I thought Mr. Perry Davis had some strong motive by his exhibiting so much interest. You [Mother] should likewise demand a fee. Your service is worth quite as much as his."[106]

Although she spent much of her time writing and reading—sometimes aloud to the Thomases—Rebecca also entertained visitors, both local residents and fellow teachers. One of her most memorable guests, Josephine Booth, was born in Hartford but moved with her family to Springfield, Massachusetts, as a child.[107] Her father, Alfred Booth, was a physician, who may have moved in the expectation of attracting patients better able to pay for services. Josephine attended Springfield's Central High School, became a teacher, and like Rebecca traveled South to teach after the war.[108] For a time she conducted a school in Oxford, Maryland, sponsored by the Baltimore Association, and visited occasionally in Royal Oak. After one such visit, Rebecca wrote, "Mr. and Mrs. Thomas look upon her as a very peculiar being, he says he does not think her equal can be found and I think he's about right—they both like her very much."[109] In Baltimore, the general opinion was much the same: "They all see there's something to her although she's so odd."[110] Josephine provided amusing stories and highly quotable statements relayed in Rebecca's letters:

> She . . . makes a practice of asking every one to read that comes to the house Sundays and she says some are taken quite by surprise and don't know what to make of it—but she excuses none. . . . I judge the people think she's an enigma not easily solved. I guess some of their habits do not suit her any more than they do me.[111]

When a box of supplies mailed from Hartford did not arrive until long after it was expected, Josephine remarked, "You know it takes longer for these heavy bodies to move south of Mason & Dixon's line than it does north of it." Reporting this, Rebecca added, "She deems the whites here only half civilized."[112] Josephine Booth's remarks often seem to express Rebecca's opinions.

Along with sketches of individuals, Rebecca, like the other letter writers, provided unknown or forgotten details of everyday life. When she asked whether her mother had put the hens to roost, we remember that nineteenth-century city dwellers retained rural ways; when we read about Rebecca changing her dress in mid-April, we recognize a custom now almost unimaginable:

> I have attired myself in a calico dress this A.M. it being the first that I've worn since Dec. I tell Mrs. Thomas it seems good to

put on a clean, whole dress once more, I've worn my woolen one all winter and I can tell you it's about thread bear now and full of dust & dirt.[113]

Note the phrase "thread bear" and the fact that even the daughter of a dressmaker owned just one everyday winter garment. Another revelation: when a box from home brought pies that had become moldy for lack of not-yet-invented refrigeration, Rebecca simply cut off the mold and warmed them in the oven.[114] In another letter, she reminds us of the complications of nineteenth-century banking: "I could not get my note cashed in Balto because none were acquainted with the bank in New York on which it is made. I shall therefore enclose it in this having endorse[d] it, & will you please get it cashed in Hartf'd."[115] Thanks to Andrew Jackson, the United States had no central bank.

Rebecca knew from the beginning that her mission was not a permanent assignment. Once the new schoolhouses were in place, the teachers would return North, and local black communities were expected to support the schools. Accordingly, by 1869, the Federal Freedmen's Bureau redirected its dwindling education resources to training black teachers. The Hartford Freedmen's Aid Society formally dissolved itself on the first of June of that year, and the Baltimore Association found it increasingly difficult to raise funds. Overall, as the decade wound down and Reconstruction unraveled, public attention moved away from the needs of the newly freed. In her last letter, July 3, 1869, Rebecca wrote at length about her school's annual exhibition and in passing remarked that her "brain and hands [were] full in closing up our affairs." That is her only comment on the fact that she would shortly leave Royal Oak for the last time.[116] Today's reader of her letters can wish that she had written of her feelings at leaving, her thoughts about her own future and that of the Primus Institute, but all we know for certain is that in July 1869 her great adventure—and her home weeklies—came to an end.

As a coda to her departure, Charles Thomas sent a letter to Mehitable expressing his great admiration for her daughter. He thanked "Mrs. Primus" for arranging the Fair that raised two hundred dollars toward the cost of Rebecca's school and its teacher:

The lady-like deportment, sterling ability, and real personal worth of your highly esteemed daughter, late in charge of our flourishing school, has been highly commended by all classes, and has been particularly spoken of by our white friends, and she has left us with many deep regrets.

Wishing you much and continued success in your future life, and many years yet to live,

> I beg leave to subscribe myself
> Your humble servant,
> Charles Thomas[117]

If Rebecca had taught Charles Thomas to read and write, she had done an outstanding job. Even if he had only dictated its contents, he shows a decided flair for language.

How did Mehitable react to the letter? Did she read anything into his high opinion of Rebecca's "sterling qualities"? What did Rebecca say about it? About him? At this point, we can assume only that Rebecca was satisfied with the work she had done in Royal Oak, very likely sorry it was over, and at the same time happy to return to familiar surroundings: home, family, church, and friends. Her next mission was to find her place in community life.

8

Addie Brown

The Working Girl in Hartford

Dearest friend & only Sister . . . you say you put my picture under your pillow I wish I had the pleasure laying along side of you. . . . Dear Sister I am very much delighted to hear you say that you like Mr. Tines if I should marry him I hope to have some pleas[ure] and comfort for he likes you very much.[1]

The most striking revelation of Addie Brown's letters is the intense and loving friendship she shared with Rebecca Primus, a friendship we know of only because Rebecca saved those letters. Not named in the census, not listed in the city directory or any other local record, Addie Brown herself would have been lost to history without them. In all, Rebecca saved one hundred and twenty postings over a nine-year period.

Addie came to Hartford sometime in the 1850s, and by 1859 she and Rebecca were intimate friends, exchanging letters even when they were both in Hartford. In 1865, when Rebecca left on her mission South, as it was called, Addie was devastated. A letter from Henrietta to Rebecca written a week later describes an inconsolable Addie, whose gentleman friend brought her home early in the evening because she could not stop crying over Rebecca's departure.[2] Addie's letters, which began in 1859, were half of a conversation with Rebecca, at first entirely dominated by the ups and downs of the intense relationship they shared. As she became accustomed to Rebecca's absence, Addie wrote more about her own life in Hartford, describing her days as a domestic worker, the struggle against her employers'

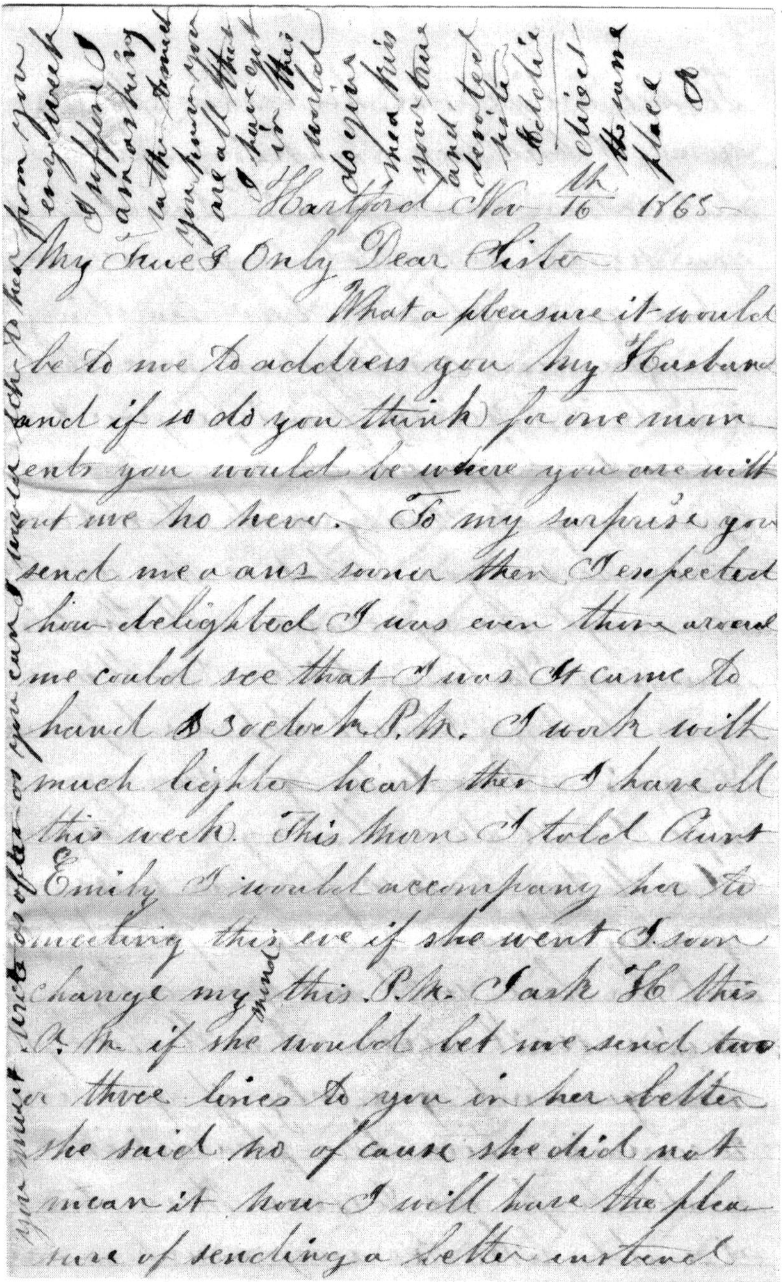

FIGURE 8.1. Sample page of an Addie Brown letter to Rebecca Primus. *Credit:* The Connecticut Historical Society.

unending demands, and her worries over money. Chronicling her days, she wove in vignettes of Hartford residents black and white, with observations on social gatherings, major political events, concerts, plays, lectures, and a series of young men who courted her. By 1866, when she wrote the sentences quoted above, Addie knew that her own future welfare hinged on marriage to a man.[3]

Her views of people and events add dimension and spice to the picture of daily life in the city in the 1860s. When Nelson and Rebecca wrote about Hartford, both were elsewhere; Addie was *there*, reporting on her particular Hartford. In 1867, when the newsworthy fair raised money for Rebecca's school, Nelson sent three paintings to be sold, and afterward Rebecca rejoiced that the event netted two hundred dollars. But Addie Brown took us into the hall, commenting on the decorations, listing the women who presided at the refreshment tables, and telling which one made the best ice cream. She noted which night the "colored band" played and described Bathsheba Champion's stunning purple dress. She pointed with pride to the presence of the white pastor of the Fourth Congregational

FIGURE 8.2. Hartford's Main Street in the late 1860s, looking north from Central Row, showing tracks of the horse trolleys, with a mix of former homes converted to commercial use and newer structures built to accommodate business concerns and apartments. *Credit:* The Connecticut Historical Society.

Church and, as a small nudge to her friend, listed the admirers who saw her home each night.

Addie's colorful language enlivens her letters and offers a distinctive third voice to the Primus trio. Like Nelson, she wrote and spoke a more colloquial English than Rebecca's, and her grammar generally conforms to the characteristics of Black English. In that dialect, verbs and nouns follow a different though regular pattern of agreement ("they has") and tense ("I have neglect reading the Bible"), and the verb *to be* can be suppressed ("It a rather pretty church").[4] Often she wrote hurriedly, omitting or shortening words and jamming different subjects together. Sometimes at the beginning of her letters she tried to match Rebecca's proper English but soon reverted to her own freewheeling style. Like the other Primus writers, she made use of phrases and expressions no longer in use. When the veterans of Connecticut's black Twenty-ninth Regiment returned to Hartford, Addie wrote that they looked "hard enough" after a two-month journey from New Orleans.[5] To register her dislike of segregated seating, she wrote: "I am no *advocate* for white churches they have seats expressly for colored people and I do not like them."[6] Hurriedly closing a letter because of waning daylight, she blamed Raphael Sands's frugality: "You know Mr. Sands is very choice of his gas."[7] Explaining why a friend had put off writing a letter, Addie wrote that Selina "thought she would have plenty of time just like coloured people time."[8] An expression still in use, "colored people's time" refers to a disregard for the promptness demanded by industrialized society. In an early letter, lamenting her separation from Rebecca, Addie complained: "man appoint and God disappoint," a wittier version of the maxim "man proposes and God disposes."

Along with recording her version of the speech of the time, Addie's letters trace a gypsy-like existence that took her to cities in Pennsylvania, New York, and Connecticut. She spent at least some of her early years with an aunt in Philadelphia.[9] Visiting the city years later, she wrote that she "did not see but one or two that I was acquainted with in my childhood and they had forgotten me."[10] The only member of her immediate family she mentioned was her brother, Ally, who served in the Civil War and wrote to her occasionally.[11] She spent time with him when she was in New York, but they did not keep in touch when she returned to Hartford. When, why, or how Addie distanced herself from her family and what brought her to Hartford remains unknown. Nor do we know how she became acquainted with the Primuses. The apparent ease with which she was folded into the family circle suggests that she might have worked at the restaurant owned by Jeremiah Jacobs and Raphael Sands, brothers-in-law of Holdridge.[12] Her acceptance by the family reinforces the conclusion that Hartford's black middle class was by no means a closed society. In fact, Farah Griffin, editor of the two women's letters, refers to the "fluidity of class and the precarious nature of middle-class status in the African American community."[13]

For Addie, friendship with Rebecca established a reliable underpinning to her hand-to-mouth existence. For scholars, that friendship has been a revelation. According to Farah Griffin, "We cannot underestimate the historical significance of these documents."[14] Historian Karen Hansen concurs, stating that Addie's correspondence "fills a gap in the literature about African-American women of the nineteenth century."[15] The friendship of Addie Brown and Rebecca Primus replicates the highly sentimental same-sex relationships between white women described by Carroll Smith-Rosenberg and Lillian Faderman.[16] Addie expresses the same romantic ideals, the same longing, the same need for reassurance, and uses the same endearments as those found in letters of white middle-class young women in the nineteenth century.[17]

In the early years, Addie portrayed herself as heartsick whenever she and Rebecca were separated. In 1859, working in Waterbury she wrote: "My Loving Friend: I realy did not know what to make of your long silence. I come to conclusion that you had just forgotten me. I was more than please to received your long look[ed] for letter and at last it arrived."[18] Later, after visiting Rebecca in Hartford she wrote: "Dearest Dearest Rebecca my heart is almost broke I don't know that I ever spent such hours as I have my loving friend it goes harder with me now then it ever did."[19] In letter after letter, her affection spilled out: "You are the first Girl I ever love so . . . you are the last one . . . I can see you now casting those loving eyes at me if you was a man what would things come to? They would after come to something very quick what do you think?"[20] In another letter she wrote, "What a pleasure it would be to me to address you <u>My Husband</u>."[21] Perhaps her most heartfelt lament was written when Rebecca had been absent for some six months: "You have been more to me then a friend or sister. My Idol Sister God being the judge I do not and never did doubt your constancy or your affections. . . . have I ever ain't trust you . . . I wish that I could express my feelings to you."[22]

While Rebecca's letters have not been found, Addie's offer evidence that the attachment was mutual. In the quote above, she describes Rebecca casting "loving eyes" and often refers to idyllic times the two shared.[23] In one of the early letters, she answers expressions of doubt on Rebecca's part—an example of the "need for reassurance":

I'm now going to comply to your request you would like to know my feelings toward you . . . it seems strange that you should ask such a question did you think that I did not <u>love</u> you as much as I profess or what was it? . . . Rebecca there is one thing no one on the face of this earth that love any more than I do and you are the only that I love or ever try to love nobody will come between us . . .[24]

Studies of friendships between young white women show that this need typically gave rise to jealousy, which in fact surfaced when Addie casually flirted with Nelson. Rebecca's reaction called for a chastened declaration:

Dear Rebecca . . . , I shall not be as friendly with your brother as I have been I know you don't like it and I also understand another member of the family don't like it. You know I like your family very much and sometime like to [be] in there society very much but for the future I will treat him as I would any other young man acquaintance I hope you will forgive what I have pen here I did not do it to hurt your feelings in no way.[25]

It is not clear which family member objected—surely Holdridge or Mehitable in view of Addie's alarm—or why, but Addie had not only upset her dearest friend; she had also jeopardized her standing with the Primus family. Her apology reflects her dependence on both relationships.

As much as the friendship between Addie and Rebecca resembles those studied between white women, it differs with respect to age, class, and education. For the most part, the relationships previously studied were between white classmates who met at boarding school when the young women were in their early teens and both roughly the same age. In 1859, Rebecca was twenty-three years old and Addie eighteen. Moreover, young white girls at boarding schools would have shared similar backgrounds as members of middle-class or bourgeois families. Addie's lack of skills and her separation from her birth family situated her in the working class, while Rebecca as a teacher had professional standing and membership in a prominent, relatively comfortable middle-class family. Aware of these differences, Addie tried very hard to live up to the Primus standards. She became faithful in church attendance and pointedly wove into her letters references to books she was reading and news events she was following. Addie's struggle toward refinement points up the third difference between them: education. Addie, as Griffin notes, was intelligent and showed "intellectual proclivities," but her interests and writing style betray a sketchy educational background.[26]

In its general outlines, however, the Addie–Rebecca romance incorporated most of the elements, emotional and physical, found in the studies of white women. Addie's letters, especially in the early years, depict a sentimental and erotic connection. In one instance, she told of a dream in which "I was seting on your lap with my head on your bosom other things connected with it," and in still another, she called Rebecca by a private name, "I wish that we could sleep together this winter I would like it very much would you not Stella."[27] Addie occasionally refers to herself as *Aerthena* and Rebecca as *Stella*, possibly after characters in a book both had read.[28] She wished "that I could exchange pen and paper for a seat by your side and my head reclining on your soft bosom and having a pleasure chit chat with thee."[29]

In recent years, depictions of romantic female friendships as platonic attachments have been challenged as scholars reinterpret the sentimental language of Victorian writers.[30] The nineteenth-century assignment of men and women to separate "spheres" created gulfs between the sexes that led to the formation of confiding, nurturing bonds with others of the same sex. Scholar Axel Nissen expands on this analysis, arguing that under Victorian protocols, "[s]exual passion of any kind was ideally to be under rigid control at every stage of an individual's life, particularly outside of marriage. When everything is forbidden," he continues, "then in a sense, nothing is forbidden. Morality loses touch with the reality of people's daily lives."[31] Sexual passion, he concludes, did not disappear; instead eroticism found a home within romanticism, and in many cases mutual same-sex attraction found physical expression.[32] Karen Hansen noted the strong erotic component in Addie Brown's letters, particularly references to "bosom sex."[33] After spending the night with a fellow employee, a white girl, Addie wrote:

> If you think that is my bosom that captivated the girl that made her want to sleep with me she got sorely disappointed enjoying it for I had my back towards her all night and my night dress was button up so she could not get to my bosom. I shall try to keep you favorite one always for you. Should in my excitement forget you will pardon me <u>I know</u>.[34]

By this time Addie was fairly certain she was going to marry Joseph Tines, but she did not hesitate to sleep with the young white woman. The specific reference to her breasts confirms the physical aspect of her friendship with Rebecca. The mention of excitement and pardon in the final sentence implies familiarity with sexual satisfaction or at least arousal.

Attachments between young women did not preclude relationships with men, including marriage, and in general men did not appear to find them objectionable.[35] Because such relationships were also maintained between men, we might assume that at least some would have found women's friendships perfectly understandable. However, Addie relates two incidents in which men expressed reservations regarding her friendship with Rebecca. In 1862, before Rebecca left the city, Addie was living and working in the home of Henry Nott, a friend of Holdridge Primus, and wrote the following to Rebecca (also in Hartford): "Mrs. Nott wanted to know if you was not going to [stay] any more nights the ans[wer] I make I did not know. She think your father has prevent you from staying she has spoke of it several time."[36] While Elizabeth Nott had no objection to Rebecca spending the night in her house with Addie, evidently Holdridge Primus did, and as a result Rebecca stopped the visits. At that time to have a bed of one's own was reserved to the elite. Women (and men) routinely slept together in the same bed. When she boarded with the Sands family, Addie shared a bed with Henrietta Primus at one time and with Sarah Sands (daughter of Emily and Raphael) at another. Such arrangements did not always make for a good night's sleep. "Sarah is my bed fellow and awful one at that she is not satisfied at kicking me she grate her teeth it makes me very nervous."[37] Addie accepted sharing a bed as a customary practice.

What then did Holdridge find objectionable about his daughter spending the night with Addie at the Nott home? Was it that their sleeping together was dictated by choice rather than necessity? Was there in his view something suspect about the intimacy of the friendship between the two women? Or did he find it unseemly for his daughter to visit the servant of another middle-class family? All we know is that this highly visible aspect of the women's friendship disturbed him.

The second instance of a man taking exception to the friendship came shortly after Rebecca left Hartford in 1865. Addie was at the Primus home reading a letter the family had received from their absent daughter when the following occurred:

> Mr. Jones came up and wanted to [know] if it was a gentleman
> letter . . . [Mrs. Primus] said I thought as much of you if you
> was a gentleman she also said if either one of us was a gent

we would marry. I was quite surprise at the remark . . . Mr.
Jones . . . says when I found some one to love I will throw you
over my shoulder. . . . I told him never.[38]

Mr. Jones was Nelson's friend (Henry) who had moved to Boston with his
wife and daughter, but he often returned to Hartford to visit. While he made
light of Addie's relationship with Rebecca, Mehitable Primus defended it. In
fact, she answered the question Addie posed to Rebecca in an earlier letter:
"if you was a man what would things come to?" And yet Addie was surprised
by the older woman's remark. The exchange suggests that Mehitable Primus
saw nothing objectionable in the friendship, while Henry Jones viewed it
with amused condescension and a hint of mistrust. Mehitable may have
seen it as an outlet for affection and experimentation with sex, a phase
that preceded or accompanied interest in courtship and marriage. There is
also the possibility that the objections of both men may have been based
on suspicions of homoeroticism.

Although the intensity of her yearning lessened over the years, Addie
continued to miss her friend and longed to be with her, even as she came
to accept the fact that they would eventually follow separate paths. After
reading Rebecca's first enthusiastic letters from Baltimore, Addie wrote: "I
have been thinking if you did return home again I dont think you would
be contented you are rec[eiving] what you[r] soul have been thursting for
you never could get it here that is to be in a society of intelligence & inter-
lectual people I know that you injoy it."[39] Addie recognized the differences
between them and saw that Rebecca's work with the Freedmen's Bureau had
moved her into a world of men and women, black and white, who were as
dedicated to education and racial justice as she was—teachers who provided
the intellectual stimulation Rebecca had not found in Hartford. Addie surely
remembered that Rebecca had previously considered moving away. As she
accustomed herself to the fact that one aspect of their relationship was
over, Addie continued to confide in Rebecca through weekly letters, but
her principal concern shifted to her own search for security.

After rejecting a series of young men who had come courting, Addie
settled on Joseph Tines, a Philadelphian she had met in New York. Tines
worked as a waiter on the *Granite State,* a steamship that ran between
Hartford and New York. With Addie's encouragement, he met Rebecca and
exchanged letters with her—thus drawing him into the Primus network.
Whatever Joseph Tines's opinion may have been regarding the friendship
between the two women, he continued his campaign to alter it. Addie's

letters show her growing fondness for Tines as she came to see him as the partner with whom she would share the future. She shared this realization with her absent friend in the same way she shared other aspects of her life in Hartford.

Addie's observations of the Primus family dynamics make clear her admiration and respect for Rebecca's parents. She viewed them as life models. Her description of an exchange between Isabella and her mother shows Mehitable's methods and her authority—and Addie's interest in family matters. One day shortly after Rebecca's departure, Isabella (Bell) invited Addie to come home with her to read a letter the family had received from their absent member. Isabella evidently asked her mother for the letter flippantly or brusquely, and Mehitable refused to give it to her. Stung, Isabella went quietly into another room. Addie had not heard the exchange but quickly realized that something was wrong, "for [Mrs. Primus] always wanted me to read her letters."[40] When Mehitable offered the letter to Addie, she refused at first to take it, thinking she may have been at fault, but she was told that Isabella had spoken impudently and the incident was at an end. Except that Mehitable had made clear her position with regard to disrespectful daughters. Generally in Addie's letters, Mehitable is portrayed as kindly, helpful, and motherly, but she had firm limits.

Holdridge, on the other hand, remains somewhat remote, although Addie provides a few glimpses of him. When Nelson's daughter Leila was in Hartford, Addie wrote, "I see your father seems to think a great deal of her."[41] When Mehitable and Isabella were overdue returning from their visit to Rebecca in Baltimore, Addie stirred up a minor tempest. "I saw your father over to the depot last night," she wrote, "I suppose he was expecting your mother and Bell they have not arrived yet."[42] It was early January 1866: imagine Holdridge Primus stamping his feet to keep warm as he looked up the tracks, snowflakes dotting the shoulders of his good black overcoat, probably tailored by William Saunders years before. Mehitable and Isabella had stopped in Philadelphia to see relatives. Five days later, Addie observed, "I suppose your mother is return by this time. Mr. Primus expect them this eve."[43] Had she seen him again on the platform, waiting for the train that would bring back the wife and daughter who now made up his immediate family? Nelson was in Boston; Henrietta was not living at home. Rebecca, reading Addie's earlier letter, wrote to Mehitable, "Why did you not write to Father again seeing you continued your stay. I guess he thought you had gone for the winter surely."[44] These quick sketches outline a grandfather, husband, and father rather than a grocery store porter, but offer no revealing anecdotes. Addie was in awe of Holdridge and Mehitable: they were the parents she would have wished for.

One of the sidelights of her connection with the family was getting to know Rebecca's two sisters, so that her letters offer insights into their personalities. When she shared a room with Henrietta in the home of Raphael Sands, Addie wrote of paying "Aunt" Emily (Mehitable's sister) $2.00 a week for board, while Henrietta paid $2.50. This pleased Addie, but it raises questions: Why did Henrietta not live in her own family home, which was on the same block? And why did Emily Sands charge her niece fifty cents a week more than she did Addie Brown, who was at best fictive kin?

Note first that if Henrietta had lived at home, she would have paid board, because household members of working age were expected to contribute to the family income.[45] In another letter, Rebecca enclosed money to pay Isabella's board.[46] As for why Henrietta did not live at home, recall that as early as the age of twelve she boarded out with a white family in town as a servant and continued to do so through her teen years.[47] Henrietta had become accustomed to living away from home, and this removal from the daily life of her family over a period of years appears to have created a certain distance and some resentment. Rebecca never, so far as is known, went out to service. During the time Addie roomed with Henrietta, she learned that "she wishes she could have the mind some folks have"—that Henrietta believed her own education was inadequate. As Addie described her, Henrietta felt overshadowed by Rebecca.[48] The two sisters exchanged letters, but they were not close. When Henrietta married Joseph Custis, Rebecca only learned of it after the fact. As for why Emily Sands charged Henrietta a higher board bill, it might have been because Addie made herself particularly agreeable, while Henrietta did not feel obliged to ingratiate herself to her aunt. On one occasion, after clearing up a minor misunderstanding, Addie wrote that Emily Sands "ought to know by this time that I think a great [deal] of her we are good friends now I shall try and keep so for the future."[49]

Addie was mindful of her need for a support network, because whatever her reasons for cutting off contact with her own family, she had in a sense orphaned herself and consequently walked an economic tightrope from one job to the next. Her employment history is a sobering look at the prospects of a black unattached, unskilled woman of the time. In the letters we follow her through a succession of jobs, always looking for less taxing work, less stressful surroundings, better wages. Between 1859 and 1867, she worked for fourteen different employers that we know of and lived at eight different addresses in Waterbury, New York City, Hartford, and Farmington, Connecticut.

In 1859, she was employed by a Mr. and Mrs. Games in Waterbury. This was the Mr. Games who wanted to kiss her.[50] Shortly afterward, she turned down the offer to continue in that household. She returned to Hartford to be near Rebecca and possibly to get away from Mr. Games. She worked briefly for a Mrs. Kellogg in Hartford, but by 1861 she was in New York City, where she lived with and worked for the extended family of John H. Jackson, who owned an "eating house" not far from his home in what is now Greenwich Village.[51] The Jackson household numbered sixteen in all, including an "Aunt Chatty" (Charity), a young woman, possibly a cousin, named Selina, and for a time Addie's brother, Ally. Addie does not mention when he left, or how things stood between them at the time, but three years later Ally wrote asking her to come to New York for Thanksgiving so as to "have us all together" once more [because] Selina [one of the Jacksons] was to marry in the spring. Addie did not go to New York and did not mention Ally again in her letters to Rebecca.

Her duties in the Jackson household included caring for numerous children, tending the sick, sewing, cleaning, and running errands. She complained that she was not always paid, but at the same time she referred to Mr. and Mrs. Jackson as *Father* and *Mother*, hinting at a blood relationship.[52] Whether or not she was related to the Jacksons, Addie was in their home as a paid servant, although her privileges included traveling to visit Rebecca occasionally in Hartford and entertaining Rebecca's sister Isabella in the Jackson home. Isabella's welcome there illustrates the openness of black networks. Nothing in the letters indicates that the Jacksons were acquainted with or related to the Primuses, yet they entertained Isabella as a guest. When she and Addie visited the Barnum Museum and other attractions in the city, various Jacksons went along. During Isabella's visit, "Aunt Chatty" wrote a letter to Rebecca, whom she had not met, after learning that Rebecca inquired after her in a letter to Addie.

In spite of the Jacksons' amiability, Addie complained of the amount of work as well as the uncertainty of payment. By September 1862, she was back to Hartford, where she stayed for the next five years, working to sharpen her skills and trying to find a balance between employer demands and her own physical limits. Her most agreeable work experience was an all-too-brief stint at Smith's Dye House, a nineteenth-century forerunner of today's dry cleaning establishments.[53] Addie wrote, "[T]hey set me to put numbers on things it took a hour, I done it so well I had to do it again today." Mr. Smith called her Miss Brown and "seem quite please with my work. This P.M. I have been working on blankets."[54] A week later, she was ecstatic:

> I get along very nicely to the Dye House I was sewing nearly all day yesterday and all this morn we was paid last night I rece[ived] $19.00 you don't know how please I felt Dear sister just look back $4.00 per month what a jump up I did not walk up.[55]

Nineteen dollars a month was a definite "jump up." She was making roughly $4.75 per week. Paying Emily Sands $2.00 a week for room and board, she cleared $11.00 a month—roughly $2.75 per week. In 1860, the *weekly* wage for female domestic workers with board included was $1.50, but in an earlier job Addie had been paid only $1.00 per week. For yet another comparison, the *daily* wage for unskilled white men at the time was $1.15, which amounted to $6.90 for a six-day week.[56]

Work at the dye house offered other advantages over domestic service. To have established work hours, reasonable assignments, and decent conditions was preferable to working in a family home, where she was on call day and night for an unlimited range of chores. That Mr. Smith called her *Miss* Brown and complimented her work makes Addie's news three weeks later all the more poignant:

> I am not at work at present we was discharged last eve no more work the business is dull with them I could cried when he told me I thought I was sure of work all winter. Rebecca don't you think my words are true that this is either a feast or a famine.[57]

Henrietta was let go at the same time and went out to service again. Addie turned to day work, sewing occasionally for white women but more often for Mehitable Primus. Much needlework was still done by hand in the 1860s: sewing machines were new, costly, and only beginning to appear in tailor shops and sewing "factories." As a seamstress, Addie made simple garments, turned collars, or assembled shirts and other items of clothing cut out by Mehitable or another dressmaker, for paper patterns were not yet in common use. Earlier, when she was in Waterbury, Addie had written, "I wish your Mother would consent to let me finish my trade with her if I could only know how to cut for my health at present will not allow me to take charge of a house but I could sew."[58] Although she wanted to improve her skills and her earning power, Addie's first priority was to make a living, which left little time for further training. In addition to paying poorly, sewing jobs did not afford lodging. Addie found the work tiring and what was worse, unpredictable.

She needed steady employment, and by February 1866 she had found it in the home of the Reverend John T. Huntington, professor of Greek Language and Literature at Trinity College. Finding that "Mrs H is rather a hard person to [get] along with," she predicted that she would not be happy there.[59] And sure enough, having been told that her wages would be $2.50 a week, Addie was paid only $2.00. "Rebecca," she wrote, "I have been working for nothing comparatively speaking now I have come to a decision stand that people shall pay me for my work I don't care colored or White."[60] Addie's style of writing made exclamation marks unnecessary. While she did not detail the ensuing confrontation, if such it was, with Professor Huntington, she wrote that "he never hesitate to give it to me." Still, even with the fifty-cents-a-week victory, Addie found the Huntington household unpleasant and the work exhausting. At half past seven one evening, she added to a letter she had started earlier:

> Dear Sister, I have just come from up stairs I have put the children to bed I believe I am done for the night. Do you know that I have five pairs of stairs to go up 20 times and sometime more[.] yesterday . . . I went up and down before breakfast six time you can judge for yourself there is a hundred and seven steps when it time for me to go to bed my limbs ache like the tooth ache I think I shall leave the second week April."[61]

That Addie left places of work she found too demanding or oppressive showed courage or perhaps recklessness, but her health may have been a factor. In her letters she complained frequently of headaches, sore back, and bone weariness. Depending on the disposition of the employer—or more often that of his wife—a live-in position could easily resemble bonded servitude. Some of Addie's complaints grew out of the racial climate of the day. She objected to the fact that "Mrs. H. wanted me to take Harry [child of the Huntingtons] to church I refuse doing so I am no advocate to take White Children out or to Church either."[62] In the same paragraph, she wrote that she had refused to "do the baby washing," a job that would have included soaking and scrubbing soiled diapers. Addie found it demeaning to appear in public as the nanny of a white child and similarly considered laundry work beneath her. She left the Huntingtons in mid-April and tried day work again. At the end of the month, she wrote:

> I have been out sewing for two weeks I guess sitting so steady is the cause of my pain yesterday I was sewing for Mrs. Mary Goodwin in High St. and I expect to go tomorrow and Friday and Saturday and the rest of the days to Mrs. Saunders. I don't think I could stand going out everyday."[63]

To sew for Mrs. Goodwin undoubtedly required reliable references and a degree of competence, which Addie could supply, having been tutored by Mehitabel Primus. The Goodwins were a large clan, descendants of one of Hartford's founding families. They held elite status as well as a great deal of prime local real estate through the nineteenth century and beyond.[64] The Saunders, as previously noted, enjoyed a prominent place in the black community. Like Mehitable Primus, Mrs. Saunders managed a sewing business, taking orders and assigning piecework to other women.

Once more Addie found day work taxing and uncertain, and in May 1866 she found a live-in job with another white family, the Crowells, where the work was less onerous and she was treated more kindly. After Thanksgiving dinner, she wrote, "Mr. Crowell says the turkey was cooked handsome. . . . Miss M was so please that I done so well that she gave me a silver dime on Saturday and a pair of gloves think her not kind."[65] She refers to Mrs. Crowell as "Miss M" or "Miss Margaret." Addie's duties at the Crowells' included cooking, a skill she had not previously mentioned. Mrs. Crowell's kindness extended to giving Addie tickets to a variety of public performances by visiting musicians, actors, and lecturers. Addie stayed with the Crowells for a full year and then left, having once again found a better job.

In May 1867, she "left Hartford Thursday 3 P.M. and arrived 6 o'clock" in Farmington, Connecticut.[66] The stagecoach must have made several stops along the way, for Farmington is just ten miles west of Hartford. Addie was to work at Miss Porter's, a boarding school for Young Ladies, daughters of well-do-do families. Founded in 1843, the school is still a prestigious presence in the town. Addie was hired as assistant to the school's cook, Raphael Sands—Holdridge Primus's brother-in-law and formerly joint proprietor of the Sands and Jacobs Saloon (restaurant) in Hartford. No doubt Sands had recommended her for the job, another example of the benefits of fictive kinship. Addie had prepared family meals at Crowell's and probably in other workplaces, but quantity cooking was new to her. "Some of the cooking utensils," she marveled, "are as large as I am."[67] After a week in Farmington, she wrote a brief sketch of what she had learned about Miss Porter's: "Saturday there is not school they do what they choose some go out riding and walking there is 17 pianos and their all going on Saturdays[.] in the winter they [have] tea [in the] evening in the week[.] summer evenings Miss Porter read to them."[68]

Miss Porter's school was a different and on the whole more agreeable environment than Addie had found in former jobs. Still, she spent most of her long days in a busy working kitchen that was as hot as her sleeping quarters were cold. There were, however, benefits. Miss Porter, seeing Addie's possibilities, gave her permission to use the school library. Miss Porter was a different and more kindly employer than any Addie had known. In January 1868, Addie wrote that she had been sick with headache and backache and had been well cared for:

> Miss Porter sent for the Dr. Sunday night and said I must keep very quiet and gave me some medicine they all was very kind to me. . . . Miss P[orter] came in three times in the day while I was sick and Miss Ran gave me my medicine. I am not intirely well yet. I am doing my work.[69]

And Miss Porter paid well. After four weeks, Addie was paid twelve dollars, an improvement over what she had made at Mrs. Crowell's.[70] While it was less than what she had earned at Smith's Dye House, at Miss Porter's she did not pay for board and room. The work at the school was interesting and in some ways rewarding, but again the physical toll made marriage to the smitten Mr. Tines ever more appealing. In these years of separation from Rebecca, Mr. Tines had become a constant in her life. During the spring she saved as much money as she could and took sewing jobs in her spare time to make more: "Your mother sent me three shirts to make."[71] Addie had decided to marry.

In the meantime, she gained competency in the kitchen and took over as head cook during Raphael Sands's absence in the summer of 1867. Realizing that she would continue to work after she married, Addie may have sought a skill that would pay more than domestic service or piecework sewing. By the following January (1868), her plans were in place, and she wrote that she expected to work sixteen more weeks before leaving.[72] Learning of her plans, Miss Porter offered to hire Addie and Joseph Tines as a couple to work at the school. Independent as always, Addie declined, evidently without consulting him: "I don't think Mr. Tines would and I am sure I would not [want to stay on as a couple]. They don't care to have me leave here. I would not stay under no consideration for I am tired already."[73] Her history of headaches and other physical ailments shows that her health was not as robust as her appetite for life.

Addie's grudging acceptance of the persistent Mr. Tines had changed to affection for "Josie," as she now called him. While she missed him in his absences, she never displayed the fervor she had shown toward Rebecca. This might indicate a lack of passion for Joseph Tines, but it could also reflect a reluctance to stress the fact that she was about to marry while Rebecca, by that time thirty-two, remained single. Addie no longer depended exclusively on her friend for affection and support, but the letters continued. As the wedding day approached, Addie confessed misgivings:

> Do not think Dear Rebecca when I say I have 16 weeks to stay that I am thinking of the change in life I expect for realy I have very serious thought and make me feel unhappy at times. I often wonder if everyone feels as I do. I realy think I should be little surprise to hear you thought of marrying too. Well you will have a nerve.[74]

Doubt is not unheard of among those about to marry. What is puzzling is the phrase "little surprise[d]"—a construction Addie uses elsewhere. In other contexts it means *more than a little*, as in "I injoy [sic] those doughnut very much I was little hungre when Bell brought them."[75] Did she think Rebecca had no intention of marrying, or perhaps that there was small chance of her having the opportunity? What is certain is that in 1868 Addie still shared her life and her inner thoughts with Rebecca.

Over the ten years her letters cover, Addie revealed a great deal about herself. In spite of her litany of complaints—long days, fatiguing duties, multiple aches and pains—she read biographies, novels, occasionally the Bible, often the *Hartford Courant*, the *Anglo-African*, and the *Independent*. She wrote not only to Rebecca but to other friends as well. She attended plays, debates, lectures, fairs, balls, banquets, taffy-pulls, and informal musical evenings. Her colorful comments bring alive the individuals with whom she came in contact, for the most part members of the black middle class. Her descriptions of people, places, and events show the social customs of the times seen through her eyes.

For Hartford's African Americans, the most important local event of 1865 was the return of the all-black Twenty-ninth and Thirty-first Regiments in November, when Addie and Henrietta Primus were working at Smith's Dye House. Henrietta, in one of her letters that were saved, dismissed some of the suggestions put forward for the troops' return:

> I must tell you what foolishness John Rodney wants when the 29 reg[iment] return of course the reception will be at the city Hall while they are eating [he wants] to have Colt Band to play for them[.] he is almost a fool if not quite he also wants 36 gallons of oysters for them he says that they want this Reg[iment] rec[eived] better than any has been rec[eived] yet."[76]

As it happened, John Rodney's plan was adopted. White Hartford rose to the occasion and cooperated with blacks to produce a gala welcome. The *Hartford Courant* reported, "The City Hall has been handsomely trimmed by the colored people, preparatory to its being used for the reception of the 29th regiment."[77] Nelson's flags may have been put to use again. Governor William A. Buckingham, local dignitaries, and Colt's Brass Band greeted the Twenty-ninth Regiment on its arrival, and the celebration included a feast for the veterans at City Hall, after which they were mustered out.[78] In a rare account of such an event by an African American civilian, Addie reported in a few packed paragraphs:

> Been nothing but excitement . . . colored people for once can say they have had the city. The 29 and 31 regiments arrived here this A.M, one at 8 and other at 11 o'clock they did look hard enough they have been coming from New Orleans two months who do you think has come to life Robison he look very thin and [happy?] to get home to his family they was telling they had nothing to eat for two days.

> I went up to meeting with Aunt Em every other person we met had niggur in his or her mouth. They was so mad to think the whites was compel to make a fuss over them. On our return home some of them said niggur to us Aunt Em ask them if that what they had for there supper. If they did could not of relish it.

The Buckingham riffle factory and the light gards receive them
the colored people [came] from all direction one of them walk
along hugging his lady in the st. Henrietta ask Mr. Smith if we
could go out to see them he said of course. We was gone from
9 to 12. I heard this P.M. that it was the fullest regiment that
has come home yet.[79]

Typically, Addie did not feel threatened, nor did she seem upset by the
racial insults. Having lived in Philadelphia and New York City, she was
perhaps inured to such outbursts. The "Robison" she mentioned may have
been Jacob Robinson, who had volunteered for the Twenty-ninth Regiment
and came home well enough to work for a living. Unfortunately, Addie
does not explain why she was surprised to see him. By 1870, Robinson
was married, with three young children, and working as a truck man. His
household included three boarders, possibly relatives of his wife. The overall
message of Addie's account is in the exultant summary "colored people for
once can say they have had the city."

The subject of race recurs in Addie's letters, sometimes out front,
sometimes as an undercurrent. In another of her more extended accounts of
a Hartford event, it is both. The fair to benefit Rebecca's school in February
1867 gave Addie material for a lengthy account. The event brought blacks
and whites together for a gathering reminiscent of the Anti-Slavery Society
reunion in Boston that Nelson had attended. Mehitable Primus and Lucinda
Saunders, the two black members of the Freedmen's Aid Society, organized
and coordinated the fair.[80] Addie wrote about it with evident pride and
included for Rebecca's consideration the names of the gentlemen who saw
her home each night:

Tuesday night we had the colored band it made it very lively
and great many would like to participate fantastic time. I will
tell you who was the table tenders doubtless you would like to
know. Misses Champion and Sands (Primus in-laws), Harden.
Mason. Hamer Bell [Primus] and Julia, Addie [Brown], O
yes Mrs. Andrew Mitchell. . . . Your aunt Mrs. C[hampion]
look very pretty indeed O a royal purple dress and a white
apron with a ruffle on and that was fluted she put some of us
in the shade that night. Mrs. C. Freeman [Charlotte, wife of
Alexander Freeman, a Prince Hall Mason] made the [ice] cream

> it was very good but the last two nights Mrs. Hammer [Hamer, wife of the Talcott Street Church pastor] made it and it excellent. . . . Mrs. F[reeman] tried to find fault but she could not get any one to agree with her. Eliza Smith and Miss Daniels up from Middletown. . . . Your mother must be tired out she was the most prominent person. Tuesday night Mr. Walter Mitchell took Addie home, Wednesday Charles Jackson and Thursday Mr. Daniel Davis."[81]

One assumes that Mr. Tines's boat was not docked in Hartford those nights.

Addie opens up Hartford's black community in ways that Nelson and Rebecca do not. Her narrow focus on particular incidents yields a detailed if subjective picture of daily life. One important component of her social life, typical of the age, was "calling"—described by one observer as "that endless trooping of women to one another's homes for social purposes."[82] Calling had definite uses in Edith Wharton's society, and it served some of the same purposes among African Americans in Hartford and Royal Oak. It was the most effective way of disseminating news of births, marriages, deaths, sickness, need, and of course gossip. But beyond the social component, for anyone seeking a job, or a better job, as Addie often was, calling was networking in the modern sense. Shortly after Smith's Dye House let her go, when she was doing piecework sewing, on a Sunday afternoon Addie wrote, "about 1 p.m. Bell [Primus] Bell Sands and I went out to make calls we made ten calls we intended to go up in five str[reets but] It began to snow and quite fast too," cutting short what might have been a communication marathon and no doubt a job search.[83]

Evening visits differed from daytime calls in that men were present and music played a prominent part. Both men and women played the guitar, many men also played the fiddle, and most women played piano. The Primus family piano figured in frequent informal gatherings:

> Friday Eve I spend quite pleasantly two of the girls from the shops came down to the [Sands'] house I took the liberty of taking them in No. 20 [the Primus home]. Several was in their while I was injoying the sweet notes there came a knock at the door who should it be but Eliza. I was about to ask her in when she told me she brought a lady to see me I look and it was Miss Ward from N[ew] H[aven].[84]

Addie was pleased and only mildly surprised by this last arrival. Miss Ward had not done anything unusual in coming by train from New Haven for a quick visit in Hartford. Before the automobile, the same overlapping rail lines that carried Rebecca from Hartford to Baltimore allowed friends in different locations to see one another fairly often.

As for other customs of the time, the letters of all three writers show that the main meal was at midday and that the evening meal was often *tea*. "[L]ast Monday P.M.," Addie wrote, "I spen[t] with your Mother & Bell I also staid to tea second time since you have been gone."[85] She and Mr. Tines were invited to tea when they visited Sarah Cummings, a friend in New Haven.[86] In Philadelphia, she reported taking tea with the Tines family.[87] Nelson described his satisfaction over sitting with all the family around the tea table during a visit to Hartford.[88] Rebecca wrote of returning to her hotel in Baltimore one evening at "just about tea time 7½ o'c[loc]k."[89] During the summer when Addie was acting cook at Miss Porter's school, she wrote of making "ice cream and biscuits for tea."[90] Preparing young ladies for their future responsibilities as homemakers, Miss Porter made sure they were familiar with tea service. A distinctly British custom had survived the Revolution and other hostilities as a class marker that gained widespread use, possibly because it bespoke refinement.

Along with social events, church activities and worship services played a large part in Addie's life. She seems not to have favored one denomination over the other, and indeed her religious impulse itself was intermittent. In Waterbury in 1859, pining for Rebecca, she wrote that she had "found a Friend this is Jesus."[91] She had attended a revival meeting with an unnamed pious young woman and was caught up in the spirit of the moment. Her zeal faded, possibly in the light of Rebecca's disdain for revivals. In Hartford a few years later, Addie wrote "I am afraid that you will be some disappointed on religion I don't feel as I use to and I have tried to do as you . . . my mind is far from it. Sometime I feel very unhappy I have also neglect reading the Bible regular."[92] After Rebecca left, Addie wrote: "I do my dear occupy your seat [in the Talcott Street Church] and . . . I also use your Hymn Book."[93] However, when Joseph Tines's boat was docked in Hartford, Addie attended services at the A.M.E. Zion church with him.

She frequently mentioned fairs and balls to raise money for benevolent purposes, and both black churches provided venues for lectures, speeches, and debates on civil rights and other topics. Addie attended an event at which "the debate was if the Black Man will have any rights that the white man [is] bound to respect."[94] The proposition uses the exact wording of Chief Justice Taney's decision in the Dred Scott case of 1859, in which he declared that blacks, being "intrinsically" inferior, were not citizens and did not have rights. Addie named the four debaters, at least three of them members of Hartford's black middle class: Isaac Cross, shoemaker, was a deacon of the Talcott Street Church, and with Holdridge Primus a member of the temperance society. Edwin Freeman, a laborer, had taught in the black schools during the 1850s and subsequently directed the Talcott Street Church choir. Albert Cleggett, a shoemaker, owned real estate and served on the church governing committee. Less easy to trace, Oliver Holden was a cook, according to the 1860 census. Addie wrote that a good crowd came out for the debate, including Mehitable Primus, Mrs. John Rodney, and other "prominent women." She added that "some of the young ladies carried on [and] they were spoken to twice."[95] Such homely details throughout Addie's letters create a sense of immediacy and establish the authenticity of the scenes she records. This particular incident illustrates the mixed uses of such programs. The young women who giggled and gossiped had come for social rather than educational purposes.

On another occasion, Addie reported on a lecture given at the AME Zion Church by a white man, Colonel Trimble, who had been

> raised in the South with all the prejudices of the southerners was against the colored race he did not think them fit for any thing but servitude or capable of any great mental or moral improvement. Since the war his opinion has changed he thinks they are the equal with the white he also spoke of Garnett Douglass and other distinguished men[.] the day would come when states would allow every man [to] vote he also said that [when that day came] he was going back to Tennessee and take two blackest men one on each arm and go up to the ballot line.[96]

Henry Highland Garnet, a popular and powerful speaker, was a supporter of abolition and black rights in the mode of Hosea Easton. Garnet eventually migrated to Liberia. Frederick Douglass was by far the best-known and most popular spokesman for African American rights.

In another letter, Addie wrote of a lecture by another white speaker, a Mr. Fairbanks, who spoke at both black churches, describing his sometimes successful attempts to free slaves from bondage before the war. For this offense, he had served a total of seventeen years in prison. Addie noted, "After he got through they took up a collection for him he received $16.00 and some cents which he seem to be very much please[d]."[97]

Her earliest comment specifically on race was in a letter from New York in 1861, when she was living and working at the Jackson home. Looking out the window one afternoon, she saw

> [a]cross the street from us a set of col[ored] people playing and dancing there is quite a mob gathered around them it is no wonder that our race is so degraded since Ive been in NY and get to thinking and see the actions of our people I wish that I did not belong to the race but it cant be help now so I will have to make the best of it."[98]

Addie's reaction again anticipates W. E. B. Du Bois's analysis of the twoness of being black and American. It also shows a pragmatic acceptance of reality. Wishing not to be black was a momentary response, and indeed the next sentence of her letter jumps to an entirely different subject.

Her letters also reveal opinions on class and echo the views of Rebecca and Nelson. Addie joined them in the belief that racial uplift depended on blacks achieving a measure of refinement, education, and respectability. She was bent on following that path herself. Whenever the opportunity arose, she attended plays, concerts, and lectures of various kinds, partly for the spectacle or the subject, but also because she was a social being, interested in seeing and being seen. Still, on one occasion she turned down an invitation to the theater. "Yesterday a.m. Mr. Asher ask me if I would go to Allyn Hall. I did not go for they has the minstrels."[99] Addie objected to whites in blackface portraying African Americans as buffoons, while Eldridge Asher, nephew of Holdridge Primus, had no such compunction. Later, at Miss Porter's School, she witnessed another incident that involved whites in blackface. At a Masquerade Ball for the students, one of the "young ladies" came costumed and presumably in blackface, as Topsy, the rough-edged, unlettered, independent black child who served as foil for Little Eva in *Uncle Tom's Cabin*. Topsy signified the evil effects of slavery on the enslaved but was popularized in stage versions of the story as evidence of the innate inferiority of African Americans. "Mr. Sands," Addie wrote, "was quite anger about [it and] was not going to let [his daughter] Sarah see them."[100] Addie did not offer her own opinion, but her earlier comment on the minstrels suggests that she let Raphael Sands's reaction stand for hers, just as Rebecca cited Josephine Booth's pithy pronouncements when they represented her own views.

Addie took note of how many blacks were in the audience when she attended public performances. "Mrs. Crowell gave me a ticket for the concert at the Allyn Hall on Friday so Bell and I went and was very much please we took a reserved seat. . . . It rained the eve and was not a great many there . . . : circle was full we was the only colored up there."[101] Addie took pride in being able to enjoy an evening's entertainment in a public hall on an equal basis with whites. On another such occasion, she wrote: "Went to Allyn Hall Friday night. Not a very full house quite a number of colored their."[102] When a new milliner's shop opened, Addie found Hartford's Main Street crowded with fashion-conscious women and observed, "I saw [a] few colored Ladies."[103] After a visit to the state prison in Wethersfield, she recorded the number of African Americans that in comparison to the number of whites would be quite extraordinary today: "I felt very sorry for the prisoners there was 184 out of that number was 7 colored."[104] Counting was and is a way to measure progress in the struggle for equality. In his 1993 autobiography, tennis champion Arthur Ashe explains, "Like many other blacks, when I find myself in a new public situation, I will count. I always count. I count the number of black and brown faces present."[105] Addie lacked the time, the energy, and the inclination to crusade for equal rights, but she was alert both to racial slights and to signs of advancement toward equality.

At Miss Porter's school, she socialized with white employees, although she wrote to Rebecca: "I am not very fond of White I can assure you."[106] Like Nelson and Rebecca, she reported racial slights. Besides the name-calling incident on the day the black regiments returned, she informed Rebecca of another experience when she visited a furniture-making subsidiary of Colt's arms enterprise. "In one of the rooms we were insulted," she wrote, and consequently, "I did not take any pleasure the Man that took us around had to speak to them."[107] She was visiting the shop where craftsmen from Austria made willow furniture, popular at the time. Colt had built a dike along the Connecticut River to protect his arms factory from the frequent spring floods and planted willow trees on it to prevent erosion. A canny entrepreneur, he imported workers to make use of willow branches as they were pruned. Evidently anxious to become Americans, the Willow workers had absorbed the prejudices of their new countrymen.

Addie chronicled news that interested her and that she knew would interest Rebecca: "Tomorrow there will be a debating at Talcott church . . . [C]olored ladies and gents had a ball at Talcot & Post [Hall] night before last. . . . Aunt Emily [Sands] gone up to the church, festival there, proceeds to aid the sick; . . . Thomas Sands & wife and I are invited to a candy pull to Mrs McQuire [Magira]. . . . Methodists had a festival last week two nights got to fighting and four was taken to the watch home. . . . Talcott St. Church give a Festival on Wednesday eve here. Music both sacred and secular reading and dialogue I think I shall go as you know I am very fond of music. . . . Mrs. Nott dead. Laid her in ice house."[108]

Her accounts center on members of middle-class black families, associates of the Primuses, and active promoters of community solidarity. Some of her accounts highlight customs long forgotten, as in her reference to Mrs. Nott dying in a time before embalming was common, but she also includes less flattering views of the community. While she did not mention drunkenness in connection with the fight at the Methodist fair, elsewhere she made clear the task of the black Temperance Society:

> I understand they had a ball Thanksgiving night. Lydia Jackson and her husband was there and both inebriated. Jim Nott was there and fell down three pairs of stairs and never hurt him he laid so quite that they suppose he was dead. Some of them afraid to go down to him. He ask for his umbrella and that his mother gave it to him and did not wish to [lose] it[.] Mr. Harris inform Bell and I of it as we was going home it really strang[e] that he don't kill himself it would break my heart if I had a dear friend like James Nott.[109]

James Nott had reason both to celebrate and to mourn. His father had died in 1864 and his mother followed in May 1866, leaving the family home and some three thousand dollars to James and his brother, Peter.

Addie wrote her last saved letter on February 5, 1868. She was to leave Miss Porter's school in April to marry Joseph Tines. Rebecca, certainly her first choice for bridesmaid, was in Royal Oak, so she chose a New Haven friend, Sarah Cummings, for that honor.[110] If the wedding went according to plan, it was held in Hartford at six in the evening, and the couple left at seven—presumably for Philadelphia, Mr. Tines's home city.[111] Addie had been well received by his parents, and his father intended to have a room built onto the family home for the couple.[112] The Tines' warm welcome pleased Addie so that in spite of her misgivings she looked forward to her marriage.[113] Her departure from Farmington was the beginning of a new life. She had found help, guidance, and friendship within the Primus circle, and her feelings would have been mixed at leaving, but she had achieved her goal of marrying a man who cared for her and who offered the companionship and support she needed.

EXPECTATIONS DEFERRED

9

Growth and Decline

The first-person revelations of Nelson and Addie Brown come to an end in 1868 and those of Rebecca in 1869: after that, the silence that surrounds the lives of "ordinary" people. The rest of the story depends on public records, accurate for the most part but lacking the particularity and the overtones of personal communication.

In 1868, Reconstruction had not yet entered its ultimate reversal, and the uneasy nation had not yet found a path to reunion. In Hartford, the slow, steady gains that fed expectations in the black community slowed and by 1880 faded away. In 1860, thirty-five blacks owned property. By 1870, the number dropped to twenty-eight; by 1880 to twenty-two. At the same time, the number of African Americans grew from 709 to 1280. Literacy, at 98 percent in 1860, by 1880 fell to 82 percent. The number of black households increased, but so did their average size. In 1860, the average black household counted five individuals; in 1880 it was seven, indicating the presence of boarders or second-generation members of a family unable to afford separate lodgings.[1]

Occupational opportunities changed only slightly and not for the better: between 1860 and 1880, the percentage of entrepreneurs and skilled workers fell by 1 percent, while the number of semi- and unskilled workers rose correspondingly.[2] The number of black professionals in Hartford never reached 1 full percent. The figure that rose markedly in those years, the number of African Americans in the city, brought its own problems.

This decline took place in the so-called Gilded Age—title of the book in which Mark Twain and Charles Dudley Warner satirized the glitter of Progress that came to characterize the waning years of the century. In the popular memory, the triumphs of the super-rich overrode the economic volatility and societal disruption that marked those times. Westward expansion, industrialization, and the golden spike that linked East and West by rail all seemed to promise expanding good times and continuing progress. In 1880, attempting to summarize developments of the year just past, the editors of Hartford's city directory were at a loss: "The changes taking place in cities during any year," they wrote, "are almost incredible."[3] In the half century between 1830 and 1880, Hartford grew from a narrow settlement facing the Connecticut River to a metropolis covering most of the eighteen square miles of the township. In the downtown area, four-story buildings edged out the family homes that had lined Main Street since colonial times. The railroad overtook the Connecticut River as the main carrier of travel and commerce so that the front entrance of the State House, facing the river, became its back door. The building itself was now dwarfed by a monstrous new Federal Post Office built in the former courtyard. Moreover, the State House lost its governmental function, shared with New Haven

FIGURE 9.1. By 1880 Connecticut had a new capitol building, and the former state house (shown here), as Hartford's City Hall, shared its former front yard—facing the river—with a grandiose Post Office. The side of the building that faced Main Street became its main entrance. *Credit:* The Connecticut Historical Society.

MAIN STREET, HARTFORD, NORTH FROM MULBERRY STREET, 1880

From a Photograph						*Collection of James B. Moore*

FIGURE 9.2. Main Street, 1880, had fewer of the old homes in place; the gaslights were gone. Notice the electric wires. *Credit:* Separated copy of a page from the publication *The Connecticut River Banking Company, 1825–1925, One Hundred Years of Service,* from the Hartford National Corporation Records in Archives and Special Collections at the Thomas J. Dodd Research Center, University of Connecticut Libraries.

since 1818. As of 1875, Hartford became the state's sole state capital. The new state house, a high Victorian Gothic edifice crowned with a Roman dome, stood at the edge of Bushnell Park on the former site of Trinity College, which in turn was building a resplendent Victorian Gothic campus in the city's South End. Hartford embraced, with mixed results, the ideal of the City Beautiful.

Change had various faces, but city fathers chose to emphasize the positive. They rejoiced that by 1884, electric streetlights replaced gas lamps. The best-known product of the industrial sector was Samuel Colt's revolver: his factory was said to be the world's largest individually owned plant.[4] After his death in 1862, his wife took over the business as it continued to expand. By 1880, it was joined by the Sharps Rifle Manufacturing Company; the Hartford Machine Screw Company; P. Jewell and Sons, supplier of industrial belts; and the Weed Company, producers of sewing machines—the product that changed the nature of home sewing. The new industries hired few blacks, and those only as janitors, drivers, or clerks—the latter a nebulous title that carried responsibility beyond that of a janitor or driver but no possibility of promotion within the company.

During the same fifty-year span, insurance became a trademark enterprise of the city, represented by Aetna, The Hartford, Phoenix, and Travelers—names that persisted into the next century and beyond.[5] Among the publishing houses, Case, Lockwood & Company dominated the field, thanks largely to its stellar client, Mark Twain, who moved to Hartford in 1871.[6] Celebrating his success, he built a showplace mansion mixing Gothic revival and Swiss Chalet with overtones of Mississippi steamboat. His neighbors in the district called Nook Farm were Calvin and Harriet Beecher Stowe; Charles Dudley Warner, author and editor-in-chief of the *Hartford Courant*; and Senator Francis Gillette, father of the actor-playwright William Gillette, who famously played Sherlock Holmes on stage. Thanks to the horse-drawn trolley, the residents of Nook Farm lived in sylvan surroundings but were not isolated from city life.[7]

As butler for his ornate showplace, Twain hired George Griffin, a former slave from Maryland who came one day to wash the mansion's many windows and stayed on in a position that lent him stature among whites and blacks. His colorful expressions and occasionally impertinent sense of humor charmed the author, while his adept management skills and thoughtful manner made him a favorite of the whole family.[8] Twain and Griffin came to Hartford under entirely different circumstances, but their relationship lasted even after both men left the city.[9]

In the fifty years since 1830, the city's total population grew fourfold from 9,789 to 42,551, and with the growth came other changes. By 1880, immigrants from abroad represented a quarter of the city's population. Lured by the promise of factory work, they overran the city's housing stock and strained municipal services. More than half of the migrants were Irish, the new despised minority. The Saint Patrick's Day riot in New York that attracted Nelson's attention in March 1867 provides an example of the volatile relations between the Irish and established whites—and the extent of the prejudice against the newcomers.

In the same fifty years, Hartford's black population experienced a steady if less spectacular growth, from 495 in 1830 to 1,280 in 1880—not quite threefold. In 1860, as the Civil War began, Hartford counted 32 Southern-born blacks. By 1880, there were 352, an elevenfold increase. As percentages of the black population, transplanted Southerners amounted to 5 percent in 1860 and 28 percent in 1880. The newcomers from the South found city life curious and sometimes intimidating. Most of the migrants were newly freed slaves who followed the pattern of the fugitives, traveling directly north. Those in Hartford came mostly from Virginia, Maryland, and Washington, DC. Some were looking for relatives, some were heading for Canada, and some had tried New York and found it too large and confusing. Some simply sought a new place to explore their freedom. They were themselves a mixture—skilled and unskilled, hardworking and indolent, savvy and rustic. Just as the Irish were not a comfortable fit in the white population, these black newcomers came with cultural, regional, and family backgrounds that had little application to life in a Northern city.

Their welcome in Hartford was mixed at best. Whites, including the elite abolitionists, rarely saw even the most educated, genteel blacks as equals. Trying to accommodate the influx of European immigrants, Hartford's city fathers associated all the newcomers with disorder and crime and saw them, black and white, as an added burden on the city's resources.[10] Hartford's established blacks, especially those striving for racial uplift, were scarcely more welcoming. In a study of Hartford blacks in the late 1800s, James A. Miller points to "turn-of-the-century tensions between settled Black Hartford residents and Southern migrants."[11] As we have seen, the writers of the Primus letters offered a sampling of responses to contact with the freedwomen who came North in 1866 and 1867. The Primus reactions suggest that members of the black middle class found Southern culture unrefined if not repellant and that they reacted to it variously. Mehitable Primus offered the Southerners training and help. Nelson dismissed them as hopeless. Rebecca gradually overcame her disapproval by concentrating on her mission to educate. To be sure, many African Americans in the city were descendants of slaves who, like Gad Asher, had served in the American Revolution, and most knew of the more recent struggles of fugitives like the Reverend Pennington. At the same time, with their Yankee background firmly in place, they feared that the unlettered, unskilled newly freed men and women would be seen as confirmation of the white belief that people of color were inferior—again the twoness cited by W. E. B. Du Bois.

Many years later, a white woman remembered her own impressions of the transplanted Southerners. Writing in 1928, Helen Post Chapman recalled a scene from her childhood, redolent of Southern life transported to a Hartford neighborhood in the 1880s:

[The houses] had about them all of the atmosphere of the South. There were willow trees in front under which they chopped their wood and in the evening they would bring out there [sic] musical instruments and play tunes and sing their spirituals. There were two angles from which these houses might have been viewed but mine was the viewpoint of youth and must be forgiven. These people interested me and pleased my childish fancy.[12]

The scene impressed her more deeply than she realized. Fifty years later, she still felt the need to apologize for having found it attractive. She had seen a place where work and leisure blended in unaccustomed harmony. Surely there were children playing or singing along with their parents. If it looked like Eden to little Helen Post, her own people saw the newcomers' neighborhood as a threat. They imprinted on their children the necessity of separation from such degraded ways. Nevertheless, as a curious and open-minded youngster, Helen stored away the memory of a harmonious scene that stayed with her, a furtive doubt as to the correctness of racism.

Another contemporary white response to the black newcomers was inadvertently recorded in the Hartford census returns for 1870 and 1880. In spite of its intended objectivity, in the column marked "color," the census provides clues to the relative status of blacks in Hartford, specifically in the assignment of B for black and M for mulatto. Although the records do not show that mulattoes in Hartford enjoyed any great advantage in property ownership or occupation, scholars agree that light skin has historically been favored by both blacks and whites.[13] At the same time, it is clear that Hartford's census enumerators were relatively casual about recording color or its variations. As an example, in 1860 Jeremiah Jacobs and his family were not marked as either black or mulatto in spite of the fact that the Jacobs family was widely known even among whites as African Americans with a long history in the city. Because the color column on the census form was left blank in the case of whites, this omission was most likely an oversight. There must have been others.

However, by 1880 the census offers a new perception. A substantial number of middle-class individuals previously recorded as "Black" were now designated "Mulatto." Those so transformed included Henry Champion, Isaac Cross, Edwin Freeman, Robert Gibbs, Andrew Mitchell, Ralph Mitchell, Isaac Scott, and Lloyd Seymour, along with their families. The Primus family was also seen with new eyes: in 1880, Holdridge and Mehitable became mulatto. Their daughter Isabella, by then married and living in a separate household, also acquired that distinction.

Of course, this assignment of color and status was and remains subjective. "Census marshals," historian James O. Horton points out, "were given few instructions to help them assign racial designation . . . Each census taker was likely to record the race of a person in accordance with his perception of the person's racial group."[14] Another variable: the enumerators of 1880 were not necessarily those of 1860. What may be significant is that in 1880, white Hartford census marshals found themselves listing 352 people of color whose origins, accents, and manners bespoke Southern ways. Twenty years earlier there had been only thirty-two such outliers. We can speculate that established middle-class African Americans were part of the known Hartford landscape, while the Southerners were migrants from an alien region, so that, without giving it much thought, the marshals rewarded those they knew by upgrading them to "Mulatto." Color was in the eye of the beholder.

Black and white newcomers, migrants and immigrants, had in common their alienation from the existing respective black and white societies. Socially, they had little encouragement to mingle with their corresponding groups, and in matters of religion they chose not to. Those from Ireland and Germany, and later from Italy, were for the most part Catholic and insisted on their own priests, rites, and parishes.[15] Other groups had equally firm preferences. By 1880, Hartford's proliferating houses of worship included three Roman Catholic churches, a synagogue, a Presbyterian church, and a Universalist Society.

Among blacks, something similar happened. The black migrants sought the reassurance of their familiar style of Baptist worship and in 1871 founded Hartford's third black church. The Rev. King T. Hayes writes that the "Union Baptist Church had its humble beginning . . . in a box car on Spruce Street in downtown Hartford. It is said that the members walked many miles home, swinging their lanterns in the night walking as far away as Wethersfield, Connecticut."[16] Hayes includes a photograph of the Erie Lackawanna railroad car in which the founding "migrants from Virginia" held services.[17] Like the protesters of 1819, they first formed a nondenominational society, Hope Chapel, which ultimately divided, forming the Union Baptist and the Shiloh Baptist churches. The fact that migrants wanted their own house of worship suggests a level of discomfort with the two existing black churches. They preferred to assemble with like-minded newcomers for social contact and familiar rites—including immersion. Their first place of worship indicates shared poverty as well as outsider status and shows that class, regional, and cultural differences were as clear to the newcomers as they were to the black and white Yankees. Their separation isolated them from the established black churches, and because churches functioned as social, educational, and political as well as religious centers, the division between established and newer residents became more pronounced.

At the same time, by 1880 the two original black churches were showing signs of stress. After the departure of the Reverend Pennington in 1848, the tenure of pastors at the Talcott Street Church was brief—two or three years for most, and at times no pastor was listed. In 1880, a "supply" preacher, that is, a seminary student not yet ordained, conducted services at the Talcott Street Church. Part of the difficulty was the requirement that Congregational ministers have seminary training and pass examination by an ecclesiastical council of ministers and lay delegates. Few African Americans could meet those standards. Pennington studied at Yale, but only as an auditor; he was not allowed to sit in the classroom with the white students—he had a desk in the hall—nor could he take books out of the library.[18] The AME Zion church also experienced difficulty from time to time in retaining its pastors.[19] Such transience reflected a variety of problems: difficulties within the congregations, an inability to provide adequate salaries, and the general condition of blacks in the city. King Hayes states that the Talcott Street Church had twenty-seven pastors between 1819 and 1900, and the AME Zion church had twenty-two from 1836 to 1900. The two older churches as well as the newer Baptist denominations survived to the present through mergers and renewed outreach.

The passage of time brought other changes. By 1880, a new generation was beginning to take up the work of church support and management. In 1880, the AME Zion Church listed twelve officers, of whom only three had been active in 1860: Robert Mason, Eldridge Asher, and W. B. Champion (son of Henry Champion). Continuity was more evident in the Talcott Street Church, where Holdridge Primus continued as treasurer, serving along with six members of the Church Society who had been active in 1860: James C. Patterson, O. O. Jackson, Isaac Cross, A. O. Cleggett, Ralph Mitchell, and E. C. Freeman. But the original group of activists was aging, and younger men and women would face the new challenges.

One more development in church management is open to different interpretations: while officers of both churches in earlier years were exclusively male, the appointment in 1870 of Rebecca Primus as assistant to the superintendent of the Talcott Street Church Sabbath School broke new ground. She left that post temporarily in 1873, and in her absence a

Mrs. A. Robinson replaced her. This was probably Angeline Robinson in the household of Isaac Cross, possibly his daughter-in-law. Rebecca returned to her post in 1881, and in the same year the AME Zion church named its first female officer, Bathsheba Champion (sister of Mehitable Primus), as treasurer of its Sunday School. Thus, two members of the Asher/Primus/Jacobs network became the first women to serve as officers of Hartford's original black churches. The women's movement may have penetrated Hartford's black society, or perhaps as racial barriers hardened, gender barriers softened.

Both external and internal forces contributed to the decline of black fortunes: the Panic of 1873, the aging of the original black leaders, the coming of migrants from the South, and the out-migration of many of the younger generation—Nelson Primus, Henry Jones, the Nott brothers, and others. The most damaging development, however, was the surge of virulent antiblack sentiment nationwide in the wake of the war. During Reconstruction, the passage of civil rights legislation and three constitutional amendments seemed to assure African Americans of citizenship, equality, and voting rights. But making those long-sought rights legal did not bring an end to race prejudice, nor did it guarantee black equality. Lynch mobs in the South enforced Jim Crow laws, while in the North an unwritten but no less effective distancing between the races took place. By the early twentieth century, according to historian Eric Foner, racism "had become more deeply embedded in the nation's culture and politics than at any time since the beginning of the antislavery crusade and perhaps in our entire history."[20]

If the coming of the freed people frayed the homogeneity of the black community and sharpened class distinctions, the resurgence of racism affected all African Americans. Isaac Scott, a middle-class homeowner in 1860, had worked as a mariner before the war. As outlined earlier, he saw action in four major battles, and afterward served in Texas. He returned to Hartford in October 1865 with numerous injuries and "general debility."[21] For a time he worked as a laborer, but by 1888, no longer a homeowner and unable to earn a living, he moved in with his son.

Opportunities that had enabled the elder Scott to buy a home and support his family were not available to the younger Scott. Even with the help of the father's pension, the family did not prosper. By 1916 when a government inspector came to the son's home to verify that Isaac Scott was still alive and in need, he found the veteran "washing clothes for his son's family."[22] When he died in 1919, his daughter-in-law wrote to the government pension office asking for help in paying his funeral expenses of $161.50:

I am poor and my Husband died just two month before his father and I don't know no way that I can pay it the post master said [Scott's pension check] had come but I had to writ to Washing[ton] and find out if I could receive it. I am his daughter in law he has lived with me 28 years and I have taken care of him when he has been sick he hasen saved any money he died July fifteenth.

Oblige
Mrs. Eva Scott
32 Martain Street[23]

Another life affected by the postwar changes was that of Rebecca's eccentric friend Josephine Booth. Raised in Hartford and educated in Springfield, she reportedly spoke three languages. She taught in Louisville, Baltimore, New York, and Brooklyn as well as in Oxford, Maryland, not far from Royal Oak. In the 1860s, Rebecca described her as independent and quirky. By the 1880s in Hartford, Josephine was known as a town character, collector of paper and rags, and "a remarkable specimen of street life," according to a feature column in the local paper.[24] She spent her days on the street collecting household discards for sale to a local dealer, averaging thirty to sixty cents a day. Rejecting all offers of charity, including her brother's attempts to provide for her, she lived alone in a cluttered apartment near the river. She died in 1894 at the age of fifty-two without explaining her reasons for living as she did.

What drove Josephine Booth from the ranks of the respectable middle class? A strong possibility is anger. When the funding for the Freedmen's Bureau schools ended, like Rebecca she returned to Hartford to find that Connecticut classrooms had been integrated, but only white teachers were hired. If the public school administration found it unthinkable to hire black teachers, Josephine found it unthinkable to quietly accept the loss of her chosen career. She turned her back on the whole society, certainly on the whites who were unable to accept even educated, informed blacks as fellow beings and also on the blacks who continued the futile struggle against the blank face of prejudice. Josephine acted on the anger that other African Americans were able to contain, at whatever cost.

In 1880, Holdridge and Mehitable still owned the house on Wadsworth Street, but in their sixties and still working, they took in boarders to meet expenses. Some of the other Primus relatives had not fared so well. Raphael

Sands, brother-in-law and neighbor, no longer owned his house and in fact was no longer in the area. Over the years, he held a succession of jobs in Hartford and elsewhere: restaurant proprietor, cook, baker, and barber. Born on one of the Cape Verde Islands, Sands had a variety of skills but somehow never lasted long in any position. He and his wife, Emily—Mehitable's sister—had moved to Farmington when Miss Porter hired him as cook at her school, and later they moved on to Saratoga Springs, New York, where Raphael's son, Thomas Sands Pennington, lived. In later years, Emily kept in touch with Mehitable, and Rebecca visited the family in "the Springs."

As the distance between black and white grew, the social gains of earlier years dwindled. When the Freedmen's Society disbanded, Mehitable and Lucinda Saunders no longer had contact with the elite whites who had previously welcomed them. The veterans of the Colored Regiments found themselves greatly outnumbered and minimally tolerated in the Connecticut National Guard after the war. In the pattern that characterized the founding of Hartford's first black churches and schools, the black veterans organized a separate post.[25] The Hartford unit of the Fifth Battalion, Colored, met in the Hartford Armory with Lloyd Seymour as captain and Charles S. Jackson, another middle-class veteran, as orderly and secretary. Seymour's son, L. Eugene, served as second lieutenant and probably assisted his father, whose disabilities were considerable. Members of the unit understood and respected the needs of a comrade with whom they had served.

The lives of other members of the middle class group show a mix of persistence, loss, and removal. The sons of Henry Nott left town, seeking opportunities elsewhere: Peter moved to Boston, where he occasionally saw Nelson; James later moved to Worcester, Massachusetts. Nelson's friend Benajah Plato finished his medical training and in 1870 was listed as a physician in Hartford. By 1880, he was employed as a clerk. A black doctor would have attracted no white patients, and Benajah's fellow blacks, nearly all in menial jobs, could ill afford professional medical care. Edwin Freeman, the former schoolteacher, by 1880 worked in an insurance office as clerk. He had left teaching years earlier because the salary was inadequate. The dead-end office job was no doubt better paying and more secure. Among the few women who owned property in 1860, Harriet Wells had died, and her daughter, Ann, succeeded her as householder, but not as property owner. George Camp, a property owner in 1860, had died, and in 1880 his widow, Mary, neither a householder nor a real estate owner, was a washerwoman living in the household of Charles Phillips, most likely a relative. Ezekiel Augustus, a laborer in 1860 who nevertheless owned property, had died, and in 1880 his widow Emeline no longer owned the home. She and her ninety-year-old mother, Nancy Morris, lived in a boarding house. Property ownership was hard to come by, and on the earnings of an elderly widow impossible to retain. For many, the sale or foreclosure of the family home mocked the successes of earlier years.

Placed against the upward arc of the city's fortunes in the last decades of the nineteenth century, the black losses seem doubly bitter. Able to vote but unable to gain election to office, free to buy real estate but unable to afford it, entitled to schooling for their children but helpless to shelter them from discrimination, blacks learned they could not break down white prejudice through their own efforts. In the words of historian Patrick Rael, "the experience of the Civil War and Reconstruction suggested that black leaders' analysis of prejudice had simply been wrong."[26] Years of costly bloody war had freed the slaves, but the shackles of race prejudice persisted and hardened.

The following chapter traces members of the Primus family through these same postwar decades that challenged their resilience, their beliefs, and the way of life that had seemed so promising in the antebellum years.

10

Loss and Persistence

When she headed home from Royal Oak for the last time in 1869, Rebecca Primus left behind a well-built schoolhouse and a population of proudly literate black townspeople on whose habits of dress, speech, and behavior she'd had small effect. No matter: they'd won her over, and she them. Her Royal Oak adventure was at an end. The Freedmen's Bureau had redirected its educational efforts and its funding to the training of black teachers; the Hartford Freedmen's Society had disbanded; and the Baltimore Association no longer commanded donations needed to sustain its many schools.

It was an easy walk from the Railroad Station to Wadsworth Street; her trunk would come a day or two later. In the absence of any firsthand account, her homecoming has to be imagined. Her mother was surely there, along with Isabella, now twenty-six and living at home, and Thronieve—the little adoptee Rebecca called Dolly Dutton. Nelson's daughter Leila, by then four years old, may have been there too. Unless it was Sunday, Holdridge was at work in the grocery store; Henrietta was in Farmington with her husband, Joseph Custis, at Miss Porter's in the positions Addie had refused for herself and Joseph Tines. Nelson was still in Boston. Addie was in Philadelphia, married. A new presence in the Primus household, Julia Heehee, was a thirty-year-old dressmaker born in Jamaica. Rebecca certainly knew her story, but to us she is known only through a listing in the 1870 census, which gives her race as white, making her another of the unknowns about the Primus family.

Settling in, Rebecca unpacked and no doubt enjoyed sleeping in her own bed again. Her Aunt Emily and Uncle Raphael Sands no longer lived down the block, but she would have visited other relatives and friends, telling about her work in Royal Oak and the building of the school, perhaps describing the curiosities of life in the South. As her contribution to the household, she joined Isabella in sewing with Mehitable. She would have kept in touch with some of the teachers she had met through the Baltimore Association, with Charles and Sarah Thomas, and certainly with Addie Brown Tines.

Looking around the city, she would have seen how postwar developments altered the face of Hartford, but the change that affected her personally, as it did Josephine Booth, was the integration of the public schools—though not the teaching staff. She knew before she left Royal Oak that her career was at an end, but within six months she suffered a loss she could not have foreseen. On the back of one of Addie's envelopes, preserved along with the letters, is a note penciled in Rebecca's hand: "Addie died at her residence, Philadelphia 7th Jany 1870 at 11 o ck am." When the news came, she must have gone to the letters and reread the rambling sentences, remembering. She would have written to Joseph Tines, sharing his grief. Two great losses: her dearest friend and her chosen profession.

Along with her parents, Rebecca remained a stalwart of the Talcott Street Church. To be named assistant principal of the Sunday School in 1871 was gratifying, but her great desire to teach came closest to fulfillment in conducting a Sunday School class for young men she called her "boys."[1] She would hardly have limited her sessions to simply reading the Bible. Surely her "boys" were expected to recite verses word for word, but they may also have been assigned papers explaining lessons contained in the stories of Adam and Eve, Cain and Abel, Noah's flood, and Jonah's whale. She may have followed the lead of the Rev. Pennington in discussing the importance of education and the need for racial justice. Life fell into a rhythm, but in 1872 it took a new turn.

The appearance in Hartford of her Royal Oak landlord, Charles Thomas, was presumably not a surprise to Rebecca. While he certainly explained to her and to the family how it was that he was no longer married to Sarah, no record has been found of his wife's death or of a divorce. Had Rebecca known when she left Royal Oak that he would follow her to Hartford? His arrival provides extra context to the amount of space she devoted to Charles in her letters, passing along his witticisms, his likes and dislikes; worrying when he was sick; and welcoming his skill and assistance in the construction of her schoolhouse. The two had struck up a friendship beyond their mutual interest in the school. The fact that on his arrival in Hartford Thomas boarded at the Primus home signals acceptance by the family, but his presence may have caused a sensation in the community in view of Rebecca's long-standing status as spinster schoolteacher—by then she was thirty-seven years old.

Surprisingly or not, the two married on March 25, 1873, and moved into a rented house on Wolcott Street, some five blocks from the Primus home.[2] If we now wonder about the fate of Sarah Thomas, surely the Primuses' neighbors and friends were curious at the time. What did the community think of this match? Were there rumors of scandal? If so, none have survived. All we know is that the prim schoolteacher and the genial Southern migrant willingly embarked on a life together.

Charles Thomas's removal from the Eastern Shore to Hartford was the reverse of Rebecca's journey in 1865 and involved a comparable adjustment. Having known Rebecca over a four-year period, he was aware of the differences he would encounter, but he was not without resources. His skills were in horse training, farming, carpentry, and management (of a sawmill). He had bought his own freedom and owned a piece of land. He was familiar with the geography of Baltimore and the politics of Royal Oak. Moreover, marrying Rebecca connected him to the Primus family networks and eased his entry into Hartford's black community. It may have helped him find work, first as a farmhand and later as a gardener on the Blue Hills property of Albert Day, an influential white landowner.[3] Years later, his obituary described him as "one of the most widely-known colored citizens of Hartford," mentioning his "large frame" and his gold-bowed glasses. Over time, his genial nature won him a place in the community, but in spite of his competencies and his connections, his skills did not translate well to life in an industrializing northern city.

Another family wedding took place around 1873. Isabella, youngest of the Primus offspring, married William B. Edwards, a young, Virginia-born migrant who clearly meant to become a part of the established black middle class. The outlines of his life suggest that he took Holdridge Primus as a model. Possibly born a slave, Edwards first appeared in Hartford in 1870, working as a coachman in a white household. He declared personal holdings of $100, an impressively large sum for a recent arrival. No record or letter tells how he met Isabella, and so far no information has been found about their wedding, including its date. At the time, "ordinary" people married with just a simple ceremony, but we might envision a gathering at the Primus home with Rebecca and Charles Thomas, Henrietta and Joseph Custis, Holdridge and Mehitable, and a thrilled six-year-old Thronieve Primus gathered to wish the newlyweds well. Nelson may have come from Boston for the event, since Isabella was the sibling to whom he was closest. If his portrait work was prospering, he may have brought Amoretta and Leila.

Unfortunately, in May 1873, around the time of Isabella's marriage and not long after his own, Charles Thomas sustained an injury that left him intermittently disabled for the rest of his life. The newspaper account of the incident stated that a white man threw a sharp stone that hit Thomas near his right temple and left "an ugly wound."[4] Years later, Thomas's obituary described the head wound as an accident, the result of a stone thrown presumably at someone else, with disastrous lifelong effects.[5] Recurring episodes of debility—whether mental or physical—cast Rebecca as more than partial breadwinner. She worked with her mother and Isabella, so that three of the Primus women were in the needle trade. Holdridge continued at the grocery store.

Family events continued to occupy the Primus clan through the 1870s. By 1875, in addition to Leila, Holdridge and Mehitable had another granddaughter: Nellie, the child of Isabella and William Edwards. In June of that year, Rebecca added a third grandchild, Ernest Primus Thomas.[6] To give birth for the first time at the age of thirty-nine is no longer considered high risk, but in the nineteenth century, childbirth at any age was a dangerous undertaking, doubly so for a woman in her late thirties. That the baby lived seemed a blessing. While his middle name memorialized his mother's line, his first name, Ernest, named a quality the infant might aspire to. In the practice of the time, Rebecca would have been confined to inactivity for as long as a month, so that Ernest's birth placed financial responsibility solely on Charles Thomas. Clearly in need, he sold his remaining piece of Royal Oak property that year. With no letters recording the baby's progress, the brief newspaper notice in February of the following year conveys the shock but not the full impact of Ernest's death at seven months, nineteen days. He died of pneumonia, to the unimaginable sorrow of his mother.[7]

In an unhappy coincidence, 1876 was a year of loss to the Boston branch as well. In July, two weeks after giving birth to a stillborn infant, Nelson's wife, Amoretta, died of peritonitis, an inflammation of the lining of the abdomen often associated with childbirth in the eighteenth and nineteenth centuries.[8] Leila, twelve years old, lost her mother as well as the prospect of a sibling. There is no account of church services or burial for the mother and child; no letter from Nelson tells us of his grief. As it happened, at this time his work was beginning to gain notice, and in 1876 he was again able to maintain a studio. Gratifying certainly, but hardly recompense for his loss.

Meanwhile, Charles Thomas, at least temporarily free from his recurring debility, found much-needed work, but in a distant city. A letter in the Primus Papers from "your loving Cousin Emma" in Philadelphia assures Rebecca her that her husband was "looking fine now he has got fix up nicely again he says he is doing a good business."[9] Emma was a daughter of Bathsheba (Mehitable's sister) Champion. She wrote that Charles Thomas was working at the Philadelphia Centennial Exhibition, a fair celebrating the past and the future of the country, running from May to December 1876.[10] Thomas's departure so soon after the baby's death points to urgent need, and it is possible that he found the job in the fair's Connecticut building through the Primus network. He left knowing that Rebecca was surrounded by family, and she must have encouraged him to go. Emma's phrasing hints that he had been unwell and that an unnamed difficulty, perhaps caused by the head wound, was in abeyance. In November, Rebecca and her mother traveled to Philadelphia to visit him.[11] They may have done so to reassure themselves that Charles Thomas was well and enjoying some success and maybe also to let him know that he was missed. Then, too, the Centennial Exposition itself was a notable event, celebrating the anniversary of the Declaration of Independence. This was the fair at which Nelson's first Boston mentor, Edward Mitchell Bannister, won a medal for his painting *Under the Oaks*, to the embarrassed surprise of the white judges. When the fair closed in December 1876, Thomas returned to Hartford and to the problem of finding work.

A year later, Nelson had good news for the family. He had found a new wife. It was the first marriage for Mary G. Wheeler, a thirty-five-year-old native of Nantucket who had been in Boston since 1860, working as a nurse for a wealthy family.[12] Her father, Henry T. Wheeler, a Quaker innkeeper on the island, had helped organize an antislavery reading room before the war.[13] Coming from an activist tradition, Mary Wheeler was remarkably unlike Amoretta, and in time she proved a distinct asset in Nelson's quest for recognition. Mary took an active interest in his art and used her public speaking skills to enhance his career. Her background as a nurse promised more reliable and higher-paid work than domestic service. If Leila was still unable to walk, Mary would have been an ideal stepmother. The new Nelson Primus family took up residence in Somerville, a suburb northwest of Boston.

The artist himself was gaining a reputation as a painter of landscapes and portraits. In January 1877, the *Hartford Daily Courant* noted that Mr. N. A. Primus had just finished a "life-size oil painting of the beautiful and accomplished little actress, Lizzie May Ulmer. It is pronounced by critics to be the finest painting ever seen in Boston." The fulsome article reminds readers that "the artist is the son of Mr. Holdridge Primus of this city."[14] The Connecticut Historical Society now owns the portrait, one of the dozen or so of his works so far identified (see Plate 1). In the 1880s, Nelson secured commissions for portraits of a number of prominent Bostonians, including Hugh O'Brien, the city's first Irish mayor; and William Wells Brown, the nationally known leader who had offered Nelson work as an agent for his book on black soldiers in the Civil War. Another reported client was the Reverend Phillips Brooks, rector of Trinity Church, best remembered as the author of the lyrics to the carol "O Little Town of Bethlehem." These three works have not been found, but at the time they added luster to the artist's reputation.

An unexpected find is a patent granted in 1883 to Nelson A. Primus of Somerville, Massachusetts.[15] His on-and-off relationship with carriage painting had evidently piqued his interest in carriages themselves, and in his design for an improved coupling for the shaft (thill) he reveals an interest in the working parts of a carriage as well as the designs that enhance its appearance. No evidence has been found that his addition of an india-rubber block to cushion the shaft head caught on among carriage makers, but it opens up another area of his interests.

One of the many reasons to regret the lack of Primus letters in these later years is the fact that the artist Charles Ethan Porter lived in Hartford around 1880, boarding for a time at 21 Wadsworth Street across the street from the Primus home. A reluctant specialist in still-life studies of flowers, fruits, and vegetables, Porter tried landscapes and other subjects, but his accomplished still-life work was so popular that it became his mainstay. As a neighbor, he would have become acquainted with Holdridge and Mehitable, and because Nelson came home from time to time, the two men surely met. In addition to his considerable talent, Porter had an advantage Nelson lacked: he had studied at the National Academy of Design in New York and later in Paris, where he arrived with letters of introduction from leading citizens, including Mark Twain.[16] While Porter maintained studios from time to time in New York and Hartford, by 1889 he was no longer able to survive on his earnings and returned to his parents' home in Rockville, Connecticut.[17] He struggled in his lifetime, but examples of Porter's work are collected and exhibited in art centers throughout the country today. His biographer attributes his failure to prosper in Hartford,

New York, and Rockville to race prejudice.[18] He and Nelson Primus had in common a lifelong dedication to art and the ultimate realization that their art would not support them. They would have welcomed the chance to compare experiences. Both men had imagined a different and better future that would allow black talent to find fulfillment. Both dared to step outside the safety of a life like that of Holdridge Primus on the strength of that hoped-for future.

In the 1880s, the event that most affected the family was not related to race or the economy. In April 1884, Holdridge suffered a stroke and died a few weeks later. We can imagine that Mehitable met her loss with dignity and that her daughters did their best to follow her example. Members of the Jacobs, Asher, and Primus families certainly visited, wrote, and offered condolences and assistance. Nelson, still in Boston, probably came home for the funeral. Holdridge Primus had been in the city since the 1830s, and after nearly fifty years as a porter in the Main Street store he was a familiar local figure. The city's newspapers devoted space to his memory and in their way eulogized him:

> The well-known colored man, Holdridge Primus, died at his residence on Wadsworth Street, yesterday afternoon, at the age of 69 years, after a month's illness, the effects of a paralytic stroke. . . . All the old residents of Hartford knew "Primus" as he was generally called. . . . He had a remarkable memory. . . . He was never known to use an order book, although he could read and write. He was a man who always kept his word and could always be depended upon. He was well known to most of the first-class families of the city, often waiting on table and doing similar duties at weddings and parties. . . . Everyone . . . would go to him when they wanted a girl, and he could always find one, but he would never recommend anyone whom he was not sure was suitable. During his illness dozens of persons called at Seyms & Co. to see him in regard to procuring help . . . He leaves a wife and four children. His son is a portrait painter in Boston, and has established quite a reputation for himself . . .[19]

Shortly afterward, Holdridge's longtime associates at the Talcott Street Church published the following announcement, at once a tribute to the man and a counter to the tone-deaf obituary:

In Memory of Holdridge Primus

At an adjourned meeting of the Talcott Street Congregational church society, last Wednesday evening, the following resolutions were passed:

Whereas: It has pleased an All wise Providence to remove from our midst our esteemed friend and fellow member, Holdridge Primus, late treasurer of this society: and

Whereas, The Faithful and intelligent devotion to the interests of this society which has characterized his relations with it for nearly fifty years, make it eminently proper that we give some expression of our feelings of appreciation of his services and regret for his loss; Therefore

Resolved, That by the death of Holdridge Primus, this society loses a most efficient and valued officer whose wise counsel, cheerful words, and inspiring energy will be sorely missed.

Resolved, that we extend our deepest sympathy to the bereaved family and friends of the deceased, hoping that even in the sorrow of their great affliction they may be in some sort consoled that the knowledge of his sterling qualities and the value of his great and disinterested services are properly appreciated.

E. C. Freeman
I. Cross
A. O. Cleggett[20]

The white-written obituary described him as a compliant, useful servant, noting without irony that those who inquired after him during his illness did so because they needed his expertise in "procuring help." His ability to read, his remarkable memory, and his utter dependability recommended him as outstanding—for a black man. His friends at the Talcott Street Church answered this racial arrogance by stating his dignity and worth as a family man and a faithful church member devoted "to the interests of this society." The three signers of the document were old friends and members of the group identified as middle class in 1860: Edwin C. Freeman, the former schoolteacher, and Isaac Cross and A. O. Cleggett, shoemakers.

Holdridge's estate included his father's small woodlot in Branford and notes on loans, one to his brother-in-law Jeremiah Asher, Mehitable's brother, for $213.16; and the other to his son-in-law Charles Thomas for $150. Mehitable inherited the Wadsworth Street house and contents. The amount of cash on hand after the settlement of bills was $43.69. Only by careful budgeting and judicious spending had he and his wife managed to live comfortably and maintain their middle-class standards over half a century. As an added tribute, their children, in their different lives, absorbed their parents' views and echoed their ways.

In the next generation, it was William Edwards, Isabella's husband, who most closely followed the example of his father-in-law. By 1880, Edwards owned a house at 24 Wadsworth Street, a few doors from the Primus home at Number 20. By 1880, he and Isabella had three daughters. According to the census, Isabella kept house, suggesting adherence to the ideal of the woman as homemaker and nurturer. At the same time, the city directory listed her as a dressmaker. She was doing as her mother had done: to the census enumerator, a white man, she gave her occupation as homemaker; for local consumption, indeed as notice to possible clients, she was a dressmaker. This may throw light on William Edwards's listings in the City Directory as a porter and in the census as a janitor. Much later, in 1920, he worked as a messenger for the Hartford Fire Insurance Company and served as sexton of the (white) Center Church. He had made friends with the white elite, as his father-in-law had, and with similar success.

Rebecca's life was less comfortable than Isabella's, although Charles Thomas did enjoy some success in Hartford. For the 1885–1886 session of the state legislature, he secured an appointment as doorman, charged with delivering notices to the lieutenant governor, who presided over the State Senate. A political plum, the job entailed Thomas's daily attendance in uniform. A newspaper account describes him announcing "a message from his excellency the governor" or from "a committee from the House" in a voice that proclaimed the "importance of the occasion."[21] Letters in the Primus Papers show that his attempts to find similar appointments in Washington did not succeed. In spite of his injury, his interest in politics continued. In 1888, he was elected vice president of the Colored Republican Club of Hartford, where he served along with members of the Mitchell, Freeman, Davis, and Jackson families.[22] In Hartford, he was "a familiar figure on the

streets and through his service at the Capitol was known all over the state."
And yet he and Rebecca lived in a succession of rented lodgings, and in
his final years he was unable to work at all.

Charles Thomas died in August 1891 of convulsions attributed to
the head wound that had affected his health for so many years. His funeral
was held at the Talcott Street Church, and his obituary included a brief
biography citing his origins as a slave, his marrying Rebecca Primus, and
his "service at the Capitol." The account concludes, "Having been long
without work he died destitute."

After his death, Rebecca moved to the family home on Wadsworth
Street, joining her mother and Thronieve, who by that time was in her late
twenties. Isabella and William Edwards and their daughters lived on the
same block. All four of the women sewed, in effect constituting a family
"shop." At one time this would have been a promising arrangement, but
the nature of the business had changed as Yankee ingenuity mechanized
the sewing trade. Indeed, by this time Mehitable herself owned a home
sewing machine, perhaps made by the Weed Manufacturing Company of
Hartford or by that of Isaac Singer, who was fast taking over a growing
market. Individual dressmakers like the Primus women found themselves in
competition with factories that turned out cheap ready-to-wear garments.
No letters tell how their business fared, but subsequent events do not indicate that it thrived.

In contrast to family losses and the general decline among blacks,
Nelson reached the high point of his Boston career in 1890, when he
brought to Hartford his mural-sized painting, *Christ before Pilate*, a work
acclaimed as a remarkable achievement. It was a copy. The original by
Mihaly Munckacsy, a Hungarian artist, was shown in New York, Boston,
and other cities around the country in 1886 and 1887.[23] In an imagined
courtroom scene, Pilate is seated on a raised platform. Christ stands before
him surrounded by more than thirty soldiers and spectators. In size and
scope alone, the work represented a challenge to Nelson's skill.[24] Estimates
of the size of the painting vary from eight by twelve feet to eighteen by
twenty-four feet.[25] Munckacsy's original received mixed reviews from critics,
but an enthusiastic public came in large numbers to see it. Nelson Primus,
inspired by the grand work, determined to make a copy, possibly with
Mary's encouragement. In view of the popularity of the original, she may
have seen an opportunity to exhibit it to a paying public. His experience
painting outsized signs, as she might have pointed out, equipped him for
such an undertaking. It proved a breakthrough. The *Hartford Courant* took

note of its success, and the Somerville, Massachusetts *Sentinel* declared that: "critics who saw both versions favor that by Mr. N. A. Primus, a colored gentleman of this city, over Munckacsy's original." The article assured the public that "it is doubly worth the small price of admission."[26]

Before the advent of moving pictures, large paintings like *Christ Before Pilate*—Frederic Church's rendering of Niagara Falls, for example—were exhibited to paying customers in a theatrical setting with dramatic "special effects."[27] Such a work, if it proved popular, could generate a stream of income. An eyewitness wrote that Nelson's work was "exhibited under subdued light amid loud claps of thunder and flashes of lightning." Viewers "heard its merits explained by Mrs. Primus who in a lecture told of both the work and her husband's career as a painter."[28] The chronicler explains that he was describing Nelson's second effort: the first copy of *Christ Before Pilate* on exhibit in Boston's Horticultural Hall was lost in a fire in December1888. Surely a daunting loss, but friends in Boston and Hartford contributed money to enable Primus to make a second copy, which was finished and shown to the public in 1890. This second version again was "pronounced by many critics to be superior in expression and brilliancy of coloring to the Munckacsy original.[29] The popular response to the drama surrounding the painting and the painter may have sparked the idea of taking it to Hartford, where it was displayed in the Foot Guard Armory and reportedly well received. In light of the work's success, Nelson, or possibly his wife, may have considered exhibiting it in other locations, as Munckacsy had done. Still, if Leila was still unable to walk, it would have been difficult either to take her along or leave her. However, Nelson and Mary did not have to make that choice: On October 12, 1893, at the age of twenty-eight, Leila died of pneumonia.[30] Mary may have supported the idea of taking the painting on tour as a change of scene to help Nelson work through his grief. His only child, Leila had her father's devotion from her infancy.

Mary and Nelson left Boston with the great painting in 1895. Whether they set out for certain destinations or simply took their chances on bookings we don't know, but eventually they reached the West Coast, certainly by rail rather than by ship as Holdridge had traveled in 1849. They spent some time in Seattle, and several portraits of local residents have been identified as Nelson's work, but so far no evidence of the couple's lodging in the city has been found. They settled in San Francisco around the turn of the century, some fifty years after the ship *Pacific* sailed into the bay with Holdridge Primus aboard. By 1900, San Francisco was no longer the ragged trading post of 1849. It had grown tenfold into a metropolis of 342,000, characterized by extremes of wealth, poverty, crime, reform, political turmoil, swagger, and discrimination—notably against the Chinese, but also against African Americans.[31] In 1895, the blacks of San Francisco numbered 1,600, little more than half of 1 percent of the population, but they had formed a community similar to those found elsewhere. Whether Nelson and Mary remained by design or simply lacked the money to return East, the West Coast became their home.

Mehitable had the company and support of Rebecca and Isabella in her final years. When she died in 1899, the *Courant* described her as "one of the best known colored women of the city," mentioning her children by name: "Nelson A. Primus, the artist who lives in Seattle; Mrs. Rebecca Thomas, Mrs. Henrietta Custis, Mrs. William B. Edwards of this city and Mrs. Phrone Harris of Boston."[32] Thronieve, who grew up as a Primus, had married and moved to Boston. The *Courant* continued its tribute days later with a description of the funeral at the Primus home, identifying the hymns sung and naming prominent white women who had sent flowers. At the graveside service at the family plot in Zion Hill Cemetery, a quartet from the Talcott Street Church sang "Asleep in Jesus," and a sheaf of wheat with a wreath of ivy leaves, given by Rebecca and Isabella, was placed on the casket.[33] The omission of Henrietta's name is not explained.

Afterward, Nelson wrote from Seattle resigning as executor of his father's will, and because Mary signed the note as witness, we know that she had survived the trip West. The house on Wadsworth Street was sold, and Rebecca, then sixty-three, went to live with Isabella and William Edwards and their three daughters. Nelson remained on the West Coast and Thronieve in Boston. While the Primus siblings were never together again, those on the East coast kept in touch. Well into the twentieth century, Thronieve and her husband hosted frequent gatherings of family members.

Henrietta's path through life has been hard to follow, as she disappears for a time from the public records; she may have spent some years out of the state, and her marriage to Thomas Custis ended, although whether by divorce or his death is unknown. Sometime after 1900 she married Theodore P. Mitchell of the William Mitchell family in Hartford. We know of the marriage only because court records reveal a dispute over Mitchell's mental state. In 1913, with the assistance of William Edwards—Isabella's husband—Henrietta had Mitchell declared "an incapable person" because of the "excessive use of alcohol." Subsequently, when Mitchell claimed to be recovered and capable of handling his own affairs, Henrietta challenged his statement. Both parties died in 1920, their dispute unresolved.[34] Henrietta was buried alongside her mother and father in the Primus family plot in Zion Hill Cemetery—as Henrietta Primus. In the end, her ambivalence toward the family was resolved by the kindness of her brother-in-law and surely the concern of her sisters.

By 1900, Nelson and Mary were living in San Francisco in a neighborhood that overlapped Chinatown. Assuming that she was with him when he settled in the city, they lived for several years in a neighborhood of artists, writers, and activists, and according to one source Nelson became known as "Primus of Boston," a "distinguished artist."[35] The city directory identified him as a portrait painter.[36] He was beginning again to enjoy some success, but he and Mary were among the thousands who witnessed the city's watershed event. The earthquake of 1906 destroyed lives and homes as well as irreplaceable works of art. Vital records were lost in the fire that swept through neighborhoods after the earthquake. The neighborhood

FIGURE 10.1. Stunned San Franciscans make their way through the rubble after the earthquake and fire of 1906. *Credit:* Untitled photograph of damage after 1906 San Francisco Earthquake and Fire; Naval Districts and Shore Establishments Record Group 181, Historian's Subject Files; National Archives at San Francisco.

around Chinatown was affected by the devastation, and the 1910 census lists Nelson as a widower. Mary Wheeler Primus may have died in the fire.

The census enumerator who informs us of Nelson's marital status was mostly correct in listing him as a black, literate fifty-two-year-old male (although he was sixty-eight), and a "servant" in the household of delicatessen owner John Wilfred McEvers. In an unusual but no doubt accurate listing, the occupation of this "servant" is given as Artist; his profession as Portrait Painting. The 1914 city directory confirms he was a clerk in McEvers's delicatessen. He had finally been forced to take full-time work to support himself, but he continued to paint. In fact San Francisco challenged his abilities with new subjects.

Two interviews conducted in the 1970s offer more clues to Nelson's later life. In the first, George Blaikie, stepson of the couple who owned the delicatessen where Nelson worked, cautions that, at the age of ninety-four, "[t]he only things I can tell you are the things that were related to me about him." He said that Nelson came to his parents' store sometime before 1906 and that Nelson was from Boston and in need of a place to live. Blaikie's mother, who ran the deli, gave him a job "cleaning up and different things like that" and a place to live. At night he painted, and one of his subjects was Blaikie's sister, whose portrait has survived.[37] Nelson's pursuit of art was "a spiritual thing . . . he was a very spiritual man, a very religious man. He had some dealings with Mammy Pleasant . . . and she was a spiritualist, and she raised his thoughts to what she thought would be a higher being in painting and he seemed to have painted from that." Mary Ellen Pleasants, a civil rights pioneer and freethinker, was a controversial figure in San Francisco history, marvelously indifferent to public opinion.[38] She was rumored to practice voodoo, but among her documented accomplishments was a successful suit against the North Beach and Mission Railroad Company on behalf of the rights of African Americans to ride on its cars.[39]

Some of George Blaikie's recollections can be confirmed, while others are not consistent with known facts. For example, he was certain that his sister was sixteen when Nelson painted her portrait. Using the 1910 census as a guide to her birth year, the portrait would have been painted in 1897: it was dated 1904. Nevertheless, Blaikie does confirm the accuracy of the unusual designation of the servant who was an artist.

The second interview was conducted in 1972 with Laura Tooms Scott, whose deceased aunt had known Nelson Primus and owned one of his paintings.[40] Mrs. Scott said that in Chinatown, "the Chinese were kind to him." He was poor, she said, and sometimes worked as a model at the

PLATE 10.1. Nelson A. Primus, *Lizzie Mae Ulmer*. Boston, 1876, oil on canvas, 27⅛ × 22 in. The Connecticut Historical Society.

PLATE 10.2. Nelson A. Primus, *Unknown Woman*. Boston, 1881, oil on canvas, 20 × 24 in. Collection of Walter and Linda Evans.

PLATE 10.3. Nelson A. Primus, *Unknown Gentleman*. Possibly Seattle, 1899, oil on canvas, 24 × 21¼ in. Collection of Walter and Linda Evans.

PLATE 10.4. Nelson A. Primus, *Going to Meet Papa*. San Francisco, 1908, oil on canvas, 16 × 14 in. Courtesy of Harriet Kelley, The Harmon and Harriet Kelley Foundation for the Arts.

PLATE 10.5. Nelson A. Primus, *Fortune Teller*. San Francisco, 1898, oil on board, 12½ × 8½ in. The Walter O. Evans Collection at the SCAD Museum of Art.

Plate 10.6. Nelson A. Primus, Untitled. San Francisco Chinatown, 1900, oil on canvas, 10¼ × 9½ in. Collection of the Oakland Museum of California. In Loving Memory of Eugene Parcel, Oakland Building Inspector, 1957–1980. 2007.51.1.

Hopkins Institute of the San Francisco Art Association, which was housed on Nob Hill in the former estate of railroad magnate Mark Hopkins.[41] This arrangement would have allowed him to "sit in" on art classes—to hear the instructor's comments and watch the student artists working—as close as he ever came to academy training.

Nelson disappeared from the San Francisco city directory after 1914, although in that year he produced one more large painting, which surfaced briefly in 1968. A California artist/upholsterer bought a rolled-up canvas at a Concord, California, auction—Nelson Primus's last-known work, *Christ Being Lowered from the Cross*. "Cracked and smudged from long neglect," it measured twelve by fifteen feet.[42] Although the new owner was reportedly having it restored, its ultimate fate is unknown.

Of Nelson's final years, we know only that he died of tuberculosis on May 29, 1916, in San Francisco Hospital and was buried in Cypress Lawn Cemetery. His death certificate correctly identifies him as a widower but gives his birth date as 1866 (he was born in 1842); it states the names of his parents as Aldrich and Matheba and his occupation as laborer.[43] The inaccuracies reveal that Nelson died alone, three thousand miles from where he started, his life story and his real occupation unrecorded, even though he had advanced as an artist in that adopted city. He did his best work there. Recent interest in his work has come too late to satisfy his hunger for recognition, but in some sense it justifies his stubborn refusal to give up his quest.

Rebecca sought a different and in the end equally unreachable goal, but like her brother she kept her commitment. She poured her zeal for teaching into her Sunday School classes. She also kept up her interest in the wider world, subscribing to a literary magazine, the *Cottage Hearth*, and attending meetings of the Progressive Union Society. In the 1970s, historian David White interviewed individuals in Hartford who remembered Rebecca simply as the kindly woman who taught "Aunt Becky's boys" in the Talcott Street Church. Late in life she was known as a grandmotherly figure, the "nearest thing to being a saint."[44] She must have taken pride in the fact that by 1900 her niece Nellie, eldest daughter of Isabella and William Edwards, was working as a schoolteacher.

Firstborn of the Primus children, Rebecca outlived them all. Nelson died first; Henrietta and Isabella both died in 1920. By the time Rebecca died in 1932, she was ninety-six years old, and her brief obituary makes no mention of her great adventure: founding the Primus Institute of Royal Oak, Maryland. She had outlived the memory of her proudest work. The school itself closed in 1929. Only one of the bearers at Rebecca's funeral represented the middle class of the 1860s in Hartford.

≈

Holdridge and Mehitable Primus were members of a black community that found courage, purpose, and expression in the common bond of race. Through most of a century of upheaval, war, and massive change, they lived circumspect lives, conforming to the doctrine of racial uplift. Two of their children dared to try for more. Rebecca and Nelson combined their parents' passive resistance to racial oppression with optimism supported by the evidence of black success in the antebellum period to seek goals that in the end eluded them.

Viewed from a later perspective, Holdridge's way can be seen as meek, cowardly, or pragmatic. He followed the pattern that had allowed his father, Ham, and his mother's father, Gad Asher, to live decent, quiet lives in a society that assigned them neither value nor membership. Perennial porter, tireless server, faithful employee, what did he do with the anger that his wife, his daughter, and his son reveal in occasional outbursts? Holdridge Primus listened to exhortations to action by Hosea Easton, Frederick Douglass, and William Lloyd Garrison; he sat in church as J. W. C. Pennington described the difference between his experiences in England and his treatment in the United States. James Mars must have approached him to sign petitions to vote. He saw Josephine Booth change from feisty to barely rational; saw his own children's prospects fade. What cannot be known about Holdridge Primus is contained in his silence.

Even with their letters to read, we have limited access to the writers. Was Nelson dedicated and steadfast or inflexible and parochial? He traveled far from Hartford, but in a sense he never left home. He rejected the caution that marked his father's way of life but honored his advice. Years later and thousands of miles away, Nelson wore a three-piece suit to his job in the delicatessen; at night he painted. He never reached the height of his ambition, but neither did he give it up. Nor did he present himself as anything but a respectable citizen.

Rebecca showed the same dedication in following her ambition. Like Nelson, she was forced to lower her sights, but she found a way to continue teaching as a contribution to racial uplift. One of the few tangible mementos of her life is a dress in the costume collection of the Wadsworth Atheneum.[45] A two-piece gown with fringed sleeves and peplum, covered buttons, a bustle, and a train; stylish but not showy—possibly her wedding

FIGURE 10.2. Sometime after 1900, a smartly dressed Nelson Primus, right, worked in a San Francisco delicatessen by day, painted at night. *Credit:* National Gallery.

dress. She and her mother must have cut the fabric, closed the seams, added the fringe, and arranged the bustle. The losses and disappointments of her later life make her achievements in Royal Oak, as preserved in her letters, all the more meaningful. One last photograph shows her in 1922, standing tall among the members of the Talcott Street congregation. Taken together, the letters and photographs of Rebecca and Nelson attest to the stubborn, unpretentious dignity that sums up the Primus answer to white hegemony.

Addie Brown was on the way to the fulfillment of her ambition before 1870. Striving for betterment, torn between her love for Rebecca and a hard-eyed analysis of her situation, she chose—and chose to love—Joseph Tines. After two years of marriage, she was still working, but no longer alone in the world. Her early death cut short the full impact of increasing race separation, as it robbed her of whatever good or ill her future may have held.

When their ambitions proved unattainable, the teacher and the artist continued in the way of life their parents exemplified. The working girl with

FIGURE 10.3. Like the Primus letters, this dress worn by Rebecca was preserved as a family keepsake. In the style of the time, beautifully made, it may have been her wedding dress. *Credit:* Unknown (American) Dress, c. 1868. Wadsworth Atheneum Museum of Art, Hartford, CT. Gift of Edward A. Singleton, 1933.99 A–C.

FIGURE 10.4. With the church building as background, the members of Hartford's Talcott Street Church assembled for this wide-angle depiction of the survival and the solidarity of their congregation. Rebecca Primus, with the large hat, is in the center of the cutout, second row. *Credit:* Copy in the Prudence Crandall Museum Collection, Connecticut Department of Economic and Community Development. Location of original unknown.

her own version of uplift meant to pursue in her marriage that same way of life. Respectability was the bedrock of their common identity: black and middle class. The outward signs—a way of dressing or of speaking, respect for religion and learning, willingness to serve their community—expressed their insistence on membership in the human race, on citizenship in the United States. Their triumph was to survive with their standards intact. The letters, the public record, the memories, and the images bring to light the Primus family story, revealing one of the resilient, persistent patterns that make up African American history.

The looked-for change has been slow in coming. From Gad Asher's kidnapping to the Emancipation Proclamation, from the collapse of the great expectations to *Brown v. Board of Education*—more than two centuries of struggle, and the goal is not yet reached.

Epilogue

One morning, as I checked in at the Connecticut Historical Society to continue reading the letters, the woman at the desk asked if I wasn't the one who was interested in the Primus Papers. I said I was, and she told me to go into the boardroom across the hall, where a member of the Primus family was looking at the Nelson Primus painting. Here were two revelations: a Primus descendant, although I had looked in vain to find one, and one of Nelson Primus's works right here in Hartford hanging on the wall. My coming in that morning and the alert woman at the desk combined to open yet another approach to the Primus past.

The man in the boardroom looking at the portrait of Lizzie Mae Ulmer was Jesse Harris, a grandson of Thronieve, the little child Holdridge and Mehitable adopted in 1867. Jesse was visiting from Boston, hoping to learn more about his family. We have been in touch off and on since then, and he generously gave me a copy of a family photograph now in the hands of another relative of his in Hawaii. It is one of a series of pictures of annual or biennial gatherings of members of the Harris/Primus clan at the Harris home in Cambridge.

Rebecca (Aunt Beckie) is on the left at the top of the picture, which dates from about 1910. Next to her are Jesse Houston Harris (Papa) and Thronieve (Mamma). Jesse writes that his grandfather and family were "very close." Another family memory he passed along is that his family "insisted that my grandmother (Thronieve) was a Pequot princess."

Bessie and Edna Edwards, daughters of Isabella Primus and William Edwards, extend the Primus family into the twentieth century, and the Jesse Harris I met in the Historical Society brings it into the twenty-first. According to the present-day Jesse Harris, the others in the photo are his aunts, Marjorie Elizabeth, Ruth Dwight, Louise Thornton (with Helen on her lap), and Hortense, who must have moved as the picture was taken. Also, Jesse's uncles Elmer and Nathaniel.

FIGURE E.1. One of a series of Harris/Primus family gatherings in and around Boston, this one, around 1900, includes Rebecca Primus (Aunt Beckie). *Credit:* Courtesy of Jesse Harris.

In his message supplying this background, Jesse adds that the family moved a few years later to Everett, where his father was born—the son of Jesse Houston Harris. The present-day Jesse will surely follow up on these connections. His letter closes with this: "Looks like a Sunday to me, grandpa was rather religious I understand."

Appendix A

Blacks in Hartford 1830–1880

Hartford City and Town	1830	1840	1850	1860	1870	1880
Total Hartford Population	9,789	12,793	17,966	29,152	37,743	42,551
Hartford Black Population	495	577	615	709	963	1280
% Black	5	4	3	2	2	3
# Black Householders	85	84	82	111	153	155
# in Black Households	336	372	478	569	671	1070
Average Household Size	3.8	4.4	5.8	5.13	4.38	6.88
% in Black Households	68	65	78	80	69	83
# Black Holders of Real Estate	n.a.	n.a.	22	35	28	22
% of Householders	n.a.	n.a.	27	31	18	14
# Blacks over age 20	n.a.	n.a.	342	411	608	871
# Illiterate Blacks	n.a.	n.a.	24	8	100	80
% Illiterate - Black Population	n.a.	n.a.	7	2	16	17
# Blacks Born in CT	n.a.	n.a.	429	525	565	684
# Born South	n.a.	n.a.	49	32	231	352
% Blacks Born in CT	n.a.	n.a.	70	74	59	53
% Born South	n.a.	n.a.	8	5	24	28
Occupation listed for:	n.a.	n.a.	139	302	437	621
# Professional	n.a.	n.a.	4	4	3	7
# Entrepreneur/skilled	n.a.	n.a.	28	42	62	83
# Semi & unskilled	n.a.	n.a.	107	256	372	533
% Professional	n.a.	n.a.	3	1	0.6	1
% Entrepreneur/skilled	n.a.	n.a.	20	14	14	13
% Semi & unskilled	n.a.	n.a.	77	85	85	86

Figure on Black Holders of Real Estate is from Hartford Property Tax Lists 107 – 109, Connecticut State Library.
All others are from the US Census.

Appendix B

Primus Timeline with Pertinent Historical Events

1774	Connecticut law forbids bringing any Indian, Negro, or mulatto slave into the state
1777	Gad Asher enlists in the American army for the "duration of the war"
1784	Connecticut law: no Negro or mulatto born in Connecticut after March to be enslaved after age twenty-five
	City of Hartford Incorporated
1793	First federal fugitive slave act
1800	Gabriel Prosser conspiracy discovered, Richmond, Virginia
1803	Maria Miller (Stewart) born, Hartford
1808	Congress passes law prohibiting importation of slaves to United States after January 1 of 1808
1811	Connecticut law forbids blacks voting
1812	Jeremiah Asher born
	Amos Gerry Beman born

1815   Holdridge Primus born

Mehitable Esther Jacobs born

1816   American Colonization Society organized

1818   Connecticut constitution passed—confirming white-only franchise and disestablishment

1819   Hartford blacks protest segregated seating in First Congregational Church

1820   Hartford Sunday School Union establishes Sunday School for blacks

1822   Denmark Vesey plot

1826   African Religious Society of Hartford organized

1828   Jeremiah Asher migrates to Hartford

1829   David Walker's *Appeal*

1830   Hartford's blacks request separate school

Colonization Society opens African Mission School, Christ Church

1831   Nat Turner Rebellion

The Liberator begins publication

Maria W. Stewart speaks and writes on women's rights, black self-improvement

1832   Prudence Crandall admits black student to her school

Amos Beman begins teaching in Hartford

Jeremiah Asher marries Abigail Stewart of Glastonbury

1833   Talcott Street Church established as a Church of Christ Congregational

Talcott Street Church hosts lecture on slavery by Arnold Buffam

North African School opens at Talcott Street Congregational Church

Hosea Easton named pastor of Talcott Street Church

State law forbids establishment of schools for "colored persons belonging to other states and countries"

Britain declares slavery unlawful in the empire

1835   Holdridge Primus and Mehitable Jacobs marry

Three-day race riot in Hartford

Gad Asher dies

1836   Rebecca Primus born

Hartford Colored Methodist Episcopal Zion Church founded by Hosea Easton

1838   Henrietta C. Primus born

Frederick Douglass escapes from slavery

1839   *Amistad* incident

Railroad comes to Hartford

Jeremiah Asher leaves Hartford for Providence to study

Amos Beman leaves Hartford for New Haven

1840   Rev. James W. C. Pennington named pastor of Talcott Street Church

Second African School opens at Zion Methodist Church, Elm Street

1841   Ann Plato's book published

Addie Brown born

1842   Nelson A. Primus born

1843   Isabella Primus born

1844   Augustus Washington comes to Hartford

Negroes denied privilege of voting in school society meetings and, as recompense, exempted from taxes

1845   *Narrative of the Life of Frederick Douglass* published

1848   Last slave freed in Connecticut

1849   January 16: Primus buys property and house on Wadsworth Street

February 17: Primus sails with C. N. Humphrey and Warburton mining company for California

1850   Fugitive slave law

1852   Hartford African Schools merge: Pearl Street facility built

Uncle Tom's Cabin published

1854   Augustus Washington leaves for Liberia

1857   Dred Scott decision

1858   Augustus Washington letter urges Primus et al. to immigrate to Liberia

1859   October 16: John Brown's attack on Harper's Ferry

Warrant for a lodge of Prince Hall Masons in Hartford, chartered by Grand Lodge, New York

1863   Emancipation Proclamation

Twenty-ninth Regiment formed

Slavery abolished in Maryland

1864   Nelson marries Amoretta Prime, moves to Boston

Leila Primus born

Calvin and Harriet Beecher Stowe move to Hartford

Black soldiers to receive equal pay with whites

1865   Lee surrenders April 9; Lincoln assassinated April 14

Connecticut Twenty-ninth and Thirty-first Regiments return to Hartford, November

Thirteenth Amendment ratified (outlawing slavery)

Freedmen's Bureau founded

Beginning of Black Codes

Rebecca Primus founds school for freed slaves at Royal Oak, Maryland

1866   First Civil Rights Act passed

Ku Klux Klan founded

1867   Primus Institute building completed in Royal Oak, Maryland

Ham Primus dies September 10, age seventy-three

Sophronia (Thronieve) Bicenter born

Reconstruction Acts passed over Johnson's veto

Constitutional conventions in Southern states

1868   Fourteenth Amendment ratified (guarantees citizenship, immunities, privileges)

Addie Brown marries Joseph Tines, April

Connecticut law integrates schools; not teaching staff

Hartford City Directory stops listing blacks separately

1869   Freedmen's Society disbanded; Rebecca returns to Hartford

1870   Fifteenth Amendment ratified (guarantees right to vote)

Addie Brown dies January 11; age twenty-eight

1871   Mark Twain moves to Hartford

1873   Rebecca Primus marries Charles H. Thomas, March 25

1875   Ernest Primus Thomas born to Charles H. and Rebecca Thomas
         Hartford becomes sole capital of the state

1876   Amoretta Primus dies, childbirth; infant dies as well

         Ernest Primus Thomas dies, pneumonia, February 11

         Charles Thomas goes to work at Philadelphia Expo (opened May
         10, closed December 31)

1877   Nelson Primus marries Mary G. Wheeler

         President Hayes's "Compromise of 1877" effectively dismantles
         guarantees of rights for African Americans

1883   Supreme Court strikes down 1875 Civil Rights Act; federal
         government cannot regulate behavior of private individuals in
         matters of race relations

1884   Holdridge Primus dies

1891   Charles H. Thomas dies

1893   Leila Primus dies

1895   Nelson and Mary (Wheeler) Primus leave Boston

1899   Mehitable Esther (Jacobs) Primus dies

         Primus home sold November 15

1916   Nelson Primus dies, San Francisco

1920   Henrietta Primus Custis Mitchell dies

         Isabella Primus Edwards dies

1932   Rebecca Primus Thomas dies

Notes

Introduction

1. David White, "Addie Brown's Hartford," *Connecticut Historical Society Bulletin* 41 (April 1976): 57–64; Karen Hansen, " 'No Kisses Is Like Youres': An Erotic Friendship Between Two African-American Women During the Mid-Nineteenth Century," *Gender and History* 7, no. 2 (August 1995): 153–182; Farah Jasmine Griffin, ed., *Beloved Sisters and Loving Friends: Letters from Rebecca Primus of Royal Oak, Maryland, and Addie Brown of Hartford, Connecticut, 1854–1868* (New York: Alfred A. Knopf, 1999).

2. Glenda Gilmore, *Gender and Jim Crow: Women and the Politics of White Supremacy in North Carolina, 1896–1920* (Chapel Hill: University of North Carolina Press, 1996), xix; Douglas Henry Daniels, *Pioneer Urbanites: A Social and Cultural History of Black San Francisco* (Berkeley: University of California Press, 1990), xvii–xviii.

3. Leon F. Litwack, *North of Slavery: The Negro in the Free States, 1790–1860* (Chicago: University of Chicago Press, 1961), 180; Nick Salvatore, *We All Got History: The Memory Books of Amos Webber* (New York: Vintage Books, 1997), 92; Gary Nash, *Forging Freedom: The Formation of Philadelphia's Black Community, 1720–1840* (Cambridge, MA: Harvard University Press, 1988), 217.

4. Leslie Harris, *In the Shadow of Slavery: African Americans in New York City, 1626–1863* (Chicago: University of Chicago Press, 2003), 173; Carla Peterson, *Black Gotham: A Family History of African Americans in Nineteenth-Century New York City* (New Haven: Yale University Press, 2011), 7.

Chapter 1. Migrant of Necessity

1. Jeremiah Asher, *Incidents in the Life of the Rev. J. Asher, Pastor of the Shiloh (Coloured) Baptist Church* (1850; repr., New York: Books for Libraries, 1971); and *An Autobiography, with Details of a Visit to England: And Some Account of the*

History of the Meeting Street Baptist Church, Providence, R.I. and of the Shiloh Baptist Church, Philadelphia, Pa. (Philadelphia, 1862).

2. Asher, *Incidents,* 14–17, and *An Autobiography,* 2–4.

3. Asher, *An Autobiography,* 4.

4. Lorenzo Greene, *The Negro in Colonial New England* (New York: Atheneum, 1969), 26–27. On Guilford harbors, see Albert E. Van Dusen, *Connecticut* (New York: Random House, 1961), 28.

5. Jeremiah Asher names Gad's purchaser as Titus Bishop in *Incidents,* 18; and as Linus Bishop in his earlier *An Autobiography,* 1. Existing records show no one by either name whose dates connect him with this purchase.

6. *Public Records of the Colony of Connecticut,* comp. Charles J. Hoadly (Hartford: Case, Lockwood & Brainard, 1877), 10: 617.

7. C. S. Manegold, *Ten Hills Farm: The Forgotten History of Slavery in the North* (Princeton: Princeton University Press, 2010), 43.

8. Ruth Balen, "Slave Ownership by Yale-Educated Clergy in Eighteenth Century Guilford, Connecticut" (unpublished manuscript, 2001), Guilford Public Library.

9. Winthrop Jordan, "Enslavement of Negroes in America to 1700," in *Colonial America: Essays in Politics and Social Development,* 4th ed., ed. Stanley N. Katz, John M. Murrin, and Douglas Greenberg (New York: McGraw-Hill, 1993), 305–309; also see Bernard Rosenthal, "Puritan Conscience and New England Slavery," *New England Quarterly* 46 (1973): 62–81.

10. Ira Berlin, *Many Thousands Gone: The First Two Centuries of Slavery in North America* (Cambridge, MA: Belknap Press, 1998), 95, 188.

11. Asher, *An Autobiography,* 1.

12. Berlin, *Many Thousands Gone,* 188.

13. Leon F. Litwack, *North of Slavery: The Negro in the Free States, 1790–1860* (Chicago: University of Chicago Press, 1992), 5. See also Berlin, *Many Thousands Gone,* 178; and Greene, *The Negro in Colonial New England,* 100–101. Jackson Turner Main had reached the same conclusion in *Connecticut Society in the Era of the American Revolution* (Hartford: American Revolution Bicentennial Commission of Connecticut, 1977), 17–18.

14. Litwack, *North of Slavery,* 4.

15. Information in this paragraph is from Venture Smith, *A Narrative of the Life and Adventures of Venture, A Native of Africa, but Resident Above Sixty Years in the United States of America, Related by Himself* (1798; repr., 1835, 1896, New London: New London County Historical Society), chaps. 1, 2.

16. Berlin, *Many Thousands Gone,* 8.

17. Asher, *An Autobiography,* 4; Arthur Zilversmit, *The First Emancipation: The Abolition of Slavery in the North* (Chicago: University of Chicago Press, 1967), 122–123.

18. Theodore Groom, "Remembering Gad Asher" (unpublished manuscript, April, 2013, Totoket Historical Society Collection, North Branford, CT), 14–18.

19. Asher, *Incidents*, 18–19; Henry P. Johnston, ed., *The Record of Connecticut Men in the Military and Naval Service During the War of the Revolution 1775–1783* (Hartford: Case Lockwood & Brainard Company, 1889).

20. Asher, *Incidents*, 19; Asher, *An Autobiography*, 5.

21. Asher, *Incidents*, 19.

22. Venture Smith, *Narrative*, chap. 2.

23. Asher, *Incidents*, 19. No record of the marriage has been found, but Temperance is named in "John Harrison's Notebook," Archives and Manuscripts Collection, Connecticut State Library. For her free status, see Asher, *Incidents*, 19.

24. "Journal of Timothy Russell Palmer 1817–1832," transcribed by Janet Gregan, Totoket Historical Society, North Branford, CT. I am indebted to Theodore Groom for this reference.

25. The northern section of Branford was separated in 1831 and named North Branford. When Gad moved there, it was still part of Branford.

26. Ruel, Maryette, Henrietta, and Temperance are named as heirs in Gad's will. Brunella is identified in the "Martha Russell Scrapbook," Branford Historical Society Archives, Blackstone Library, Record Group #1, Family Papers, Box 26, Folders 17 and 18.

27. Gloria L. Main, "Naming Children in Early New England," *Journal of Interdisciplinary History* 27, no. 1 (Summer 1996): 1–27.

28. Asher, *Incidents*, 20. Gad Asher is listed in the 1790 Branford manuscript census with eight in his household. For his real estate purchase, see Branford Land Records, book 12, p. 125, September 7, 1791.

29. Asher, *An Autobiography*, 5.

30. Asher, *An Autobiography*, 6.

31. Litwack, *North of Slavery*, 6.

32. Arthur Zilversmit, *The First Emancipation: The Abolition of Slavery in the North* (Chicago: University of Chicago Press, 1967), 123.

33. Berlin, *Many Thousands Gone*, 228–9. On the linkage between military service and abolition in the North, see James O. Horton and Lois E. Horton, "Revolution and the Abolition of Northern Slavery," in *In Hope of Liberty: Culture, Community and Protest Among Northern Free Blacks, 1700–1860* (New York: Oxford University Press, 1997), 55–76; also see Litwack, *North of Slavery*, 6–8.

34. David O. White, *Connecticut's Black Soldiers, 1775–1783* (Chester, CT: Pequot Press, 1973), 55.

35. Asher, *Incidents*, 20–21.

36. Asher, *Incidents*, 20; Asher, *An Autobiography*, 2.

37. Berlin, *Many Thousands Gone*, 191.

38. Branford Land Records, vol. 19, 224.

39. Charles Sellers, *The Market Revolution: Jacksonian America, 1815–1846* (New York: Oxford University Press, 1991), 10.

40. The 1820 US Census for Branford listed three in the Gad Asher household and eight in that of Ruel Asher.

41. North Branford Town Records, April 10, 1811. The entry misstates the bride's first name, but she is named Tempe or Temperance in subsequent records, including the Martha Russell Notebook, 5.

42. Seaman's Protection Certificate no. 86, for Ham Primus, was issued by the US Customs District of New Haven (1803–1841), according to records at the Frederick C. Murphy Federal Center, Waltham, MA. Ham's age is confirmed by his birth date, June 7, 1787, recorded in the *Branford Vital Records*, III, 411.

43. *The Life and Times of Frederick Douglass* (1892; repr., 1962, intro. Rayford W. Logan, New York: Collier Books, 1962), 198–200.

44. For Holdridge's place of birth, see the *Hartford Evening Post*, May 9, 1884, 4.

45. W. Jeffrey Bolster, *Black Jacks: African American Seamen in the Age of Sail* (Cambridge, MA: Harvard University Press, 1997), 171.

46. The children of Ham and Temperance Primus so far located are Holdridge, b. January 28, 1815, Barbour Records, Hartford Cemetery 5, 72; Nelson, b. March 19, 1817, T. Fitch's Book, *Guilford Private Records*, 1815, 1; Daughter, b. January 15, 1819, T. Fitch, 6; Maryette, b. July 24, 1821, Register of Baptisms, Christ Church, Guilford, in *Bulletin of the Connecticut Historical Society*, V, no. 3 (April 1939); Clara and Amelia (twins), private baptism, January 18, 1822, *Register of Baptisms in St. Johns Church North Guilford*, VI, no. 1, 14; Gad Asher, child of Ham Primus, b. January 29, 1823; baptized September 21, 1823, *Register of Baptisms in St. Johns Church North Guilford*, VI, no. 1, 6; Margetta, b. July 24, 1827, *Guilford Christ Episcopal Church Records*, III, no. 8.

47. Asher, *Incidents*, 20.

48. Main, "Naming Children," 26.

49. Amelia died on January 21, 1822, *Burials in North Guilford*, 6, no. 2, 14.

50. Gad Asher Primus died on October 13, 1824: Nelson Primus died on October 24, 1824. T. Fitch's Book, *Guilford Private Records*, 36; *Burials in North Guilford*, 6, no. 2, 15.

51. Listed in the Guilford census for 1820, Ham Primus does not appear in the 1830 census anywhere in the state. However, in 1830, the Gad Asher household in North Branford consisted of seven members divided into age groups—males: one 36 to 55 (Ham Primus); one 55 to 100 (Gad Asher). Females: two under 10 (Maryette and Margetta), one 10 to 24 (daughter—name not given—born in 1819), one 36 to 55 (Temperance Primus), and one 55 to 100 (Temperance Asher).

52. Bolster, *Black Jacks*, 178.

53. Charles, *The Market Revolution*, 137.

54. Sellers, *The Market Revolution*, chap. 5, "Hard Times, Hard Feelings, Hard Money," 137–171.

55. Betty M. Linsley and Elizabeth Radulski, eds., *The Diary of Malachi Linsley, Branford, Connecticut, 1821–1834* (Branford, CT: B. M. Linsley, 1993), 135.

56. The *New Haven Register*, July 15, 1886, reports that "Uncle Ham," formerly a slave of Malachi Linsley of North Branford, had died at an advanced age "several years ago." This explains the connection between the Linsley family and Holdridge's (the latter's father and grandfather were named Ham).

57. Data have been compiled by Jane Bouley, Branford historian, and Betty Linsley, genealogist (and granddaughter of Malachi Linsley), using census data, church records, and the "Notebooks of Martha Russell" in the Branford Public Library and the Totoket Historical Society, North Branford.

58. Linsley and Radulski, *Diary*, 135, 138, 140, 147, 149, 151.

59. *North Branford Land Records*, vol. I, 1831–1836, 103; microfilm reel 3438, Connecticut State Library. On Ham Primus buying land and building a house, see "Martha Russell Scrapbook," 5. The Ham Primus dwelling is marked on a nineteenth-century map: Frederick W. Beers, A. B. Prindle, and others, Atlas of New Haven County, CT (New York: F. W. Beers, A. D. Ellis & G. G. Soule, 1868), map #37.

60. The Asher farm supported the following extended family in three households: Gad and Temperance Asher; their son Ruel with his wife, Jerusha, and six children; and son-in-law Ham Primus with his wife, Temperance, and five children.

61. Dwight B. Billings and Kathleen M. Bell, *The Road to Poverty: The Making of Wealth and Hardship in Appalachia* (Cambridge: Cambridge University Press 2000), 206.

62. Linsley Radulski, *Diary*, 140, 163.

63. Jarvis Morse, *The Neglected Period of Connecticut's History*, 1818–1850 (New York: Octagon Books, 1978), 21.

64. Asher, *An Autobiography*, 16–17.

65. The time of Holdridge's arrival is based on a statement in his obituary in the *Hartford Evening Post* on May 9, 1884, stating that in his early days he worked for W. W. Ellsworth when Ellsworth was a representative in Congress (1829–1833).

66. The life of Henry C. Bowen of Woodstock, Connecticut, provides an example of a young white man forced by need to leave home. His father, a struggling storekeeper, arranged for his son to seek out silk importers in New York. Lewis and Arthur Tappan did indeed hire young Bowen. See Barbara J. Beeching, "Henry Chandler Bowen and Roseland Cottage: Success in Nineteenth Century America," *Connecticut History* 38, no. 2 (Fall 1999): 133–134.

67. Richard D. Brown, *Modernization: The Transformation of American Life 1600–1865* (1976; repr., Prospect Heights, IL: Waveland Press, 1988), 107.

68. S. G. Goodrich, *Recollections of A Lifetime of Men and Things I Have Seen*, vol. I (1857; repr., Detroit: Gale Research Co., 1967), 436. Also John Woodhull Stedman, "Hartford in 1830: Some Things That I Remember About Hartford Sixty Years Ago," reprinted in *Connecticut Historical Society Bulletin* 14, no. 5 (July 1949): 23.

69. Stedman, "Hartford in 1830," 23. Congress outlawed the importation of slaves to the United States after January 1, 1808, although evidence shows that a clandestine trade continued: Anne Farrow, Joel Lang, and Jennifer Frank, *Complicity: How the North Promoted, Prolonged, and Profited from Slavery* (New York: Ballantine Books, 2005), 110–113. On Connecticut's participation in the triangle trade, see Farrow, Lang, and Frank, *Complicity,* 49–50.

70. Glenn Weaver and Michael Swift, *Hartford, Connecticut's Capital: an Illustrated History* (Sun Valley, CA: American Historical Press, 2003), 56.

71. Stedman, "Hartford in 1830," 18–19, 6.

72. Asher, *An Autobiography,* 17.

73. Henry Leavitt Ellsworth (1791–1858), president of the Aetna Insurance Company, later held posts in Andrew Jackson's administration. Donna Holt Siemiatkoski, T*he Ancestors and Descendants of Chief Justice Oliver Ellsworth and His Wife Abigail Wolcott and the Story of Elmwood, Their Homestead* (Baltimore: Gateway Press, 1992), 23.

74. See Asher, *An Autobiography,* 1. The family name, Olford, appears in the Hartford census of 1790 and 1800, in the Kingsbury census of 1805, and in the 1838 City Directory. See *Gardner's City Directory* (Hartford: Case-Tiffany & Co., 1838).

75. Siemiatkoski, *Ancestors and Descendants of Oliver Ellsworth,* 22.

76. Holdridge Primus's place of employment is from the *Hartford Evening Post* obituary, May 9, 1884. Information on Jeremiah's is from Asher, *An Autobiography,* 16–17.

77. William W. Ellsworth would become governor of the state and later justice of the state Supreme Court. Siemiatkoski, *Ancestors and Descendants of Chief Justice Oliver Ellsworth,* 22–23. Jeremiah later worked for Thomas S. Williams, chief justice of the state of Connecticut—brother-in-law of the Ellsworth brothers.

78. Asher, *Incidents,* 36–38.

79. Nick Salvatore, *We All Got History: The Memory Books of Amos Webber* (New York: Vintage Books, 1997), quote, 181; reference to favorable treatment, 299.

80. Robert Cottrol, *The Afro-Yankees: Providence's Black Community in the Ante-bellum Era* (Westport, CT: Greenwood Press, 1982), 130.

81. Edward Strutt Abdy, *Journal of a Residence and Tour in the United States of North America, from April, 1833, to October, 1834,* vols. 1, 3 (London: John Murray, 1835).

82. Lawrence B. Goodheart, *Abolitionist, Actuary, Atheist: Elizur Wright and the Reform Impulse* (Kent, OH: Kent State University Press, 1990), 38, 39.

83. Goodheart, *Abolitionist, Actuary, Atheist,* 61–84, esp. 75. See also Leonard Richards, *"Gentlemen of Property and Standing": Anti-Abolition Mobs in Jacksonian America* (New York: Oxford University Press, 1970), 30–31.

84. Abdy, *Journal,* vol. 3, 206–207.

85. Asher, *Incidents,* 24–26.

86. Frederick Douglass, *Life and Times of Frederick Douglass* (1892; repr., intro. Rayford W. Logan, New York: Collier Books, 1962), 210–211.

Chapter 2. Growing Up with the Community

1. Edwin Pond Parker, *History of the Second Church of Christ in Hartford 1670–1892* (Hartford: Belknap and Warfield, 1892), 342, record #1690.

2. Kingsbury Negro Census of Hartford, 1805, Stowe Center Library, Archives Collection, Hartford. In 1756, Connecticut counted 101 *slaves*.

3. Jeremiah Jacobs Account Books, Stowe Center Library, Archives Collection, Hartford. Also see Hartford Land Records, vol. 36, 511.

4. See "Mortgage Burning of the Talcott Street Congregational Church, 1944" (Hartford, CT: Faith Congregational Church, 1944), 3, in the author's possession.

5. In some records, the name "Mehitable" (or "Mehitabel") is shortened to Mabel or Hetty.

6. "Mortgage Burning," 1.

7. Leon F. Litwack: *North of Slavery: The Negro in the Free States 1790–1860* (Chicago: University of Chicago Press, 1961), 196.

8. Jeremiah Asher, *Incidents in the Life of the Rev. J. Asher, Pastor of the Shiloh (Coloured) Baptist Church* (1850; repr., New York: Books for Libraries, 1971), 44. See also his *An Autobiography, with Details of a Visit to England: And Some Account of the History of the Meeting Street Baptist Church, Providence, R.I. and of the Shiloh Baptist Church, Philadelphia, Pa.* (Philadelphia, 1862), 35–36.

9. Asher, *Incidents,* 44.

10. See "Mortgage Burning," 1.

11. The earliest confirmation of Hawes's offer is in a speech by the Rev. Robert F. Wheeler at farewell services in the Talcott Street Church, March 25, 1906, reported in the *Hartford Courant,* on March 26, 1906.

12. See Robert Cottrol, *The Afro-Yankees: Providence's Black Community in the Ante-bellum Era* (Westport, CT: Greenwood Press, 1982), 58, 61, 130.

13. William D. Piersen, *Black Yankees: Development of an Afro-American Subculture in Eighteenth-Century New England* (Amherst: University of Massachusetts Press, 1988), 59; Gary B. Nash, *Forging Freedom: The Formation of Philadelphia's Black Community 1720–1840* (Cambridge, MA: Harvard University Press, 1988), 100; James O. Horton and Lois E. Horton, *Black Bostonians: Family Life and Community Struggle in the Antebellum North* (New York: Holmes & Meier, 1979), 28.

14. Leonard Curry, *The Free Black in Urban America 1800–1850: The Shadow of the Dream* (Chicago: University of Chicago Press, 1981), 244–245; for Hartford, the 1830 US Census.

15. Curry, *The Free Black in Urban America,* 191.

16. Information on the Sunday School Union is from "A Brief Historical Sketch," in "Mortgage Burning."

17. See "A Brief Historical Sketch," in "Mortgage Burning."

18. Hartford Land Records, vol. 43, 520; vol. 44, 628.

19. "A Brief Historical Sketch," in "Mortgage Burning."

20. David O. White, "Hartford's African Schools, 1830–1868," *Connecticut Historical Society Bulletin* (April 1974): 47.

21. Connecticut State Archives, RG 002, Box I, folder 8, Connecticut State Library.

22. In 1994, the historian of Faith Congregational Church, Lessie Jackson, supplied copies of several early church publications. Another was brought to my attention by Evans Seland, archivist of the Connecticut Conference, United Church of Christ, Hartford.

23. The list is from the historical sketch printed and reprinted in pamphlets of the Talcott Street Church (later Faith Congregational Church).

24. "Historical Sketch," in "Our 150th Anniversary 1826–1976," pamphlet, Faith Congregational Church (formerly the Talcott Street Church), Hartford, 1976. Sources for the information are not given.

25. Asher, *An Autobiography,* 1.

26. For Peter Magira, see James M. Rose and Barbara W. Brown, *Tapestry: A Living History of the Black Family in Southeastern Connecticut* (New London, CT: New London County Historical Society, 1979), 94.

27. Rose and Brown, *Tapestry,* 28, 111.

28. Information in this paragraph on Cook (or Cooke) is from Gurdon Wadsworth Russell, *"Up-Neck" in 1825* (Hartford: Case, Lockwood & Brainard, 1890), 82.

29. Hartford Land Records, vol. 44, 628, 654, 678.

30. The pamphlet *Passages in the Life of Jack Blackstone, a Christian Negro. By One Who Knew Him* (Hartford: Elihu Geer, 1843) is in the African American Collection, Connecticut Historical Society, Hartford, 3–11. Quotes on 3, 4.

31. *Passages in the Life of Jack Blackstone,* 13.

32. Randall K. Burkett, "'Elizabeth Mars Johnson Thomson' (1807–1864): A Research Note," *Historical Magazine of the Protestant Episcopal Church* 60, no. 1 (March 1986): 18–26.

33. Burkett, "Elizabeth Mars Johnson Thompson," 23.

34. Marilyn Richardson, ed., *Maria W. Stewart, America's First Black Woman Political Writer: Essays and Speeches* (Bloomington: Indiana University Press, 1987), 28–29, 7, 11.

35. Ibid., 21.

36. Marla R. Miller, "Mehitable Primus and Addie Brown: Women of Color and Hartford's Nineteenth-Century Dressmaking Trades," in *Dressing New England:*

Clothing, Fashion, and Identity, ed. Peter Benes, Dublin Seminar for New England Folklife Annual Proceedings (Deerfield, MA: Trustees of Historic Deerfield, 2010), 65, 72.ˑ

37. Nash, *Forging Freedom*, 234–240; Litwak, *North of Slavery*, 24–26.

38. "Historical Sketch," in "Our 150th Anniversary 1826–1976," pamphlet, Faith Congregational Church, 1976.

39. Asher, *An Autobiography*, 24.

40. Ibid.

41. Asher, *An Autobiography*, 24–25.

42. See Robert Wheeler, "Farewell to the Talcott Street Church," *Hartford Courant* 27 (March 1906): 13.

43. Stephen G. Ray, "Not All Black and White: African-American Christian History and the Politics of Historical Identity," paper presented at workshop on "The Project on Lived Theology," University of Virginia, November 10, 2003, 7.

44. "Historical Sketch," in "Our 150th Anniversary 1826–1976," pamphlet, Talcott Street Church. In 1954, the Talcott Street congregation merged with the Mother Bethel Methodist Church to become Faith Congregational Church.

45. Mehitabel Primus obituary, *Hartford Courant*, March 11, 1899.

46. "In Memory of Holdridge Primus," *Hartford Courant*, May 23, 1884.

47. Hartford Vital Records X, 121, Barbour Records, Connecticut State Library.

Chapter 3. Family Life Amid Racial Turmoil

1. Howard H. Bell, ed., "Minutes and Proceedings of the First Annual Convention," in *Minutes of the Proceedings of the National Negro Conventions, 1830–1864* (New York: Arno Press, 1969), 5.

2. Jeremiah Asher, *Incidents in the Life of the Rev. J. Asher, Pastor of the Shiloh (Coloured) Baptist Church Philadelphia, U.S.* (1850; repr., New York: Books for Libraries, 1971), 43–47.

3. Charles M. Wiltse, ed., *David Walker's Appeal, in Four Articles*, First American Century Series (New York: Hill and Wang, 1965).

4. Benjamin Quarles, *Black Abolitionists* (New York: Oxford University Press, 1969), 107.

5. Leon F. Litwak, *North of Slavery: The Negro in the Free States, 1790–1860* (Chicago: University of Chicago Press, 1961), 124, 125.

6. Quarles, *Black Abolitionists*, 107.

7. Litwak, *North of Slavery*, 124.

8. Susan Strane, *A Whole-Souled Woman: Prudence Crandall and the Education of Black Women* (New York: W. W. Norton & Company, 1990); also see Diana Ross McCain, *To All on Equal Terms: The Life and Legacy of Prudence Crandall* (Hartford:

Connecticut Commission on the Arts, Tourism, Culture, History and Film, 2004).

9. Bell, *Proceedings of the National Negro Conventions*, 1833 meeting, 5–6.

10. See Leonard Richards, *Gentlemen of Property and Standing: Anti-Abolition Mobs in Jacksonian America* (New York: Oxford University Press, 1970).

11. Two Hartford newspapers, the *Courant*, June 15, 1835, and the *Times*, June 13, 1835, reported on the riots. *The Liberator*, June 20, 1835, reprinted a third account, from the *Hartford Review*. State v. Cooper, Superior Court, Hartford County, Connecticut State Library Archives RG 3, Files, February 1835 to September 1835, New Cases, #84. Also see State v. Minor, Wilcox et al., and State v. Oliver Bannon, County Court, Hartford County, August Term 1835. Connecticut State Library Archives, RG 3, Box 426, March–August 1835.

12. The anonymous and undated description is in the *John W. Stedman Scrapbook* 1:27, MS 15763, Connecticut Historical Society.

13. The title of Leonard Richards's study of the riots, cited above.

14. See the *Hartford Review* (n.d.); reprinted in *The Liberator*, June 20, 1835.

15. *The Hartford Courant*, June 15, 1835.

16. Lawrence Goodheart, *Abolitionist, Actuary, Atheist: Elizur Wright and the Reform Impulse* (Kent, OH: Kent State University Press, 1990), 73–84.

17. Richards, "Generation of Anti-Abolitionist Violence," in *Gentlemen of Property and Standing*, 20–46, esp. 30 and 38.

18. Patrick Rael, "Dark, Deep, and Hopeless: Black Elevation, White Anxiety," in *Black Identity & Black Protest in the Antebellum North* (Chapel Hill: University of North Carolina Press, 2002), 159–173. Also see Winthrop D. Jordan, *White Over Black: American Attitudes towards the Negro, 1550–1812* (Baltimore: Penguin Books, 1969), 542.

19. George R. Price and James B. Stewart, eds., *To Heal the Scourge of Prejudice: The Life and Writings of Hosea Easton* (Amherst: University of Massachusetts Press, 1999), 3–10.

20. Price and Stewart, *To Heal the Scourge of Prejudice*, 45, n. 27.

21. Conflicting reports on its origin leave the early history of the church opaque, but the city directory states that Easton founded it in 1836. See *Geer's City Directory* (Hartford: Elihu Geer, 1853), 210.

22. Price and Stewart, *To Heal the Scourge of Prejudice*, 45, n. 27. Thomas Robbins, Hartford school inspector, recorded visits to the "Second Coloured School, Elm Street" in 1844 and 1845. Also see Thomas Robbins School Papers, Connecticut State Library Manuscript Collection.

23. Easton's "Treatise on the Intellectual Character, and Civil and Political Condition of the Colored People of the United States; and the Prejudice Exercised towards Them" is published in Price and Stewart, *To Heal the Scourge of Prejudice*, 63–121.

24. Hartford County Court Files 1713–1835, Box 427, November 1835. The accusations cited both financial and moral transgressions on Easton's part.

25. See Jennet Boardman, "Midwife Records 1815–1849, Part IV," *Connecticut Historical Society Bulletin* 34, no. 4 (October 1969), Rebecca, 120; Henrietta, 122.

26. Nichols and Company became Humphrey & Seyms in about 1851 and by 1884 was Seyms. On Holdridge's service, see the *Hartford Evening Post*, May 9, 1884.

27. Primus Collection, Connecticut Historical Society, Photo #4.

28. *Hartford Evening Post*, May 9, 1884.

29. "Death of Holdridge Primus," obituary, no date, no identification, in Connecticut Historical Society Scrapbook, III, 53.

30. *Hartford·Evening Post*, May 9, 1884.

31. Darlene Clark Hine, *Hine Sight: Black Women and the Re-Construction of American History* (Bloomington: Indiana University Press, 1994), 37–47.

32. For more on the *Amistad* affair, see Howard Jones, *Mutiny on the Amistad: The Saga of a Slave Revolt and Its Impact on American Abolition, Law, and Diplomacy* (New York: Oxford University Press, 1987). For a contemporary view, see John Warner Barber, *A History of the Amistad Captives* (1840; repr., New York: Arno Press, 1969).

33. Jones, *Mutiny on the Amistad*, 64–65.

34. "The Amistad Case and the Federal Courts," *The Court Historian* 9 (March 1998), Federal Judicial History Center, Washington, DC, http://ftp.resource.org/courts.gov/fjc/couhis09.pdf.

35. See "Mortgage Burning," 4.

36. Howard H. Bell, ed., *Minutes of the Proceedings of the National Negro Conventions, 1830–1864* (New York: Arno Press, 1969).

37. Leonard Curry, *The Free Black in Urban America 1800–1850: The Shadow of the Dream* (Chicago: University of Chicago Press, 1981), 232–236. See also Nash, *Forging Freedom*, 100–104. On an attempt by an American black to encourage colonization, see Lamont D. Thomas, *Paul Cuffe, Black Entrepreneur and Pan-Africanist* (Urbana: University of Illinois Press, 1988). See also James O. Horton, "Double Consciousness: African American Identity in the Nineteenth Century," in *Free People of Color: Inside the African American Community* (Washington, DC: Smithsonian Institution Press, 1993), esp. 156–158.

38. On the charitable society, see Randall K. Burkett, "Elizabeth Mars Johnson Thomson (1807–1864): A Research Note," *Historical Magazine of the Protestant Episcopal Church* LV, no. 1 (March 1986): 18–26. On the Literary and Religious Institution and the temperance societies, see Quarles, *Black Abolitionists*, 103, 94.

39. Henrietta Primus, Hartford, to Rebecca Primus, Royal Oak, November 15, 1865.

40. David O. White discovered receipts for the work outlined here done by "Holdridge and Mrs. Primus" in the papers of the Samuel F. Jarvis Family, IX, Manuscript #68804, Connecticut State Library.

41. Addie Brown, Hartford, to Rebecca Primus, Royal Oak, March 4, 1866.

42. Stephanie J. Shaw, *What a Woman Ought to Be and to Do: Black Professional Women Workers during the Jim Crow Era* (Chicago: University of Chicago Press, 1996); Glenda E. Gilmore, *Women and the Politics of White Supremacy in North Carolina, 1896–1920* (Chapel Hill: University of North Carolina Press, 1996).

43. Hine, *Hine Sight,* 109.

44. *Hartford Evening Post,* May 9, 1884.

45. Mrs. Jacob Newcomb, Waterbury, to Mehitable Primus, Hartford, July 15, 1867, in the Primus Papers, Connecticut Historical Society Manuscript Collection. The 1860 Hartford census counted 6,432 Irish-born residents in the city.

46. Addie Brown, Waterbury, to Rebecca Primus, Hartford, August 30, 1859.

Chapter 4. Beyond Uplift: A New Spirit of Resistance

1. *Minutes of the Proceedings of the National Negro Conventions,* "Introduction to The Conventions of the 1840s."

2. David E. Swift, *Black Prophets of Justice: Activist Clergy Before the Civil War* (Baton Rouge: Louisiana State University Press, 1989), chap. 8; "Amos G. Beman, New Haven Pastor and Connecticut Activist," 173–203. For Cesar Beman's war service, see War Department Collection of Revolutionary War Records, Group 93, microfilm M246, National Archives.

3. Swift, *Black Prophets,* 176–178.

4. Ibid., 177.

5. James Mars, *Life of James Mars, A Slave Born and Sold in Connecticut,* in *Five Black Lives* (1864; repr., intro. Arna Bontemps, Middletown, CT: Wesleyan University Press, 1971), 35–58.

6. Ibid., 58.

7. Swift, *Black Prophets,* 216–217.

8. J. W. C. Pennington, "The Fugitive Blacksmith," in *Five Slave Narratives: A Compendium,* The American Negro: His History and Literature Series, ed. William Loren Katz (New York: Arno Press, 1968), 12–40.

9. Pennington, "The Fugitive Blacksmith," 56.

10. Frederick Douglass, *Life and Times of Frederick Douglass* (1892; repr., New York: Collier Books, 1962), 204–205.

11. White, "Fugitive Blacksmith," 14; Swift, *Black Prophets,* 236–237; and James Pennington, *Covenants Involving Moral Wrong Are Not Obligatory Upon Man* (Hartford: John C. Wells, 1842). See also Christopher L. Webber, *American to the Backbone: The Life of James W.C. Pennington, the Fugitive Slave Who Became One of the First Black Abolitionists* (New York: Pegasus Books, 2011), 237.

12. Jennet Boardman, "Midwife Records 1815–1849, Part IV," *Connecticut Historical Society Bulletin* 34, no. 4 (October 1969): 119–126, 125.

13. *Amos Beman Scrapbooks,* Beinecke Rare Book and Manuscript Library, Yale University, vol. 1, 35, 56.

14. White, "Fugitive Blacksmith," 11; Swift, *Black Prophets*, 217.

15. White, "Fugitive Blacksmith," 18.

16. Ann Plato, *Essays, Including Biographies and Miscellaneous Pieces, in Prose and Poetry* (1841; repr., foreword by Henry Louis Gates, Schomburg Library of Nineteenth-Century Black Women Writers, New York: Oxford University Press, 1988).

17. Ron Welburn, *Hartford's Ann Plato and the Native American Borders of Identity* (Albany: State University of New York Press, 2015).

18. David White, "Hartford's African Schools, 1830–1868," in *Connecticut Historical Society Bulletin* 39, no. 2 (April 1974): 48–49.

19. Plato, *Essays*, James W. C. Pennington, "Foreword," xviii–xx.

20. Gayle Tate, "Free Black Women in the Antebellum Era," in Darlene Clark Hine, *Black Women in America* (New York: Oxford University Press, 2005), I, 482.

21. The three women who can be placed in Hartford were Louisa Sebury (1816–1838), Eliza Loomis Sherman (1832–1839), and Elizabeth Low (1818–1838). Sebury and Sherman were born in Hartford; Low came from Cooperstown, and all were described as church members. Their families appear in the Hartford census variously between 1820 and 1850.

22. Swift, *Black Prophets*, 231, quoting the *Christian Freeman*, October 26, 1843.

23. The incident is related, with the quotation, in Swift, *Black Prophets*, 232–233.

24. *Colored American*, January 11, 1841, copy in the Beman Scrapbooks, Beinecke Rare Book and Manuscript Library, Yale University, 1, 38.

25. Swift, *Black Prophets*, 239.

26. David White, "Hartford's African Schools, 1830–1868," *Connecticut Historical Society Bulletin* 39, no. 2 (April 1974): 49. Augustus Washington taught in 1844 and 1845; Selah Africanus from 1847 to 1850.

27. David White, "Augustus Washington, Black Daguerreotypist of Hartford," *Connecticut Historical Society Bulletin* 39, no. 1 (January 1974): 14–19.

28. White, "Hartford's African Schools," 51.

29. Ibid., 52.

30. Ibid., 52–53.

31. White, "Augustus Washington," 18; *Hartford Courant*, "A Rare Glimpse at Augustus Washington," September 10, 1999.

32. *New York Tribune*, July 3, 1850.

33. *Hartford Courant*, September 27, 1858.

34. *Hartford Courant*, December 21, 1841. Henry R. Wilson is described as a native of Barbados and Mrs. Wilson as a native of Brooklyn, Connecticut, in the pamphlet "Mortgage Burning," 3.

35. David O. White, "Augustus Washington, Black Daguerreotypist of Hartford," *Connecticut Historical Society Bulletin* XXXIX, no. 1 (January 1974): 18.

36. White, "Augustus Washington," 18.

37. White, "African Schools," 48–49. On Africanus's birthplace, see Horatio Strother, *Underground Railroad in Connecticut* (Middletown, CT: Wesleyan University Press, 1969), 90.

38. The *New Haven Palladium*, September 15, 1849, in the Amos Beman Scrapbook, IV, 11,
    Beinecke Rare Book and Manuscript Library, Yale University.

39. See Connecticut State Archives, Rejected Bills, African Americans, RG 002, Box 2, Folders 11, 13, 15, 16.

40. See Connecticut State Archives, Rejected Bills, African Americans, RG 002, Box 2, Folder 20.

41. Ibid.

42. Eric Foner, *Gateway to Freedom: The Hidden History of the Underground Railroad* (New York: W. W. Norton, 2015), 30; and Barbara Donohue, "A Walk Along the Underground Railroad," in *African American Connecticut Explored*, ed. Elizabeth Normen et al. (Middletown, CT: Wesleyan University Press 2013), 171–173.

43. Webber, *American to the Backbone*, 158–169.

44. Swift, in *Black Prophets*, 238–239, cites James Pennington to Mr. Soul (of the British and Foreign Anti-Slavery Society), November 17, 1847. A.L.S. in Rhodes House, Department of Manuscripts, Oxford, England, MS British Empire C159–194 (microfilm copy in Carter and Ripley, eds., *BAP*, reel 4, item 296).

45. Swift, *Black Prophets*, 238–239.

46. Webber, *American to the Backbone*, 1.

47. John Hooker, *Some Reminiscences of a Long Life* (Hartford: Belknap & Warfield, 1889), 37–40.

48. *Autobiography of James L. Smith* (Norwich, CT: Press of the Bulletin Company, 1881), reprinted in *Five Black Lives*, intro. Arna Bontemps (Middletown, CT: Wesleyan University Press, 1971), 147–240.

49. Reprinted in *The Liberator* XX, no. 42, October 18, 1850, 167.

50. Ibid.

51. See Mars, *Life of James Mars*, 35–58. For his role in freeing Nancy, 55–56.

52. Swift, *Black Prophets*, 226–228.

53. The court case is outlined in Swift, *Black Prophets*, 226.

54. Mars, *Life of James Mars*, 56.

55. Chief Justice Williams was the brother-in-law of the Ellsworth brothers, who had hired Jeremiah Asher and Holdridge Primus upon their arrival in Hartford. Asher subsequently also worked for Williams.

56. Mars, *Life of James Mars*, 56.

57. *Hartford Courant*, October 24, 1850.

58. Frances A. Hoxie, "Connecticut's Forty-Niners," *Western Historical Quarterly* V, no. 1 (January 1974): 18.

59. Holdridge Primus obituary, source not given, in the Mary Morris Scrapbook of Obituaries, vol. 3, 53, Connecticut Historical Society. Another obituary, in the Hartford *Evening Post*, May 9, 1884, also mentions Primus going to California with a Hartford mining company.

60. Jacob D. B. Stillman, *Seeking the Golden Fleece* (San Francisco: A. Roman and Company, 1877), 280–281;

Charles R. Schultz, "The Gold Rush Voyage of the Ship *Pacific*: A Study in Ship Management," *The American Neptune: A Quarterly Journal of Maritime History* LIII, no. 3 (Summer 1993): 190. The incident involving Primus is related in the same source. The name of the company is supplied by Frances A. Hoxie, in "Connecticut's Forty-Niners," *Western Historical Quarterly* V, no. 1 (January 1974): 19.

61. Hartford Land Records, vol. 75, 495; vol. 77, 117. In a complicated transaction involving the American Asylum for the Deaf and Dumb as well as John Robinson, the price to Primus came to $1,750. The purchase was encumbered by Robinson's note for $500 to the American Asylum for the Deaf and Dumb—a note that Primus assumed as part of the agreement.

62. See Hartford Land Records, vol. 83, 583.

63. Schultz, "The Gold Rush Voyage of the Ship *Pacific*," 190. Much of the information here regarding incidents on the voyage comes from the same source. See also Hoxie, "Connecticut's Forty-Niners," 19. The date of departure is confirmed in the *New England Weekly Gazette*, January 27, 1849.

64. Hoxie, "Connecticut's Forty-Niners"; Stillman, *Seeking the Golden Fleece*, 280–281; Schultz, "The Gold Rush Voyage," 194–195; and Addison S. Clark, "Journal, 22 Jan. to 5 Dec. 1849 of a Voyage from New York to San Francisco in the Ship *Pacific*" (New Brunswick, NJ: Rutgers University Libraries).

65. Schultz, "The Gold Rush Voyage," 194–195.

66. Ibid., 195.

67. Stillman, *Seeking the Golden Fleece*, 81–82.

68. Schultz, "The Gold Rush Voyage," f.n. 25.

69. Primus obituary, *Hartford Evening Post*, May 9, 1884; also see Hoxie, "Connecticut's Forty-Niners," 24, 28. For the date of arrival in San Francisco, see *Hartford Courant*, October 11, 1849.

70. Hartford *Evening Post*, May 9, 1884.

71. Quarles, *Black Abolitionists*, 156.

Chapter 5. A Black Middle Class Takes Shape in a Time of War

1. In the 1850 census, Henrietta, aged twelve, was listed as residing in the household of a white man, James Babcock, and attending school.

2. David White, "Hartford's African Schools," *CHS Bulletin* 39, no. 2 (April 1974): 53.

3. Talcott Street Church pamphlet "Mortgage Burning of the Talcott Street Congregational Church, 1944" (Hartford: Faith Congregational Church, 1944) notes the visit by Garrison, and the daguerreotype exists.

4. Information from the 1830 and 1860 US Census.

5. For the Boston figure, see James O. Horton and Lois E. Horton, *Black Bostonians: Family Life and Community Struggle in the Antebellum North* (New York: Holmes & Meier, 1979), 13; for Providence, Robert J. Cottrol, *The Afro-Yankees: Providence's Black Community in the Ante-bellum Era* (Westport, CT: Greenwood Press, 1982), 117.

6. Horton and Horton, *Black Bostonians*, 13.

7. See Jean Boydston, "The Pastoralization of Housework," in *Women's America: Refocusing the Past*, ed. Linda K. Kerber and Jane Sherron De Hart (Oxford: Oxford University Press, 1995), 142–153. Also see the discussion of the "cult of domesticity" in Eric Foner, "Free Labor and Nineteenth-Century Political Ideology," in *The Market Revolution in America: Social, Political, and Religious Expressions, 1800–1880* (Charlottesville: University Press of Virginia, 1996), 99–127, 114–116.

8. Charles H. Proctor, *The Life of James Williams, Better Known as Professor Jim, for Half a Century Janitor of Trinity College* (Hartford: Case, Lockwood & Brainerd, 1873). Also see Williams obituary, May 21, 1878, in "Brocklesby Scrapbook," Watkinson Library, Trinity College.

9. Proctor, *The Life of James Williams,* 61; on his Masonic affiliation, see John E. Rogers, J. Elmer Dixon, and Leroy E. Fitch, comps., *History of Most Worshipful Prince Hall Grand Lodge of Connecticut, Inc., F. & A.M.*, paperback (Connecticut: The Lodge, 1973), Bronson Library, Waterbury, CT, 36.

10. In all, thirty-five blacks owned property in 1860. The forty individuals listed are a sampling of middle-class householders.

11. Jeremiah was the grandson of Reese Jacobs, who had come to Hartford with his family as a free man in 1769. See the Kingsbury Census, Stowe Center manuscript collection. Jeremiah's father, also Jeremiah, had been a shoemaker and homeowner.

12. Holdridge Primus Estate, Probate Inventory, Hartford County, city of Hartford, May 29, 1884. On the emblems of middle-class status, see Richard L. Bushman, *The Refinement of America: Persons, Houses, Cities* (New York: Vintage Books, 1993), 273, 434.

13. Bushman, *The Refinement of America*, 232. Citing the work of historian Stuart Blumin, Bushman describes pianos as "emblems of middle-class living." See Bushman, *The Refinement of America*, 232, 434.

14. Mehitable Primus, Hartford, to Rebecca Primus, Royal Oak, November 10, 1867.

15. The letters of Rebecca and Nelson Primus provide this information.

16. The letters of Addie Brown during the late 1860s detail informal social events in the Primus home, often featuring music. She names local and out-of-town visitors who occasionally appear at such gatherings. See Chapter 6.

17. *Hartford Evening Post*, May 9, 1884. Genealogist Colleen Cyr brought this clipping to my attention.

18. Cottrol, *The Afro-Yankees*, 143.

19. Civil War Pension Records, Bureau of Pensions, Department of the Interior, National Archives, Washington, DC, Application 302292; Certificate 420368, and a second, filed by his widow, Nancy, Application 904511, Certificate 772517.

20. Geer's City Directory, 1853; *Hartford Times*, January 19, 1903.

21. Hartford *Courant*, May 17, 1859.

22. Rogers, Dixon, and Fitch, *History of Most Worshipful Prince Hall Grand Lodge of Connecticut,* 36–37.

23. David Gray, *Inside Prince Hall* (Lancaster, VA: Anchor Communications, 2004), 104.

24. Nick Salvatore, *We All Got History: The Memory Books of Amos Webber* (New York: Vintage Books, 1997), 61.

25. *The Liberator* 4, February 22, 1834, 4.

26. *Hartford Evening Press*, September 20, 1862, in Amos Beman Scrapbooks, Beinecke Rare Book and Manuscript Library, Yale University, 2, 88. See also *Hartford Courant*, January 11, 1866; and Addie Brown, Hartford, to Rebecca Primus, Royal Oak, November 3, 1866.

27. Addie Brown, Hartford, to Rebecca Primus, Royal Oak, January 21, 1866.

28. A copy of the talk is in the Rebecca Primus file, Primus Papers, Manuscript Collection, Connecticut Historical Society. See Chapter 7 for the text.

29. See Stephanie J. Shaw, *What a Woman Ought to Be and to Do: Black Professional Women Workers during the Jim Crow Era* (Chicago: University of Chicago Press, 1996); and Glenda Elizabeth Gilmore: *Women and the Politics of White Supremacy in North Carolina, 1896–1920* (Asheville: University of North Carolina Press, 1996).

30. *Anglo-African*, September 21, 1861; quoted in James McPherson, *The Negro's Civil War: How American Blacks Felt and Acted During the War for the Union*, Vintage Civil War Library (New York: Vintage Books, 1993), 40–41.

31. Frederick Douglass's *Monthly* IV (July 1861), 486; quoted in McPherson, *The Negro's Civil War*, 38.

32. Nelson Primus, Boston, to mother, Hartford, April 25, 1865.

33. Bethuel Hunter, *No Man Can Hinder Me: Black Troops in the Union Armies During the American Civil War*, exhibition catalog (New Haven: Beinecke Rare Book and Manuscript Library, 2003), 13.

34. Diana Ross McCain, *Connecticut's African-American Soldiers in the Civil War, 1861–1865* (Hartford: Connecticut Historical Commission, 2000), ll. Also see the brochure "One Hundred Seventy-fifth Anniversary Faith Congregational Church," Hartford, 1994, 6.

35. McPherson, *The Negro's Civil War*, 175–176.

36. McPherson, *The Negro's Civil War*, 176. Also see Richard Slotkin, *No Quarter: The Battle of the Crater, 1864* (New York: Random House, 2009).

37. Hunter, *No Man Can Hinder Me*, 16.

38. McPherson, *The Negro's Civil War*, 176–177. After hostilities ceased, "a handful of black soldiers were awarded commissions." See also Hunter, *No Man Can Hinder Me*, 17, 19–20.

39. Hunter, *No Man Can Hinder Me*, 23–25.

40. Addie Brown, New York City, to Rebecca Primus, Hartford, July 22, 1861.

41. Addie Brown, New York City, to Rebecca Primus, Hartford, September 17, 1861.

42. See Richard Slotkin, *No Quarter: The Battle of the Crater, 1864* (New York: Random House, 2009), 256. Also see Hunter, *No Man Can Hinder Me*, 32–35.

43. McCain, *Connecticut's African American Soldiers*, 21.

44. I. J. Hill, *A Sketch of the Twenty-ninth Regiment Connecticut Colored Troops* (Baltimore: Daugherty, Maguire & Co., 1867), 7, quoted in McCain, *Connecticut's African-American Soldiers*, 24.

45. See Lloyd Seymour, Application 302292; Certificate 42036, Civil War Pension Applications, National Archives.

46. Ibid.

47. Worthy H. E. Brewster, Application 207415, Certificate 176966, Civil War Pension Records, National Archives.

48. Isaac Scott, Application 996145, Certificate 792679, Civil War Pension Records, National Archives.

49. Thomas Sands Pennington enlisted in the Twentieth Regiment, USCT. New York State Archives, Civil War Service Record 6007. See Webber, *American to the Backbone*, 247–248.

50. Lancaster County Historical Society, Lancaster, PA, Document Collection, Archives, Box 17, folder 16, contains a handwritten biography of the Rev. J. W. C. Pennington by Thomas Sands Pennington, which states that Pennington adopted Thomas Sands "at the time of his second marriage" in 1847.

51. Patrick Rael, *Black Identity and Black Protest in the Antebellum North* (Chapel Hill: University of North Carolina Press, 2002), 288.

52. Historian David O. White, "Addie Brown's Hartford," *Connecticut Historical Society Bulletin* 41 (April 1976): 57–64.

Chapter 6. Nelson Primus: The Artist in Boston

1. Nelson Primus, Boston, to mother, Hartford, April 25, 1865. Nelson refers to the Arlington Congregational Unitarian Church, 351 Boylston St.

2. Ibid.

3. Nelson Primus, Boston, to mother, Hartford, July 10, 1865.

4. James A. Porter, *Modern Negro Art*, intro. David C. Driskell (1943; repr., Washington, DC: Howard University Press, 1992), 19.

5. Porter, *Modern Negro Art*, 30.

6. Alexis de Tocqueville, *Democracy in America* (1831; repr., New York: Vintage Books, 1990), 2: 48.

7. Sharon F. Patton, *African-American Art*, Oxford History of Art (Oxford: Oxford University Press, 1998), 71.

8. Nelson Primus, Boston, to mother, Hartford, July 10, 1865, and February 3, 1867.

9. Nelson Primus, Boston, to Isabella, Hartford, March 27, 1867.

10. Amos Gerry Beman, "A Visit to Hartford," *Weekly Anglo-African*, October 25, 1862, in the Beman Scrapbooks, Beinecke Rare Book and Manuscript Library, Yale University, II, 2. E. M. Thomas was a black intellectual who wrote of black achievements.

11. Juanita Marie Holland, "'Co-Workers in the Kingdom of Culture,' Edward Mitchell Bannister and the Boston Community of African American Artists, 1848–1901" (PhD diss., Columbia University, 1998), 12. Holland quotes Bannister's account as told to George Whitaker, author of "Edward M. Bannister," undated typescript, Edward Mitchell Bannister Papers, Archives of American Art, Washington, DC, 4–5.

12. Patton, *African-American Art*, 102.

13. Nelson Primus, Boston, to Isabella, January 27, 1867.

14. Jennet Boardman, "Midwife Records 1815–1849, Part IV," *Connecticut Historical Society Bulletin* 34, no. 4 (October 1969): 119–126.

15. Nelson Primus, Boston, to mother, Hartford, July 10, 1865.

16. Nelson Primus, Boston, to Isabella, Hartford, March 18, 1867.

17. H. W. French, *Art and Artists in Connecticut* (1879; repr., New York: Penguin Books, 1996), 46–47.

18. Ibid., 169. Mrs. Jerome's background is outlined in her obituary in the *Hartford Daily Courant*, April 25, 1910.

19. *Hartford Courant*, September 28, 1859, and October 20, 1859.

20. French, *Art and Artists in Connecticut*, 155.

21. Walter O. Evans, collector of black art and print materials, provided a copy of this valuable find.

22. Amoretta's birthplace is given on the death certificate of her second born: Commonwealth of Massachusetts, 1876, vol. 284, p. 164, no. 221; her parents are named on her own death certificate: Commonwealth of Massachusetts, 1876, vol. 284, p. 165, no. 238. Her name is sometimes recorded as "Prince."

23. Hartford Marriage Records microfilm 1863–1865, 492. Connecticut State Library, Hartford. Newspaper announcements of the marriage give her last name as "Prince."

24. Information on the likelihood of survival for a premature infant at the time is from Dr. Theodore Johnson, ob-gyn, retired. Interviewed by the author by telephone on January 4, 2007, and in person on January 6, 2007.

25. Nelson's first letter was dated April 25, 1865.

26. For more on Bannister, see Holland, " 'Co-Workers in the Kingdom of Culture,' " 13–55ff. Also see Porter, *Modern Negro Art*, 44–47; and Patton, *African-American Art*, 86–90.

27. Nelson Primus, Boston, to mother, Hartford, July 10, 1865.

28. Holland, "Co-Workers in the Kingdom of Culture," 49.

29. From 1862 to 1873, the Boston city directory listed Stetfield as an artist in the Studio Building. Information on Stetfield supplied by Cecile W. Gardner, Fine Arts reference librarian, Boston Public Library.

30. The six-inch-by-eight-inch lithograph, published by J. Mayer & Co., Boston, is attributed to C. E. Stetfield by Andrew Sutherland of Heritage Fabrications, Newark, Delaware.

31. Nelson Primus, Boston, to mother, Hartford, February 3, 1867.

32. Holland, "Co-Workers in the Kingdom of Culture," 55–59.

33. Patton, *African-American Art*, 91–98.

34. Nelson Primus, Boston, to father, Hartford, January 28, 1866.

35. Nelson Primus, Boston, to mother, Hartford, February 3, 1867.

36. Nelson Primus, Boston, to mother, Hartford, October 27, 1867.

37. Nelson Primus, Boston, to mother, Hartford, July 10, 1865.

38. Nelson Primus, Boston, to mother, Hartford, April 25, 1865.

39. Nelson Primus, Boston, to mother, Hartford, October 27, 1867; and Nelson Primus, Boston, to father, Hartford, May 23, 1866.

40. Nelson Primus, Boston, to father, Hartford, May 23, 1866.

41. Nelson Primus, Boston, to mother, Hartford, September 21, 1865; and Nelson Primus, Boston, to Isabella, Hartford, July 31, 1866.

42. Nelson Primus, Boston, to mother, Hartford, November 29, 1866.

43. Nelson Primus, Boston, to Isabella, Hartford, January 27, 1867.

44. Nelson Primus, Boston, to Isabella, Hartford, February 6, 1867.

45. Nelson Primus, Boston, to Isabella, Hartford, January 27, 1867.

46. *Historical Statistics of the United States: Colonial Times to 1970* (Washington, DC: US Bureau of the Census, 1975), Part 1, Series D, 728–734, p. 165.

47. Frank Moore, *Women of the War: Their Heroism and Self-Sacrifice* (Hartford: S. S. Scranton & Company, 1866).

48. Nelson Primus, Boston, to Isabella, Hartford, March 13, 1867.

49. Nelson Primus, Boston, to Isabella, Hartford, March 13, 1867.

50. Nelson Primus, Boston, to mother, Hartford, March 22, 1867.

51. Nelson Primus, Boston, to mother, Hartford, March 22, 1867. William Wells Brown's *The Negro in the American Rebellion: His Heroism and His Fidelity* was published by Lee & Shepard in Boston in 1867.

52. Nelson Primus, Boston, to mother, Hartford, March 22, 1867.

53. Nelson Primus, Boston, to mother, Hartford, April 28, 1867.

54. Nelson Primus, Boston, to mother, Hartford, April 28, 1867.

55. Nelson Primus, Boston, to Isabella, Hartford, November 30, 1867.

56. Nelson Primus, Boston, to Isabella, Hartford, July 3, 1866.

57. Nelson Primus, Boston, to Isabella, Hartford, September 6, 1867.

58. Both quotes in Nelson Primus, Boston, to Isabella, Hartford, July 31, 1866. Mrs. Tredwell is the wife of the barbershop owner who hired Nelson to paint a sign and who joined him for sessions of music making.

59. Nelson Primus, Boston, to Isabella, Hartford, March 7, 1868.

60. Nelson Primus, Boston, to Isabella, Hartford, July 7, 1866. Babies normally learn to walk between nine and fifteen months.

61. Nelson Primus, Boston, to Isabella, Hartford, March 13, 1867.

62. Ibid.

63. Joanne M. Martin and Elmer P. Martin, *The Helping Tradition in the Black Family and Community* (Silver Spring, MD: National Association of Social Workers, 1985), 1–2, 16, 36–43. See also Salvatore, *We All Got History*, 295.

64. Nelson Primus, Boston, to mother, Hartford, April 28, 1867.

65. Nelson Primus, Boston, to Isabella, Hartford, January 27, 1867.

66. Nelson Primus, Boston, to Isabella, Hartford, January 27, 1867.

67. On the Rev. Grimes, see Horton and Horton, *Black Bostonians*, 44, 47; also Benjamin Quarles, *Black Abolitionists* (New York: Oxford University Press, 1969), 146, 206–209, 242.

68. Nelson Primus, Boston, to mother, Hartford, July 10, 1865. The *Anglo-African Magazine* ceased publication in 1865, its mission accomplished.

69. Nelson Primus, Boston, to mother, Hartford, April 28, 1867.

70. This unfound portrait is reported in a George Forbes typewritten manuscript, "Bannister and Other Artists," in Boston Public Library Rare Books and Manuscripts collection.

71. Nelson Primus, Boston, to father, Hartford, January 28, 1866.

72. Both Rebecca Primus and Addie Brown mention Clara, Charles, and other members of the Mitchell family in their letters.

73. On Charles Mitchell, see John Daniels, *In Freedom's Birthplace: A Study of the Boston Negroes* (New York: Negro Universities Press, 1914), 98, 99.

74. Nelson Primus, Boston, to mother, Hartford, October 27, 1867.

75. Nelson Primus, Boston, to mother, Hartford, March 22, 1867.

76. See the *New York Times*, March 19 and 25, 1867.

77. Quote is from Elizabeth Pleck, *Black Migration and Poverty: Boston 1865–1900* (New York: Academic Press, 1979), 25.

78. Ibid., 28.

79. Nelson Primus, Boston, to mother, Hartford, October 27, 1867.

80. Nelson Primus, Boston, to mother, Hartford, April 28, 1867.

81. Rebecca Primus, Royal Oak, to family, Hartford, June 1, 1867.

82. Addie Brown, Hartford, to Rebecca Primus, Royal Oak, December 16, 1866.

83. Addie Brown, Hartford, to Rebecca Primus, Royal Oak, January 1, January 7, February 18, February 25, and March 11, 1866.

84. Addie Brown, Hartford, to Rebecca Primus, Royal Oak, January 18, 1866.

85. Nelson Primus, Boston, to father, Hartford, May 23, 1866.

86. Rebecca Primus, Royal Oak, to family, Hartford, April 7, 1866.

87. Addie Brown, Farmington, to Rebecca Primus, Royal Oak, June 23, 1867.

88. Nelson Primus, Boston, to father, Hartford, May 23, 1866.

89. Nelson Primus, Boston, to Isabella, Hartford, January 27, 1867. See David M. Ludlum, *Early American Winters II: 1821–1870, History of American Weather* (Boston: American Meteorological Society, 1968), 72–73.

90. Nelson Primus, Boston, to mother, Hartford, April 28, 1867.

91. Nelson Primus, Boston, to mother, Hartford, October 18, 1867.

Chapter 7. Rebecca Primus: The Teacher in Royal Oak

1. Rebecca Primus, Royal Oak, to family, Hartford, April 7, 1866.

2. Forty-eight of Rebecca's letters to her parents and Isabella have been preserved; undoubtedly some were lost.

3. Jennet Boardman, "Midwife Records 1815–1849, Part IV," *Connecticut Historical Society Bulletin* 34, no. 4 (October 1969): 120.

4. The two essays are in the Primus Papers in the Connecticut Historical Society, Hartford.

5. Addie Brown, Waterbury, to Rebecca Primus, Hartford, August 2, 1859. Also see letters to Rebecca from Addie Brown, New York, January 10, 1862; from Hartford, December 9, 1862; January 8, 1864; and November 28, 1866.

6. "Second Annual Report of the Baltimore Association for the Moral and Educational Improvement of the Colored People" (Baltimore: J. B. Rose and Co., 1866), 7.

7. Based on the US Census, the average age of blacks who married in Hartford in 1860 was twenty-four.

8. Addie Brown, Hartford, to Rebecca Primus, Hartford, October 28, 1862.

9. *Hartford City Directory,* 1866; also the *Hartford Courant*, June 11, 1866. Stowe and his wife moved to Hartford in 1864.

10. Richard Paul Fuke, "The Baltimore Association for the Moral and Educational Improvement of the Colored People 1864–1870," *Maryland Historical Magazine* 46, no. 4 (Winter 1971): 369–404.

11. *Hartford Courant*, June 11, 1866. Other teachers sponsored by the program included Carrie Loomis and Rebecca H. Elwell, according to an unidentified clipping, dated 1869, in the Primus Papers, Connecticut Historical Society.

12. Rebecca Primus, Baltimore, to family, Hartford, November 8, 1865.

13. Ibid.

14. "Second Annual Report of the Baltimore Association, 14–16, 7.

15. James O. Horton and Lois E. Horton, *In Hope of Liberty: Culture, Community and Protest Among Northern Free Blacks, 1700–1860* (New York: Oxford University Press, 1997), xi.

16. Richard Paul Fuke, "Land, Lumber, and Learning: The Freedmen's Bureau, Education, and the Black Community in Post-Emancipation Maryland," in Paul A. Cimbala and Randall M. Miller, *The Freedmen's Bureau and Reconstruction: Reconsiderations* (New York: Fordham University Press, 1999), 289.

17. "Second Annual Report of the Baltimore Association," 16, 18. Rebecca's salary was paid at first by the New England Society and later by the New York Society.

18. Information on Freedmen's Bureau schools in Eric Foner, *Reconstruction: America's Unfinished Revolution: 1863–1877* (New York: Harper and Row, 1989), 144–145.

19. Rebecca Primus, Baltimore, to family, Hartford, November 8, 1865.

20. Fuke, "Land, Lumber, and Learning," 293–294. Also see the "Second Annual Report" of the Baltimore Association, 4.

21. Sandra E. Small, "The Yankee Schoolmarm in Freedmen's Schools: An Analysis of Attitudes," *The Journal of Southern History* 45, no. 3 (August 1979): 398.

22. Rebecca Primus, Royal Oak, to family, Hartford, October 6, 1866.

23. Royal Oak and Hartford censuses of 1860.

24. The 1860 Royal Oak census.

25. Charles Thomas's middle initial is given variously over the years as N., H., and M. His middle name is not given.

26. Rebecca Primus, Royal Oak, to family, Hartford, November 8, 1868.

27. Rebecca Primus, Royal Oak, to family, Hartford, April 28, 1867.

28. Charles Thomas obituary, *Hartford Courant*, August 3, 1891.

29. Rebecca Primus, Royal Oak, to family, Hartford April 7, 1866.

30. Rebecca Primus, Royal Oak, to family, Hartford, December 1, 1866.

31. Rebecca Primus, Royal Oak, to family, Hartford, June 2, 1866.

32. Rebecca Primus, Royal Oak, to family, Hartford, May 18, 1867.

33. Rebecca Primus, Royal Oak, to family, Hartford, April 11, 1869.

34. Farah Jasmine Griffin, ed., *Beloved Sisters and Loving Friends: Letters from Rebecca Primus of Royal Oak, Maryland, and Addie Brown of Hartford, Connecticut, 1854–1868* (New York: Alfred A. Knopf, 1999), 260.

35. Primus Papers, Connecticut Historical Society. While branches of the Thomas family appear in the Royal Oak census for 1860, 1870, and 1880, Sallie Thomas is not among them.

36. For the quote, Foner, *Reconstruction*, 146; see also Small, "Yankee Schoolmarm," 393.

37. Rebecca Primus, Royal Oak, to family, Hartford, February 16, 1867.

38. Rebecca Primus, Royal Oak, to family, Hartford, February 8, 1867.

39. Rebecca Primus, Royal Oak, to family, Hartford, February 8, 1867.

40. Rebecca Primus, Royal Oak, to family, Hartford, February 23, 1867.

41. Rebecca Primus, Royal Oak, to family, Hartford, April 13, 1867.

42. Rebecca Primus, Royal Oak, to family, Hartford, May 18, 1867.

43. Charlotte Forten, *The Journals of Charlotte Forten Grimke*, ed. Brenda Stevenson (New York: Oxford University Press, 1988), 402.

44. Forten, *The Journals of Charlotte Forten Grimke*, 423–424.

45. Forten, *The Journals of Charlotte Forten Grimke*, 393, 425.

46. Rebecca Primus, Royal Oak, to family, Hartford, November 8, 1868.

47. Rebecca Primus, Royal Oak, to family, Hartford, March 10, 1867.

48. Foner, *Reconstruction*, 147.

49. Rebecca Primus, Royal Oak, to family, Hartford, October 1, 1866.

50. Ibid.

51. Rebecca Primus, Royal Oak, to family, Hartford, March 30, 1867.

52. Rebecca Primus, Royal Oak, to family, Hartford, December 1, 1866.

53. Rebecca Primus, Royal Oak, to family, Hartford, December 1, 1866.

54. Rebecca Primus, Royal Oak, to family, Hartford, October 6, 1866.

55. For this and the quote that follows, Rebecca Primus, Royal Oak, to family, Hartford, February 23, 1867.

56. Rebecca Primus, Royal Oak, to family, Hartford, December 8, 1866.

57. Rebecca Primus, Royal Oak, to family, Hartford, December 8, 1866.

58. Fuke, "The Baltimore Association," 384, f.n. 53.

59. Primus Papers, Connecticut Historical Society.

60. Rebecca Primus, Royal Oak, to family, Hartford, May 11, 1867.

61. Rebecca Primus, Royal Oak, to family, Hartford, May 25, 1867.

62. Rebecca Primus, Royal Oak, to family, Hartford, April 4, 1868.

63. Richard Paul Fuke, "The Baltimore Association, 399–400. See also Small, "Yankee Schoolmarm," 395–396; and Foner, *Reconstruction*, 146.

64. Rebecca Primus, Royal Oak, to family, Hartford, October 6, 1866.

65. Rebecca Primus, Royal Oak, to family, Hartford, December 8, 1866.

66. The *Hartford Courant*, February 7, 1867.

67. The *Hartford Courant*, February 7, 1867.

68. Addie Brown, Hartford, to Rebecca Primus, Royal Oak, February 16, 1867.

69. Rebecca Primus, Royal Oak, to family, Hartford, March 2, 1867.

70. Rebecca Primus, Royal Oak, to family, Hartford, March 2, 1867.

71. Rebecca Primus, Royal Oak, to family, Hartford, March 16, 1867.

72. Rebecca Primus, Royal Oak, to family, Hartford, March 16, 1867.

73. Rebecca Primus, Royal Oak to family, Hartford March 16, 1867.

74. Rebecca Primus, Royal Oak, to family, Hartford, March 30, 1867.

75. Rebecca Primus, Royal Oak, to family, Hartford, April 18, 1867. The Freedmen's Bureau supplied used lumber for schoolhouses.

76. Rebecca Primus, Royal Oak, to family, Hartford, May 11, 1867.

77. Rebecca Primus, Royal Oak, to family, Hartford, May 18 and 25, 1867.

78. Rebecca Primus, Royal Oak, to family, Hartford, September 30, 1867.

79. The original specifications called for dimensions twenty by twenty-five by sixteen feet in height, but the Baltimore Association revised these to the measurements shown above. See Rebecca Primus letter, Royal Oak, March 2, 1867; and Rebecca Primus statement of her "mission South," September 1, 1867.

80. Rebecca Primus, Royal Oak, to family, Hartford, September 30, 1867.

81. The *Hartford Evening Press*, November 7, 1867.

82. Rebecca Primus, Royal Oak, to family, Hartford, April 8, 1868.

83. David O. White, "Rebecca Primus in Later Life," in Griffin, *Beloved Sisters*, 280.

84. Griffin, *Beloved Sisters*, 269.

85. Rebecca Primus, Royal Oak, to family, Hartford, May 25, 1867.

86. Rebecca Primus, Royal Oak, to family, Hartford, June 2, 1866.

87. Rebecca Primus, Royal Oak, to family, Hartford, April 8, 1866.

88. Rebecca Primus, Royal Oak, to family, Hartford, June 2, 1866.

89. Ibid.

90. See Fuke, "Land, Lumber, and Learning," 296, 297, 305. Also see O. O. Howard, *Autobiography of O. O. Howard, Major General United States Army 1830–1909* (New York: Baker and Taylor, 1907), 273.

91. See Rebecca Primus, Royal Oak, to family, Hartford, December 1, 1866.

92. Rebecca Primus, Royal Oak, to family, Hartford, April 13, 1867.

93. Rebecca Primus, Royal Oak, to family, Hartford, April 7, 1866. Harriet Hamilton, white, and Rebecca Primus were the first two teachers sent South by the Hartford Freedmen's Society, according to the *Hartford Courant*, June 11, 1866.

94. Rebecca Primus, Royal Oak, to family, Hartford, December 6, 1866.

95. Rebecca Primus, Royal Oak, to family, Hartford, December 1, 1866.

96. On the law aimed at stopping abolitionist propaganda, see Preston Dickson, *Talbot County, A History* (Centreville, MD: Tidewater Publishers, 1983), 204.

97. On the Jebusites, see Exodus 33:2.

98. Rebecca Primus, Royal Oak, to family, Hartford, February 23, 1867.

99. Bernard Schwartz, ed., *Statutory History of the United States: Civil Rights*, I (New York: Chelsea House Publishers, 1970), 199.

100. Section 2 of the bill in Schwartz, *Statutory History of the United States*, I, 199.

101. Rebecca Primus, Royal Oak, to family, Hartford, April 7, 1866.

102. The 1848 Seneca Falls convention set off agitation that finally resulted in women's suffrage in 1920. See Judith Wellman, "The Seneca Falls Women's Rights Convention: A Study of Social Networks," in Linda K. Kerber and Jan Sherron De Hart, eds., *Women's America: Refocusing the Past* (New York: Oxford University Press, 1995), 203–215.

103. Rebecca Primus, Royal Oak, to family, Hartford, December 14, 1867.

104. The name "Thumbiana" is derived from Tom Thumb, Barnum's midget protégé. Sophronia or Thronieve was named an heir in Holdridge's will.

105. See the following Rebecca Primus letters: Royal Oak: n.d. 1866; April 7, 1866; December 14, 1866; February 8, 1867; February 23, 1867; March 2, 1867; March 10, 1867; March 16, 1867; March 23, 1867; December 8, 1867; and March 16, 1868.

106. Rebecca Primus, Royal Oak, to family, Hartford, March 23, 1867.

107. Information on the Booth [or Boothe] family is from Joseph Carvalho III, *Black Families in Hampden County, Massachusetts 1650–1855* (Westfield, MA: New England Historic Genealogical Society and Institute for Massachusetts Studies, Westfield State College, 1984), 33–34.

108. See Caroline Ladd Gates, comp., "Pupils of Springfield High School, Classes of 1845–1863," vol. I, MS list, in Connecticut Valley Historical Museum, Springfield, MA.

109. Rebecca Primus, Royal Oak, to family, Hartford, March 10, 1867.

110. Rebecca Primus, Royal Oak, to family, Hartford, September 27, 1866.

111. Rebecca Primus, Royal Oak, to family, Hartford, March 16, 1867.

112. Rebecca Primus, Royal Oak, to family, Hartford, May 18, 1867.

113. Rebecca Primus, Royal Oak, to family, Hartford, April 28, 1867.

114. Rebecca Primus, Royal Oak, to family, Hartford, December 17, 1868.

115. Rebecca Primus, Royal Oak, to family, Hartford, October 1, 1866.

116. Rebecca Primus, Royal Oak, to family, Hartford, July 3, 1869.

117. Charles Thomas, Royal Oak, to Mehitable Primus, Hartford, July 8, 1868.

Chapter 8. Addie Brown: The Working Girl in Hartford

1. Addie Brown, Hartford, to Rebecca Primus, Royal Oak, January 16, 1866.

2. Henrietta Primus, Hartford, to Rebecca, Royal Oak, December 15, 1865.

3. Addie Brown, New York, to Rebecca, Hartford, February 23, 1862.

4. J. L. Dillard, "The Development of Black English," in *A History of American English* (New York: Longman Group, 1992), 60–92, esp. 65, 82.

5. Addie Brown, Hartford, to Rebecca Primus, Royal Oak, n.d. November 1865.

6. Addie Brown, Farmington, to Rebecca Primus, Royal Oak, May 19, 1867.

7. Addie Brown, Farmington, to Rebecca Primus, Royal Oak, February 1, 1866.

8. Addie Brown, New York, to Rebecca Primus, Royal Oak, March 5, 1862.

9. On Addie's birth date, see Addie Brown, Hartford, to Rebecca Primus, Royal Oak, June 5, 1866. On the unidentified aunt in Philadelphia, see Addie Brown, New York, to Rebecca Primus, Hartford, July 2, 1861.

10. Addie Brown, Farmington, to Rebecca Primus, Royal Oak, October 6, 1867.

11. Addie Brown, New York, to Rebecca Primus, Hartford, January 10, 1862; Hartford, November 10, 1865; December 10, 1865. For Ally's Civil War service, see Griffin, *Beloved Sisters*, 18.

12. David White, "Addie Brown's Hartford," *Connecticut Historical Society Bulletin* 41, no. 2 (April 1976): 57.

13. Farah Griffin, *Beloved Sisters*, 12.

14. Farah Griffin, *Beloved Sisters*, 7.

15. Karen V. Hansen, " 'No Kisses Is Like Youres': An Erotic Friendship Between Two African-American Women During the Mid-Nineteenth Century," *Gender and History* 7, no. 2 (July 1995): 153.

16. Carroll Smith-Rosenberg, "The Female World of Love and Ritual: Relations Between Women in Nineteenth-Century America," in *Disorderly Conduct: Visions of Gender in Victorian America* (New York: Alfred A. Knopf, 1985), 53–76; and Lillian Faderman, *Surpassing the Love of Men: Romantic Friendship and Love between Women from the Renaissance to the Present* (New York: William Morrow, 1981), 157–177.

17. Smith-Rosenberg, "The Female World of Love and Ritual, 53–76.

18. Addie Brown, Waterbury, to Rebecca Primus, Hartford, August 2, 1859.

19. Addie Brown, Waterbury, to Rebecca Primus, Hartford, August 30, 1859.

20. Addie Brown, Waterbury, to Rebecca Primus, Hartford, August 30, 1859.

21. Addie Brown, Hartford, to Rebecca Primus, Royal Oak, November 16, 1865.

22. Addie Brown, Hartford, to Rebecca Primus, Royal Oak, April 10, 1866.

23. Addie Brown, Waterbury, to Rebecca Primus, Hartford, August 30, 1859.

24. Addie Brown, Hartford, to Rebecca Primus, Hartford, August 31, 1861.

25. Addie Brown, Hartford, to Rebecca Primus, Hartford, September 21, 1862.

26. Griffin, *Beloved Sisters*, 32.

27. Addie Brown, New York, to Rebecca Primus, Hartford, October 2, 1861; Addie Brown, Hartford, to Rebecca Primus, Hartford, December 9, 1862.

28. Griffin, *Beloved Sisters*, 73.

29. Addie Brown, Hartford, to Rebecca Primus, Royal Oak, May 20, 1866.

30. Faderman, *Surpassing the Love of Men,* 160–177; and Smith-Rosenberg, *Disorderly Conduct,* 59–60.

31. Axel Nissen, *The Romantic Friendship Reader: Love Stories between Men in Victorian America* (Boston: Northeastern University Press, 2003), 7.

32. Nissen, *Romantic Friendship Reader,* 3–10; also see David Deitcher, *Dear Friends: American Photographs of Men Together, 1840–1918* (New York: Harry N. Abrams, 2001).

33. Hansen, "No Kisses Is Like Youres," 160–163.

34. Addie Brown, Farmington, to Rebecca Primus, Royal Oak, November 17, 1867. Addie described the girl as "English"; Farah Griffin suggests she more likely was Irish. Griffin, *Beloved Sisters,* 224.

35. Hansen, "No Kisses Is Like Youres," 172–174; and Smith-Rosenberg, "The Female World of Love and Ritual," 59.

36. Addie Brown, Hartford, to Rebecca Primus, Hartford, December 9, 1862.

37. Addie Brown, Hartford, to Rebecca Primus, Royal Oak, February 1, 1866.

38. Addie Brown, Hartford, to Rebecca Primus, Royal Oak, January 21, 1866.

39. Addie Brown, Hartford, to Rebecca Primus, Baltimore, November 16, 1865.

40. See Addie Brown, Hartford, to Rebecca Primus, Royal Oak, January 21, 1866.

41. Addie Brown, Hartford, to Rebecca, Royal Oak, March 31, 1867.

42. Addie Brown, Hartford, to Rebecca, Royal Oak, January 9, 1867.

43. Addie Brown, Hartford, to Rebecca, Royal Oak, January 14, 1867.

44. Rebecca Primus, Royal Oak, to family, Hartford, January 19, 1867.

45. Horton and Horton, *Black Bostonians,* 16–18.

46. Rebecca Primus, Royal Oak, to family, Hartford, March 23, 1867.

47. US Census, Hartford, 1850.

48. Addie Brown, Hartford, to Rebecca Primus, Royal Oak, December 3, 1865.

49. Addie Brown, Hartford, to Rebecca Primus, Royal Oak, January 21, 1866.

50. Addie Brown, Waterbury, to Rebecca Primus, Hartford, February 16, 1860.

51. Griffin, *Beloved Sisters,* 27–28.

52. Addie Brown, Hartford, to Rebecca Primus, Royal Oak, November 10, 1865.

53. George Smith's Dye House was at 37 Wells Street, a short walk from the Sands house on Wadsworth Street.

54. Addie Brown, Hartford, to Rebecca Primus, Baltimore, November 10, 1865.

55. Addie Brown, Hartford, to Rebecca Primus, Baltimore, November 16, 1865.

56. See *U.S. Department of the Interior, Statistics of the United States (Including Mortality, Property, etc.) in 1860* (Washington, DC, 1866), 512.

57. Addie Brown, Hartford, to Rebecca Primus, Royal Oak, December 1, 1865.

58. Addie Brown, Waterbury, to Rebecca Primus, Royal Oak, February 16, 1860.

59. Addie Brown, Hartford, to Rebecca Primus, Royal Oak, February 18, 1866.

60. For this quote and the account that follows, see Addie Brown, Hartford, to Rebecca Primus, Royal Oak, February 15, 1866.

61. Addie Brown, Hartford, to Rebecca Primus, Royal Oak, March 25, 1866.

62. Addie Brown, Hartford, to Rebecca Primus, Royal Oak, March 25, 1866. .

63. Addie Brown, Hartford, to Rebecca Primus, Royal Oak, April 29, 1866.

64. Glenn Weaver and Michael Swift, *Hartford: Connecticut's Capital* (Sun Valley, CA: American Historical Press, 2003), 35.

65. Addie Brown, Hartford, to Rebecca Primus, Baltimore, November 3, 1866.

66. Addie Brown, Farmington, to Rebecca Primus, Royal Oak, May 5, 1867. Miss Porter was known to advocate long walks.

67. Addie Brown, Farmington, to Rebecca Primus, Royal Oak, May 5, 1867.

68. Addie Brown, Farmington, to Rebecca Primus, Royal Oak, May 12, 1867.

69. Addie Brown, Farmington, to Rebecca Primus, Royal Oak, January 19, 1868.

70. Addie Brown, Farmington, to Rebecca Primus, Royal Oak, May 12, 1867; June 2, 1867; and April 28, 1867.

71. Addie Brown, Farmington, to Rebecca Primus, Royal Oak, June 2, 1867.

72. Addie Brown, Farmington, to Rebecca Primus, Royal Oak, January 19, 1868.

73. Addie Brown, Farmington, to Rebecca Primus, Royal Oak, January 19, 1868.

74. Addie Brown, Farmington, to Rebecca Primus, Royal Oak, January 6, 1868.

75. Addie Brown, Hartford, to Rebecca Primus, Hartford, October 28, 1862.

76. Addie Brown, Hartford, to Rebecca Primus, Royal Oak, November 10, 1865.

77. Hartford *Courant*, November 17, 1865.

78. For descriptions of the return of the Twenty-ninth Regiment, see A. H. Newton, *Out of the Briars: Autobiography and Sketch of the Twenty-Ninth Regiment* (1910; repr., Miami: Mnemosyne Publishing Co., 1969), 88. See also Alan E. Green, "The Day the 29th Came Home," *Northeast Magazine, The Hartford Courant*, May 31, 1998, 15–16.

79. Addie Brown, Hartford, to Rebecca Primus, Baltimore, November 19, 1865.

80. Mrs. Saunders, not otherwise identified, may have been Lucinda, wife of Prince Saunders, or possibly Elizabeth, sister of Prince and Thomas Saunders.

81. Addie Brown, Hartford, to Rebecca Primus, Royal Oak, February 16, 1867.

82. Smith-Rosenberg, "Female World," 61.

83. Addie Brown, Hartford, to Rebecca Primus, Royal Oak, February 1, 1866. Bell Primus was Isabella, Rebecca's sister; Bell Sands was the wife of Civil War veteran Tommy Sands, the son of Raphael and Emily Sands.

84. Addie Brown, Hartford, to Rebecca Primus, Royal Oak, November 19, 1865. The girls from the shop were probably fellow workers at Smith's Dye Shop, where Addie and Henrietta were working.

85. Addie Brown, Hartford, to Rebecca Primus, Royal Oak, February 1, 1866.

86. Addie Brown, Hartford, to Rebecca Primus, Royal Oak, January 7, 1867.

87. Addie Brown, Farmington, to Rebecca Primus, Royal Oak, September 30, 1867.

88. Nelson Primus, Boston, to mother, Hartford, October 18, 1867.

89. Rebecca Primus, Royal Oak, to family, Hartford, October 18, 1868.

90. Addie Brown, Farmington, to Rebecca Primus, Royal Oak, July 18, 1867.

91. Addie Brown, Waterbury, to Rebecca Primus, Hartford, n.d. January 1860.

92. Addie Brown, Hartford, to Rebecca Primus, Royal Oak, December 9, 1862.

93. Addie Brown, Hartford, to Rebecca Primus, Royal Oak, February 1, 1866.

94. Addie Brown, Hartford, to Rebecca Primus, Royal Oak, March 25, 1866.

95. Addie Brown, Hartford, to Rebecca Primus, Royal Oak, March 25, 1866.

96. Addie Brown, Hartford, to Rebecca Primus, Royal Oak, March 3, 1867.

97. Addie Brown, Hartford, to Rebecca Primus, Royal Oak, n.d. October 1866.

98. Addie Brown, New York, to Rebecca Primus, Hartford, September 17, 1861.

99. Addie Brown, Hartford, to Rebecca Primus, Royal Oak, January 21, 1866.

100. Addie Brown, Farmington, to Rebecca Primus, Royal Oak, December 11, 1867.

101. Addie Brown, Hartford, to Rebecca Primus, Royal Oak, October 25, 1866.

102. Addie Brown, Hartford, to Rebecca Primus, Royal Oak, November 11, 1866.

103. Addie Brown, Hartford, to Rebecca Primus, Royal Oak, April 15, 1866.

104. Addie Brown, Hartford, to Rebecca Primus, Royal Oak, January 7, 1866.

105. Arthur Ashe and Arnold Rampersand, *Days of Grace: A Memoir* (New York: Alfred A. Knopf, 1993), 131.

106. Addie Brown, Farmington, to Rebecca Primus, Royal Oak, October 27, 1867.

107. Addie Brown, Hartford, to Rebecca Primus, Royal Oak, January 7, 1866.

108. Addie Brown, Hartford, to Rebecca Primus, Royal Oak, January 21, 1866; November 10, 1865; November 19, 1865; January 1, 1866; January 7, 1866; April 15, 1866; and May 6, 1866.

109. Addie Brown, Hartford, to Rebecca Primus, Royal Oak, November 3, 1866.

110. Addie Brown, Farmington, to Rebecca Primus, Royal Oak, October 15, 1867.

111. Addie Brown, Farmington, to Rebecca Primus, Royal Oak, October 15, 1867.

112. Addie Brown, Farmington, to Rebecca Primus, Royal Oak, October 6, 1867.

113. Addie Brown, Farmington, to Rebecca Primus, Royal Oak, September 30 and October 15, 1867.

Chapter 9. Growth and Decline

1. Numbers derived from the Hartford census of years cited. See Appendix A: Blacks in Hartford 1830–1880.

2. See Appendix A.

3. Preface, *Geer's City Directory*, Hartford 1879.

4. Glenn Weaver and Michael Swift, *Hartford: Connecticut's Capital* (Sun Valley, CA: American Historical Press, 2003), 78.

5. Albert E. Van Dusen, *Connecticut* (New York: Random House, 1961), 330–332.

6. Weaver and Swift, *Hartford*, 75.

7. Ibid., 97. Trolleys were electrified in 1888.

8. "Interview with Bonnyeclaire Smith-Stewart about George Griffin, Hartford Butler of Mark Twain," *Mark Twain Journal* 53, no. 1 (Spring 2015): 114–121. Also see Moira Hagerty, former assistant curator of the Mark Twain House, report on Twain's butler, Nook Farm, October 17, 1994.

9. "Interview with Bonnyeclaire Smith-Stewart."

10. Peter Baldwin, "The Fight against the Vice District," in *Domesticating the Street: The Reform of Public Space in Hartford, 1850–1930* (Columbus: Ohio State University Press, 1999), chap. 3, esp. 71–72.

11. James A. Miller, "Relationship to Culture, Political Structure, and the Life Blood of the Black Community," in Stanley F. Battle, ed., *The State of Black Hartford* (Hartford: Urban League of Hartford, 1994), 40.

12. Helen Post Chapman, *My Hartford of the Nineteenth Century* (Hartford: Edwin Valentine Mitchell, 1928), 35.

13. See James O. Horton, "Shades of Color," in *Free People of Color Inside the African American Community* (Washington, DC: Smithsonian Institution Press, 1993), 122–144.

14. Horton, *Free People of Color*, 126.

15. Weaver and Swift, *Hartford*, 68–69.

16. King T. Hayes, "A Historical Profile of Fifteen Black Churches of Hartford, Connecticut" (Hartford, 1994), 7.

17. Spruce Street, west of the railroad depot, ran on the far side of the converging tracks entering Hartford.

18. David E. Swift, *Black Prophets of Justice: Activist Clergy Before the Civil War* (Baton Rouge: Louisiana State University Press, 1989), 213–214, 216.

19. King Hayes, manuscript, "Hartford's Black Churches: Reflections of the Gilded Age," student paper, Trinity College, 1993.

20. Eric Foner, *Reconstruction: America's Unfinished Revolution: 1863–1877* (New York: Harper and Row, 1989), 604.

21. Isaac A. Scott Pension Application 996145; Certification 792679.

22. Ibid. Scott was first granted a pension of eight dollars per month; it was later increased to twenty-two dollars.

23. Isaac A. Scott Pension Application 996145; Certification 792679.

24. Two unattributed manuscripts in the Thompson-Kinny Collection 1728–1922, Box 11, Connecticut State Library, RG69.3.

25. Geer's City Directory 1880, 289.

26. Patrick Rael, *Black Identity and Black Protest in the Antebellum North* (Chapel Hill: University of North Carolina Press, 2002), 294.

Chapter 10. Loss and Persistence

1. David O. White, "Rebecca Primus in Later Life," in *Beloved Sisters and Loving Friends: Letters from Rebecca Primus of Royal Oak, Maryland, and Addie Brown of Hartford, Connecticut, 1854–1868*, ed. Farah Jasmine Griffin (New York: Alfred A. Knopf, 1999), 281–283.

2. Hartford Vital Records, Marriages, VM1, 1863–1885, microfilm Reel 1554; LDS 1313873, Connecticut State Library.

3. Charles Thomas obituary, *Hartford Courant*, August 3, 1891.

4. *Hartford Courant*, May 5, 1873.

5. *Hartford Courant*, August 3, 1891.

6. *Hartford Courant*, June 19, 1875.

7. Hartford Vital Records, Deaths, DI 1871–1886, microfilm Reel 1550; LDS 1313869, Connecticut State Library.

8. Massachusetts Copies of Record of Death: female Primus, July 6, 1876; D004029, vol. 284, p. 164, no. 221; and Amorett M. Primus, July 18, 1876; D004030, vol. 284, p. 165, no. 238.

9. Emma Smith, Philadelphia, to Mehitable Primus, Hartford, August 19, 1876.

10. White, "Rebecca Primus in Later Life," 281–282.

11. Ibid., 282.

12. "A Colored Artist's Loss," *Hartford Courant*, January 12, 1889.

13. Information on the Wheelers was supplied by Ames Fellows Frances Karttunen and Isabel Kaldenbach of the Nantucket Historical Society.

14. *Hartford Daily Courant*, January 16, 1877.

15. Letters Patent No. 274,656, March 27, 1883. Original data: United States Patent and Trademark Office. *USPTO Patent Full-Text and Image Database*, http://patft.uspto.gov/netahtml/PTO/search-bool.html.

16. Hildegarde Cummings, *Charles Ethan Porter* (New Britain, CT: New Britain Museum of American Art, 2007), 51–52. See also Thomas P. Riggio, "Charles Ethan Porter and Mark Twain," in Helen Fusscas, *Charles Ethan Porter* (Marlborough, CT: The Connecticut Gallery, 1987), 76–87.

17. Cummings, *Charles Ethan Porter*, 93.

18. Cummings, "The Hartford Artist," in *Charles Ethan Porter*, 58–73.

19. *Hartford Evening Post*, May 9, 1884.

20. *Hartford Courant*, May 23, 1884.

21. *Hartford Courant*, August 3, 1891.

22. "Colored Republicans," *Hartford Courant*, September 8, 1888.

23. *Boston Herald and Globe* 1, April 8, 1894.

24. "The Great Painting, *Christ Before Pilate*: A Wonderful Copy of Munckacsy great work, by Nelson A. Primus," brochure, n.d., describes the work in detail. Collector Walter O. Evans provided a copy.

25. For the estimates of size, see George Forbes, "Bannister and Other Artists," typescript, Boston Public Library Rare Books and Manuscripts EMB4 MS. AM 282(9); and G. F. Richings, *Evidences of Progress among Colored People* (Philadelphia: Geo. S. Ferguson Co., 1897), 348.

26. *Hartford Courant*, December 29, 1888; *Somerville Sentinel*, December 22, 1888.

27. Sharon F. Patton, *African-American Art*, Oxford History of Art (Oxford: Oxford University Press, 1998), 73.

28. From "The Great Painting" brochure. See also the typewritten manuscript by George Forbes, Boston Public Library Rare Books and Manuscripts EMB MS. AM. 282(9). The writer cites the *Boston Herald* and *Boston Globe*, April 1–8, 1894. For this information, I am indebted to art historian Arthur Monroe, Black Arts curator, Oakland Museum, who gave me access to the museum file on Nelson Primus, June 4, 2001.

29. Albert Emerson Benson, *History of the Massachusetts Horticultural Society* (Boston: Massachusetts Horticultural Society, 1929), 279.

30. Massachusetts Death Record, 1893, vol. 437, p. 384, no. 599.

31. Douglas H. Daniels, *Pioneer Urbanites: A Social and Cultural History of Black San Francisco* (Berkeley: University of California Press, 1990), 13, 106, 107, 110–111.

32. *Hartford Courant*, March 11, 1899.

33. *Hartford Courant*, March 13, 1899.

34. Connecticut State Library Archival Record Group #4, Hartford Probate District, Theodore P. Mitchell, 1913, 1915, 1916, 1920.

35. Douglas H. Daniels, *Pioneer Urbanites*, 97; also see Elizabeth L. Parker and James Abajian, "Walking Tour of the Black Presence in San Francisco during the Nineteenth Century: A Black History Week Event," San Francisco African American Historical and Cultural Society, 1974, 1–2.

36. This address, from the city directory, is confirmed in Parker and Abajian, "Walking Tour of the Black Presence in San Francisco," 15.

37. Taped interview supplied by the Corcoran Museum of Art, Washington, DC. George and Elmo were Mrs. McEvers's children from a previous marriage; Wilfred McEvers adopted the children but did not change their names. The portrait of Elmo Blaikie, known as *Portrait of a Lady, or Lady with Golden Hair,* is in the Harmon and Harriet Kelley collection.

38. Mary Ellen Pleasant Collection, San Francisco History Center, San Francisco Public Library; also see Helen Holdredge, *Mammy Pleasant* (New York: G. P. Putnam's Sons, 1953).

39. Supreme Court of California 34 Cal. 586; 1868 Cal. Lexis 26.

40. Marjorie Arkelian and the late E. J. Montgomery, black art historians, interviewed Laura Tooms Scott for the Oakland Museum, May 15, 1972. Ms. Arkelian's notes are in the Nelson Primus file at the Oakland Museum.

41. On Primus's modeling, see Samella Lewis, *Art: African American* (New York: Harcourt Brace Jovanovich, 1978), 39.

42. *Oakland Tribune*, December 11 and August 8, 1969.

43. Department of Public Health, Birth and Mortality Division, San Francisco, certificate no. 3292.

44. White, "Rebecca Primus in Later Life," 283.

45. Textile and costume historian Lynne Bassett provided information on the fabric and construction of the dress in an e-mail to the author, June 4, 2015.

Bibliography

Primary Sources

Amos Beman Scrapbooks, Beinecke Rare Book and Manuscript Library, Yale University.

Boston Public Library Rare Books and Manuscripts Collection.

Connecticut State Library, State Archives, Hartford.

Harriet Beecher Stowe Center Manuscripts and Collections.

Hartford History Center Collections, Hartford Public Library.

Hartford Freedmen's Aid Society Records 1865–1869, Connecticut Historical Society, Hartford.

John Henry Brocklesby Scrap Book 1865, Watkinson Library, Trinity College, Hartford.

John W. Stedman Scrapbooks on Hartford History, Connecticut Historical Society, Hartford.

Mary Morris Scrapbooks, Connecticut Historical Society, Hartford.

Nelson Primus Folder, Connecticut Artists Collection, University of Connecticut Library.

Nelson Primus Folders, Oakland Museum Archives, Oakland.

Primus Papers, Connecticut Historical Society, Hartford.

Seth Terry Account Books 1825–1857. Connecticut Historical Society, Hartford.

Newspapers, Periodicals, and Annuals

Boston City Directory
Geers Hartford City Directory
Hartford Courant
Hartford Evening Post
Hartford Evening Press
Hartford Post

Hartford Times
The Independent, New York
The Liberator, Boston
Oakland Tribune, Oakland, California
San Francisco City Directory

Printed Sources

Abdy, Edward Strutt. *Journal of a Residence and Tour in the United States of North America, from April, 1833, to October, 1834*. London: John Murray, 1835.

Asher, Jeremiah. *An Autobiography, with Details of a Visit to England: and Some Account of the History of the Meeting Street Baptist Church, Providence, R.I. and of the Shiloh Baptist Church, Philadelphia, Pa.* Philadelphia, 1862.

Asher, Jeremiah. *Incidents in the Life of the Rev. J. Asher, Pastor of the Shiloh (Coloured) Baptist Church, Philadelphia, U.S.* 1850. Reprint, New York: Books for Libraries, 1971.

Baltimore Society for the Moral and Educational Improvement of the Colored People. *First Annual Report*. Baltimore, 1865.

Baltimore Society for the Moral and Educational Improvement of the Colored People. *Second Annual Report*. Baltimore: J. B. Rose and Company, 1866.

Barber, John Warner. *Connecticut Historical Collections*. 1836. Reprint, Storrs, CT: Bibliopola Press, 1999.

———. *A History of the Amistad Captives*. 1840. Reprint, New York: Arno Press, 1969.

Bell, Howard H., ed. *Minutes of the Proceedings of the National Negro Conventions, 1830–1864*. New York: Arno Press, 1969.

Boardman, Jennet. "Midwife Records 1815–1849, Part IV." *Connecticut Historical Society Bulletin* 34, no. 4 (October 1969): 119–126.

Buel, Richard, Jr., and J. Bard McNulty, eds. *Connecticut Observed: Three Centuries of Visitors' Impressions 1676–1940*. Hartford: The Acorn Club, 1999.

Catalogue of the Talcott-st. Congregational Church in Hartford, Together with Its Articles of Faith and Covenant, and Rules of Order and Discipline. Hartford: Courier Office, 1842.

Chapman, Helen Post. *My Hartford of the Nineteenth Century*. Hartford: Edwin Valentine Mitchell, 1928.

Five Black Lives, the Autobiographies of Venture Smith, James Mars, William Grimes, the Rev. G. W. Offley, James L. Smith. Introduction by Arna Bontemps. Middletown, CT: Wesleyan University Press, 1971.

Five Slave Narratives: A Compendium. The American Negro: His History and Literature Series. Edited by William Loren Katz. New York: Arno Press, 1968.

Goodrich, Samuel G. *Recollections of a Lifetime.* 2 vols. New York: Miller, Orton, and Mulligan, 1856.

Grimke, Charlotte Forten. *The Journals of Charlotte Forten Grimke.* Edited by Brenda Stevenson. Schomburg Library of Nineteenth-Century Black Women Writers. New York: Oxford University Press, 1988.

Hooker, John. *Some Reminiscences of a Long Life.* Hartford: Belknap & Warfield, 1899.

Independent Order of Odd Fellows. *Odd Fellows Directory and Guide, Contains a Complete List of Odd Fellow Lodges in New England.* Boston, 1887.

Linsley, Betty M., and Elizabeth Radulski, eds. *Malachi Linsley Diary. 1821–1834.* Branford, CT: B. M. Linsley, 1993.

Mars, James. *Life of James Mars, a Slave Born and Sold in Connecticut.* Hartford: Case, Lockwood & Company, 1864.

Moore, Frank. *Women of the War: Their Heroism and Self-Sacrifice.* Hartford: S. S. Scranton and Co., 1866.

Mortgage Burning of the Talcott Street Congregational Church. Hartford: Faith Congregational Church, 1944.

Newton, A. H. *Out of the Briars: Autobiography and Sketch of the Twenty-Ninth Regiment.* 1910. Reprint, Miami: Mnemosyne Publishing Co., 1969.

One Hundred Seventy-Fifth Anniversary, Faith Congregational Church, United Church of Christ, 1819–1994.

Passages in the Life of Jack Blackstone, a Christian Negro. By One Who Knew Him. Hartford: Elihu Geer, 1843. Connecticut Historical Society, Hartford.

Pennington, James W. C. "Sermon at the Fifth Congregational Church, Hartford, on 'Covenants Involving Moral Wrong Are Not Obligatory upon Man.'" November 17, 1842. Connecticut Historical Society, Hartford.

Plato, Ann. *Essays, Including Biographies and Miscellaneous Pieces, in Prose and Poetry, 1841.* Reprint, with foreword by Henry Louis Gates. Schomburg Library of Nineteenth-Century Black Women Writers. New York: Oxford University Press, 1988.

Proceedings of the Masonic State Convention, Free and Accepted Masons. 1873.

Richings, G. F. *Evidences of Progress among Colored People.* Philadelphia: George S. Ferguson, 1897.

Russell, Gurdon W. *Up-Neck in 1825.* Hartford: Case, Lockwood & Brainard, 1890.

Stedman, John Woodhull. "Hartford in 1830: Some Things That I Remember About Hartford Sixty Years Ago." *Connecticut Historical Society Bulletin* XIV (July 1949): 17–24; (October 1949): 30–32; and XV (January 1950): 30–32.

Stewart, Maria. *Maria W. Stewart, America's First Black Woman Political Writer: Essays and Speeches.* Edited by Marilyn Richardson. Bloomington: Indiana University Press, 1987.

Stuart, Isaac William [Scaeva pseud.]. *Hartford in the Olden Time: Its First 30 Years.* Edited by W. M. B. Hartley. Hartford: F.A. Brown, 1853.

Twenty-fifth Merger Anniversary Talcott Street Congregational and Mother Bethel Methodist 1954–1979. 1979.

Walker, David. *David Walker's Appeal to the Coloured Citizens of the World.* Boston, 1829. Reprint, with an introduction by Charles M. Wiltse. New York: Hill and Wang, 1965.

Government Publications

Anderson, Margo J., ed. *Encyclopedia of the U.S. Census.* Washington, DC: CQ Press, 2000.

Hartford Assessor's List, 1880. Archives, Connecticut State Library.

Municipal Register and City Year Book of the City of Hartford. Hartford: Case, Lockwood & Brainard, 1880.

National Archive. Civil War Pension Applications, RG 15.

National Archives. Records of the Educational Division of the Bureau of Refugees, Freedmen, and Abandoned Lands.

Record of Service of Connecticut Men in the Army and Navy of the United States during the War of the Rebellion. Compiled by the Authority of the General Assembly. Hartford: Case, Lockwood & Brainard, 1889.

US Bureau of the Census. *Fifth Census.* 1830. Manuscript. Connecticut State Library, Hartford.

———. *Sixth Census of the United States,* Hartford County, CT [microfilm].

———. *Seventh Census of the United States,* Hartford County, CT [microfilm].

———. *Eighth Census of the United States,* Hartford County, CT 1860 [microfilm].

———. *Ninth Census of the United States,* Hartford County, CT 1870 [microfilm].

———. *Tenth Census of the United States,* Hartford County, CT 1880 [microfilm].

———. *Statistical View of the United States, Being a Compendium of the Seventh Census, to Which Are Added the Results of Every Previous Census, Beginning with 1790, in Comparative Tables, with Explanatory and Illustrative Notes, Based Upon the Schedules and Other Official Sources of Information.* J. D. B. DeBow, superintendent of the US Census. Washington, DC: Beverley Tucker, Senate Printer, 1854.

———. *Statistics of the United States (Including Mortality, Property, etc.) in 1860.* Washington, DC: US Department of the Interior, 1866.

———. *Population of the United States in 1860.* Compiled by Joseph C. G. Kennedy.

———. *Statistics of the Population of the United States at the Tenth Census.* Washington, DC: Government Printing Office, 1883.

———. *200 Years of U.S. Census Taking: Population and Housing Questions, 1790–1990.* US Department of Commerce, 1989. Compiled by Frederick G. Bohme.

Secondary Sources: Books, Articles and Unpublished Papers

Alexopoulos, John. *The Nineteenth Century Parks of Hartford: A Legacy to the Nation.* Hartford: Hartford Architecture Conservancy, 1983.

Andrews, Gregory E., and David F. Ransom. *Structures and Styles: Guided Tours of Hartford Architecture.* Hartford: Connecticut Historical Society and Connecticut Architecture Foundation, 1988.

Ashe, Arthur, and Arnold Rampersad. *Days of Grace: A Memoir.* New York: Alfred A. Knopf, 1993.

Bacon, Edwin M. *The Book of Boston: Fifty Years' Recollections of the New England Metropolis.* Boston: Book of Boston Company, 1916.

Baldwin, Peter C. *Domesticating the Street: The Reform of Public Space in Hartford, 1850–1930.* Columbus: Ohio State University Press, 1999.

Balen, Ruth. "Slave Ownership by Yale-Educated Clergy in 18th Century Guilford, Connecticut." Typescript. Guilford, CT: Nettleton Room, Guilford Free Library.

Battle, Stanley F., ed. *The State of Black Hartford.* Hartford: Urban League of Greater Hartford, 1994.

Beeching, Barbara J. "African Americans and Native Americans in Hartford 1636–1800: Antecedents of Hartford's Nineteenth Century Black Community." Student paper, Wesleyan University, Middletown, CT, 1993.

———. "Henry Chandler Bowen and Roseland Cottage: Success in Nineteenth Century America." *Connecticut History* 38 (Fall 1999): 127–149.

Bentley, George R. *A History of the Freedmen's Bureau.* 1955. Reprint, New York: Octagon Books, 1970.

Berkeley, Kathleen C. *"Like a Plague of Locusts": From an Antebellum Town to a New South City, Memphis, Tennessee, 1850–1880.* New York: Garland Publishing, 1991.

Berlin, Ira. *Generations of Captivity: A History of African-American Slaves.* Cambridge, MA: Belknap Press, 2003.

———. *Many Thousands Gone: The First Two Centuries of Slavery in North America.* Cambridge, MA: Belknap Press, 1998.

Bernstein, Iver. *The New York City Draft Riots: Their Significance for American Society and Politics in the Age of the Civil War.* New York: Oxford University Press, 1990.

Billings, Dwight B., and Kathleen M. Bell. *The Road to Poverty: The Making of Wealth and Hardship in Appalachia.* Cambridge: Cambridge University Press, 2000.

Billingsley, Andrew. *Climbing Jacob's Ladder: The Enduring Legacy of African-American Families.* New York: Simon & Schuster, 1992.

Bolster, W. Jeffrey. *Black Jacks: African American Seamen in the Age of Sail.* Cambridge, MA: Harvard University Press, 1997.

Boydston, Jean. "The Pastoralization of Housework." In *Women's America: Refocusing the Past,* edited by Linda K. Kerber and Jane Sheron de Hart, 124–153. Oxford: Oxford University Press, 1995.

Brown, Lois, ed. *Memoir of James Jackson, the Attentive and Obedient Scholar, Who Died in Boston, October 31, 1833, Aged Six Years and Eleven Months, by His Teacher, Miss Susan Paul.* Cambridge, MA: Harvard University Press, 2000.

Brown, Richard D. *Modernization: The Transformation of American Life 1600–1865.* Prospect Heights, IL: Waveland Press, 1976.

Brugger, Robert J. *Maryland, a Middle Temperament, 1634–1980.* Baltimore: Johns Hopkins University Press in Association with Maryland Historical Society, 1988.

Burkett, Randall K. "Elizabeth Mars Johnson Thomson (1807–1864): A Research Note." *Historical Magazine of the Protestant Episcopal Church* LV (March 1986): 18–26.

Burns, Khephra. "Up from Obscurity: African American Art Is at Last Achieving Mainstream Recognition, Supported by the Expanding Number of Primarily Black Dealers and Collectors." *Art and Auction* (March 1995): 104–129.

Bushman, Richard L. *The Refinement of America: Persons, Houses, Cities.* New York: Vintage Books, 1992.

Butterworth, Miriam, Ellsworth Grant, and Richard Woodworth. *Celebrate! West Hartford: An Illustrated History.* West Hartford, CT: Celebrate West Hartford LLC, 2001.

Cimbala, Paul A., and Randall M. Miller. *The Freedmen's Bureau and Reconstruction: Reconsiderations.* New York: Fordham University Press, 1999.

Contributions to the Ecclesiastical History of Connecticut. Prepared Under the Direction of the General Association, to Commemorate the Completion of One Hundred and Fifty Years Since Its First Annual Assembly. New Haven: William L. Kingsley, 1861.

Cooper, Frederick. "Elevating the Race: Social Thought of Black Leaders 1827–1850." *American Quarterly* 24 (December 1972): 604–625.

Cottrol, Robert. *The Afro-Yankees: Providence's Black Community in the Ante-bellum Era.* Westport, CT: Greenwood Press, 1982.

Cummings, Hildegarde. *Charles Ethan Porter: African-American Master of Still Life.* New Britain, CT: New Britain Museum of American Art, 2007.

Curry, Leonard P. *The Free Black in Urban America, 1800–1850: The Shadow of the Dream.* Chicago: University of Chicago Press, 1981.

Daniels, Douglas Henry. *Pioneer Urbanites: A Social and Cultural History of Black San Francisco.* Berkeley: University of California Press, 1990.

Daniels, John. *In Freedom's Birthplace: A Study of the Boston Negroes.* New York: Negro Universities Press, 1914.

Deitcher, David. *Dear Friends: American Photographs of Men Together, 1840–1918.* New York: Harry N. Abrams, 2001.

Dillard, J. L. *Black English: Its History and Usage in the United States*. New York: Vintage Books, 1973.

———. "The Development of Black English." In *A History of American English*, 60–92. New York: Longman Group, 1992.

DuBois, W. E. B. *The Negro*. 1915. Reprint, with afterword by Robert Gregg. Philadelphia: University of Pennsylvania Press, 2001.

Faderman, Lillian. *Surpassing the Love of Men: Romantic Friendship and Love between Women from the Renaissance to the Present*. New York: William Morrow, 1981.

Farley, Reynolds. *Growth of the Black Population: A Study of Demographic Trends*. Chicago: Markham Publishing Co., 1971.

Farrow, Anne, Joel Lang, and Jennifer Frank. *Complicity: How the North Promoted, Prolonged, and Profited from Slavery*. New York: Ballantine Books, 2005.

Faude, Wilson H. *Lost Hartford*. Images of America Series. Charleston, SC: Arcadia Publishing, 2000.

Finkelman, Paul, ed. *Abolitionists in Northern Courts: The Pamphlet Literature*, Series 3. New York: Garland Press, 1988.

Foner, Eric. "Free Labor and Nineteenth-Century Political Ideology." In *The Market Revolution in America: Social, Political, and Religious Expressions, 1800–1880*, edited by Melvyn Stokes and Stephen Conway, 99–127. Charlottesville: University Press of Virginia, 1996.

———. *Gateway to Freedom: The Hidden History of the Underground Railroad*. New York: W. W. Norton & Company, 2015.

———. *Reconstruction: America's Unfinished Revolution: 1863–1877*. New York: Harper and Row, 1989.

Foner, Philip S., and Josephine Pacheo. *Three Who Dared: Prudence Crandall, Margaret Douglass, Myrtilla Miner—Champions of Antebellum Education*. Contributions in Women's Studies, no. 47. Westport, CT: Greenwood Press, 1984.

Fowler, William C. *Historical Status of the Negro in Connecticut: A Paper Read Before the New Haven Historical Society*. Charleston, SC: Walker, Evans and Cogswell, 1901.

Frazier, E. Franklin. *The Negro Church in America*. New York: Schocken Books, 1964.

French, Scot. *The Rebellious Slave: Nat Turner in American Memory*. Boston: Houghton Mifflin, 2004.

French, H. W. *Art and Artists in Connecticut*. 1879. Reprint, New York: Penguin Books, 1996.

Fuke, Richard Paul. "The Baltimore Association for the Moral and Educational Improvement of the Colored People 1864–1870." *Maryland Historical Magazine* 66 (Winter 1971): 369–404.

Fusscas, Helen K., ed. *Charles Ethan Porter 1847–1923*. Marlborough, CT: The Connecticut Gallery Inc., 1987.

Gates, Caroline Ladd, comp. "Pupils of Springfield High School, Classes of 1845–1863, vol. I, MS list, Connecticut Valley Historical Museum, Springfield, MA.

Gilmore, Glenda Elizabeth. *Gender and Jim Crow: Women and the Politics of White Supremacy in North Carolina, 1896–1920*. Chapel Hill: University of North Carolina Press, 1996.

Goings, Kenneth W., and Gerald L. Smith. " 'Duty of the Hour': African-American Communities in Memphis, Tennessee, 1862–1923." *Tennessee Historical Quarterly* 55 (Summer 1996): 130–143.

Goodheart, Lawrence. *Abolitionist, Actuary, Atheist: Elizur Wright and the Reform Impulse*. Kent, OH: Kent State University Press, 1990.

Gorman, Kathleen. "Servants in the Twain Household." Student Paper, Trinity College, 1994. Copy in African American Collection, Connecticut Historical Society, Hartford.

Grant, Ellsworth S. *"Thar She Goes!" Shipbuilding on the Connecticut River*. Old Saybrook, CT: Fenwick Productions, 2000.

Gray, David. *Inside Prince Hall*. Lancaster, VA: Anchor Communications, 2004.

Green, Alan E. "The Day the 29th Came Home." *Northeast Magazine, Hartford Courant*, May 31, 1998.

Greene, Lorenzo Johnston. *The Negro in Colonial New England*. New York: Atheneum, 1969.

Griffin, Farah Jasmine. *Beloved Sisters and Loving Friends: Letters from Rebecca Primus of Royal Oak, Maryland, and Addie Brown of Hartford, Connecticut, 1854–1868*. New York: Alfred A. Knopf, 1999.

Grimshaw, William H. *Official History of Freemasonry Among the Colored People of North America*. 1903. Reprint, New York: Negro Universities Press, 1969.

Groom, Theodore. "Remembering Gad Asher." Unpublished manuscript, April 2013. Totoket Historical Society, North Branford, CT.

Hansen, Karen V. " 'No Kisses Is Like Youres': An Erotic Friendship Between Two African-American Women During the Mid-Nineteenth Century." *Gender and History* 7, no. 2 (July 1995): 153–182.

Hayes, King T. "A Historical Profile of Fifteen Black Churches of Hartford, Connecticut." Hartford, 1994.

Hedrick, Joan. *Harriet Beecher Stowe, A Life*. New York: Oxford University Press, 1994.

Herskovits, Melville J. *The Myth of the Negro Past*. 1941. Reprint, Boston: Beacon Press, 1958.

Higginbotham, Evelyn Brooks. *Righteous Discontent: The Women's Movement in the Black Baptist Church 1880–1920*. Cambridge, MA: Harvard University Press, 1993.

Hinckley, Marcia D. " 'We Just Went On with It': The Black Experience in Windsor, Connecticut 1790–1950." Master's thesis, Trinity College, Hartford, CT, 1991.

Hine, Darlene Clark. *Hine Sight: Black Women and the Re-Construction of American History*. Bloomington: Indiana University Press, 1994.

Hirst, Robert H. "Who Was 'G.G., Chief of Ordnance'?" Newsletter of the Friends of the Bancroft Library, Fall 2000.

Holland, Juanita Marie. " 'Co-Workers in the Kingdom of Culture': Edward Mitchell Bannister and the Boston Community of African-American Artists, 1848–1901." PhD diss., Columbia University, 1998.

———. *Edward Mitchell Bannister, 1828–1901*. Exhibition catalog. New York: Keneleba House, Whitney Museum of Art, 1992.

Horton, James Oliver. *Free People of Color: Inside the African American Community*. Washington, DC: Smithsonian Institution Press, 1993.

Horton, James Oliver, and Lois E. Horton. *Black Bostonians: Family Life and Community Struggle in the Antebellum North*. New York: Holmes & Meier, 1979.

———. *In Hope of Liberty: Culture, Community and Protest Among Northern Free Blacks, 1700–1860*. New York: Oxford University Press, 1997.

Hosley, William. *Colt: The Making of an American Legend*. Amherst: University of Massachusetts Press in Association with the Wadsworth Atheneum, Hartford, 1996.

Howard, O. O. *Autobiography of O. O. Howard, Major General United States Army, 1830–1909*. New York: Baker & Taylor Co., 1907.

Hoxie, Frances Alida. "Connecticut's Forty-Niners." *Western Historical Quarterly* V, no. 1 (January 1974): 17–28.

Hunter, Bethuel. *"No Man Can Hinder Me": Black Troops in the Union Armies During the American Civil War*. Exhibition Catalog. New Haven: Beinecke Rare Book & Manuscript Library, Yale University, 2003.

Johnston, Henry P., ed. *The Record of Connecticut Men in the Military and Naval Service During the War of the Revolution 1775–1783*. Hartford: Case Lockwood & Brainard Company, 1889.

Jones, Howard. *Mutiny on the Amistad: The Saga of a Slave Revolt and Its Impact on American Abolition, Law, and Diplomacy*. New York: Oxford University Press, 1987.

Kusmer, Kenneth. "Black Urban Experience in American History." In *State of Afro-American History*, ed. Darlene C. Hine, 91–122. Baton Rouge: Louisiana State University, 1986.

Leonard, R. Bernice. *Twig and Turf III: The Royal Oak*. St. Michaels, MD, 1985.

Litwack, Leon F. *North of Slavery: The Negro in the Free States, 1790–1860*. Chicago: University of Chicago Press, 1961.

Main, Gloria L. "Naming Children in Early New England." *Journal of Interdisciplinary History* 27, No. 1 (Summer 1996): 1–27.

Main, Jackson Turner. *Connecticut Society in the Era of the American Revolution*. Connecticut Bicentennial Series, No. 21. Hartford: The American Revolution Bicentennial Commission of Connecticut, 1977.

Manegold, C. S. *Ten Hills Farm: The Forgotten History of Slavery in the North.* Princeton: Princeton University Press, 2010.

Martin, Joanne M., and Elmer P. Martin. *The Helping Tradition in the Black Family and Community.* Silver Spring, MD: National Association of Social Workers, 1985.

McCain, Diana Ross. *Connecticut's African-American Soldiers in the Civil War 1861–1865.* Report to the Connecticut Historical Commission, State of Connecticut, 2000.

———. *To All on Equal Terms: The Life and Legacy of Prudence Crandall.* Hartford: Connecticut Commission on the Arts, Tourism, Culture, History and Film, 2004.

McNulty, John Bard. *Older Than the Nation: The Life and Times of the Hartford Courant, Oldest Newspaper of Continuous Publication in America.* Stonington, CT: The Pequot Press, 1964.

McPherson, James M. *The Abolitionist Legacy: From Reconstruction to the NAACP.* Princeton: Princeton University Press, 1975.

———. *Battle Cry of Freedom: The Civil War Era.* New York: Oxford University Press, 1988.

———. *The Negro's Civil War: How American Blacks Felt and Acted During the War for the Union.* New York: Vintage Books, 1965.

Meier, August. *Negro Thought in America 1880–1915: Racial Ideologies in the Age of Booker T. Washington.* Ann Arbor: University of Michigan Press, 1973.

Melish, Joanne Pope. *Disowning Slavery: Gradual Emancipation and "Race" in New England, 1780–1860.* Ithaca, NY: Cornell University Press, 1998.

Miller, Herbert C. *The History of North Branford and Northford.* North Branford, CT: Totoket Historical Society, 1982.

Miller, James A. "Charles Ethan Porter and the Hartford Black Community." In *Charles Ethan Porter 1847–1923*, edited by Helen Fusscass, 88–95. Exhibition Catalog. Marlborough, CT: The Connecticut Gallery, 1987.

———. "Relationship to Culture, Political Structure, and the Life Blood of the Black Community." In *The State of Black Hartford*, edited by Stanley F. Battle, 38–44. Hartford: Urban League of Hartford, 1994.

Miller, Marla R. "Mehitable Primus and Addie Brown: Women of Color and Hartford's Nineteenth-Century Dressmaking Trades." In *Dressing New England: Clothing, Fashion, and Identity*, edited by Peter Benes and Jane Montague Benes, 64–85. Dublin Seminar for New England Folklife Annual Proceedings. Deerfield, MA: Trustees of Historic Deerfield, 2010.

Morse, Jarvis Means. *The Neglected Period of Connecticut's History, 1818–1850.* New York: Octagon Books, 1978.

Muraskin, William A. *Middle-Class Blacks in a White Society: Prince Hall Freemasonry in America.* Berkeley: University of California Press, 1975.

Nash, Gary. *Forging Freedom: The Formation of Philadelphia's Black Community, 1720–1840.* Cambridge: Harvard University Press, 1988.

Nissen, Axel. *The Romantic Friendship Reader: Love Stories between Men in Victorian America*. Boston: Northeastern University Press, 2003.

Normen, Elizabeth J., ed., with Stacey K. Close, Katherine J. Harris, William Frank Mitchell, and Olivia White. *African American Connecticut Explored*. Middletown, CT: Wesleyan University Press, 2013.

Parker, Edwin Pond. *History of the Second Church of Christ in Hartford 1670–1892*. Hartford: Belknap and Warfield, 1892.

Parker, Elizabeth L., and James Abajian. "A Walking Tour of the Black Presence in San Francisco during the Nineteenth Century: A Black History Week Event." San Francisco African American Historical and Cultural Society, 1974.

Patton, Sharon F. *African-American Art*. Oxford History of Art Series. Oxford: Oxford University Press, 1998.

Pawlowski, Robert E., and the Northwest Catholic High School Urban Studies Class. *How the Other Half Lived: An Ethnic History of the Old East Side and South End of Hartford*. West Hartford, CT: Northwest Catholic High School, 1973.

Pease, Jane, and Pease, William. *They Who Would Be Free*. New York: Atheneum, 1974.

Peterson, Carla L. *Black Gotham: A Family History of African Americans in Nineteenth-Century New York City*. New Haven: Yale University Press, 2011.

Petry, Elisabeth. *Can Anything Beat White? A Black Family's Letters*. Jackson: University Press of Mississippi, 2005.

Piersen, William D. *Black Yankees: The Development of an Afro-American Subculture in Eighteenth-Century New England*. Amherst, MA: New England University Press, 1988.

Pleck, Elizabeth. *Black Migration and Poverty: Boston 1865–1900*. Studies in Social Discontinuity. New York: Academic Press, 1979.

Porter, Dorothy B. "The Organized Educational Activities of Negro Literary Societies, 1828–1846." *Journal of Negro Education* V (October 1936): 555–576.

Porter, James A. "Four Problems in the History of Negro Art." *Journal of Negro History* 27 (January 1942): 9–36.

———. *Modern Negro Art*. 1943. Reprint, with an introduction by David C. Driskell, Washington, DC: Howard University Press, 1992.

Preston, Dickson. *Talbot County, A History*. Centreville, MD: Tidewater Publishers, 1983.

Price, George R., and James Brewer Stewart, eds. *To Heal the Scourge of Prejudice: The Life and Writings of Hosea Easton*. Amherst: University of Massachusetts Press, 1999.

Proctor, Charles H. *The Life of James Williams, Better Known as Professor Jim, for Half a Century Janitor of Trinity College*. Hartford: Case, Lockwood & Brainard, 1873.

Quarles, Benjamin. *Black Abolitionists*. New York: Oxford University Press, 1969.

Rael, Patrick. *Black Identity and Black Protest in the Antebellum North*. Chapel Hill: University of North Carolina Press, 2002.

————. "Black Theodicy: African Americans and Nationalism in the Antebellum North." *The North Star: A Journal of African American Religious History* 3 (Spring 2000): 1–24.

Ray, Stephen G., Jr. "Not All Black and White: African-American Christian History and the Politics of Historical Identity." Paper presented at workshop of The Project on Lived Theology, University of Virginia, November 10, 2003.

————. *A Struggle from the Start: Stories of Passage.* "A Struggle from the Start: The Black Community of Hartford, 1639–1960." Exhibit catalog, The Connecticut Historical Society and Charter Oak Cultural Center, Hartford, 1996.

Richards, Leonard L. *"Gentlemen of Property and Standing": Anti-Abolition Mobs in Jacksonian America.* New York: Oxford University Press, 1970.

Rogers, John E., J. Elmer Dixon, and Leroy E. Fitch, comps. *History of Most Worshipful Prince Hall Grand Lodge of Connecticut, Inc., F. & A.M.* Connecticut: The Lodge, 1973.

Rose, James M., and Barbara W. Brown. *Tapestry: A Living History of the Black Family in Southeastern Connecticut.* New London, CT: New London County Historical Society, 1979.

Rosenthal, Bernard. "Puritan Conscience and New England Slavery." *New England Quarterly* 46 (1973): 62–81.

Saint, Chandler B., and George A. Krimsky. *Making Freedom: The Extraordinary Life of Venture Smith.* Middletown, CT: Wesleyan University Press, 2009.

Salvatore, Nick. *We All Got History: The Memory Books of Amos Webber.* New York: Vintage Books, 1997.

Schor, Joel. *Henry Highland Garnet: A Voice of Black Radicalism in the Nineteenth Century.* Westport, CT: Praeger, 1977.

Schultz, Charles R. "The Gold Rush Voyage of the Ship Pacific: A Study in Ship Management." *The American Neptune: A Quarterly Journal of Maritime History* 53 (Summer 1993) 190–198.

Sellers, Charles. *The Market Revolution: Jacksonian America, 1815–1846.* New York: Oxford University Press, 1991.

Shaw, Stephanie J. *What a Woman Ought to Be and to Do: Black Professional Women Workers During the Jim Crow Era.* Chicago: University of Chicago Press, 1996.

Siemiatkoski, Donna Holt. *The Ancestors and Descendants of Chief Justice Oliver Ellsworth and His Wife Abigail Wolcott and the Story of Elmwood, Their Homestead.* Baltimore: Gateway Press, 1992.

Small, Sandra E. "The Yankee Schoolmarm in Freedmen's Schools: An Analysis of Attitudes." *The Journal of Southern History* 45 (August 1979): 381–402.

Smith-Rosenberg, Carroll. "The Female World of Love and Ritual: Relations between Women in Nineteenth-Century America." In *Disorderly Conduct: Visions of Gender in Victorian America.* New York: Alfred A. Knopf, 1985.

Steinberg, Sharon Y. "An Early American Midwife's Tale." *Hog River Journal* 1 (Summer 2003): 38–39.

Steiner, Bernard C. *History of Slavery in Connecticut*. Reprint, Baltimore: John Hopkins University Press, September–October 1893.

Stewart, James Brewer. "What Color Meant in Antebellum New England: The New Haven 'Negro College' and Conflicting Histories of 'Race,' 1776–1870. *New England Quarterly* (September 2003): 323–355.

Stillman, Jacob D. B. *Seeking the Golden Fleece*. San Francisco: A. Roman and Company, 1877.

Strane, Susan. *A Whole-Souled Woman: Prudence Crandall and the Education of Black Women*. New York: W. W. Norton and Company, 1990.

Strother, Horatio T. *The Underground Railroad in Connecticut*. Middletown: Wesleyan University Press, 1962.

Stuart, Isaac William [Scaeva pseud.]. *Hartford in the Olden Time: Its First Thirty Years*. Edited by W. M. B. Hartley. Hartford: F. A. Brown, 1853.

Swift, David E. *Black Prophets of Justice: Activist Clergy before the Civil War*. Baton Rouge: Louisiana State University Press, 1989.

Tate, Gayle. "Free Black Women in the Antebellum Era." In vol. I of *Black Women in America*, edited by Darlene Clark Hine, 482. New York: Oxford University Press, 2005,

Toll, Robert C. *Blacking Up: The Minstrel Show in Nineteenth-Century America*. New York: Oxford University Press, 1974.

Van Dusen, Albert E. *Connecticut*. New York: Random House, 1961.

Van Dusen, Glyndon G. *The Jacksonian Era: 1828–1848*. New York: Harper Torchbooks, 1992.

Vara-Dannen, Theresa. *The African American Experience in Nineteenth Century Connecticut: Benevolence and Bitterness*. Lanham, MD: Lexington Books, 2014.

Walker, George Leon. *History of the First Church in Hartford, 1633–1883*. Hartford: Brown and Gross, 1884.

Walker, Joseph A., Jr. *Black Square & Compass: Two Hundred Years of Prince Hall Freemasonry*. Revised edition. Richmond, VA: Macoy Publishing & Masonic Supply Co., 1981.

Warner, Robert A. "Amos Gerry Beman—1812–1847, a Memoir on a Forgotten Leader." *Journal of Negro History* 22, no. 2 (April 1937): 200–219.

———. *New Haven Negroes: A Social History*. New Haven: Yale University Press, 1940. New York: Arno Press, 1969.

Warshauer, Matthew. *Connecticut in the American Civil War: Slavery, Sacrifice, and Survival*. Middletown, CT: Wesleyan University Press, 2011.

Weaver, Glenn, and Michael Swift. *Hartford: Connecticut's Capital: An Illustrated History*. Sun Valley, CA: American Historical Press, 2003.

Webber, Christopher L. *American to the Backbone: The Life of James W.C. Pennington, the Fugitive Slave Who Became One of the First Black Abolitionists*. New York: Pegasus Books, 2011.

Welburn, Ron. *Hartford's Ann Plato and the Native Borders of Identity*. Albany: State University of New York Press, 2015.

Weld, Ralph Foster. "Slavery in Connecticut." Tercentenary Commission of the State of Connecticut Committee on Historical Publications #37. Pamphlet. New Haven: Yale University Press, 1977.

White, David O. "Addie Brown's Hartford." *Connecticut Historical Society Bulletin* 41 (April 1976): 57–64.

———. "Augustus Washington, Black Daguerreotypist of Hartford." *Connecticut Historical Society Bulletin* 39 (January 1974): 14–19.

———. *Connecticut's Black Soldiers 1775–1783*. Chester, CT: Pequot Press, 1973.

———. "The Fugitive Blacksmith of Hartford: James W. C. Pennington." *Connecticut Historical Society Bulletin* 49, no. 1 (Winter 1984): 5–29.

———. "Hartford's African Schools, 1830–1868." *Connecticut Historical Society Bulletin* 39 (April 1974): 47–53.

———. "Rebecca Primus in Later Life." In *Beloved Sisters and Loving Friends: Letters from Rebecca Primus of Royal Oak, Maryland, and Addie Brown of Hartford, Connecticut, 1854–1868*, ed. Farah Griffin, 279–284. New York: Alfred A. Knopf, 1999.

Wilkerson, Isabel. *The Warmth of Other Suns: The Epic Story of America's Great Migration*. New York: Random House, 2010.

Williams, Loretta J. *Black Freemasonry and Middle-Class Realities*. Columbia: University of Missouri Press, 1980.

Wilson, Joseph T. *The Black Phalanx: A History of the Negro Soldiers of the United States in the Wars of 1775–1812, 1861–65*. Hartford: American Publishing Company, 1888.

Woodson, Carter G. *Free Negro Heads of Families in the United States in 1830 Together with a Brief Treatment of the Free Negro*. Washington, DC: Association for the Study of Negro Life and History, 1925.

Woodward, C. Vann. *The Strange Career of Jim Crow*. New York: Oxford University Press, 1974.

Index

Abdy, Edward, 16–17
abolition, 16, 26, 31–32, 40–41, 47,
    129, 171. *See also* American Anti-
    Slavery Society; *Liberator*; slave
    rebellions; slavery
  and the arts, 92, 93
  backlash and reactions, 32, 36,
    57–59, 68, 76, 77, 126
  *David Walker's Appeal to the Coloured
    Citizens of the World*, 26, 32, 99, 244
  racial equality and, 16, 47, 77, 167
African Methodist Episcopal (AME/
    A.M.E.) Zion Church, 37, 70,
    75, 80, 131, 155, 156, 170, 171
African Religious Society, 17, 20–23,
    25–28, 37
Africanus, Selah, 52, 55–56, 89, 109
American Anti-Slavery Society, 16, 50
  Boston reunion, 101, 153
American Colonization Society, 16
American Indians. *See* Native Americans
Amistad, United States v. The, 40–41
Andrews, Jacob, 92
Anti-Slavery Society. *See* American
    Anti-Slavery Society
arson, 34, 37–38, 127
artist
  black artists in Boston, 87–88, 92–93
  nineteenth century views on, 85–87

Ashe, Arthur, 158
Asher, Brunella, 7–8
Asher, Edwin, 51, 60
Asher, Gad, 3–13, 40, 51, 167, 190,
    193
Asher, Henrietta, 7–8
Asher, Jeremiah, 4f, 32, 183
  African Religious Society and, 27
  churches and, 20
  education, 17
  Ellsworth family and, 15–16
  equality and, 8, 31–32
  family background, 3, 6–9, 12, 15,
    17, 19–20, 23–24, 51, 56
  Gad Asher and, 3, 6, 7, 9
  in Hartford, 15
  memoirs and autobiography, 3, 6, 8,
    12
  work and employment, 4f, 8, 12,
    13, 15–16, 23, 72
Asher, Jerusha Olford, 15, 23
Asher, Marietta, 7–8
Asher, Ruel, 7–10, 12, 16–17, 51
Asher, Temperance (wife of Gad), 7,
    10
Asher (Primus), Temperance. *See*
    Primus, Temperance Asher
Augustus, Emeline, 174
Augustus, Ezekiel, 70, 173

Baltimore Association for the Moral
and Educational Advancement of
Colored People, 110, 112, 113,
121, 123–25, 132, 133, 175
books used in classrooms, 121
Bannister, Edward Mitchell, 87–89,
91–92, 99, 179
Baptist churches
black, 99–100, 169, 170
white, 20, 21, 32
Beman, Amos Gerry, 9, 45, 47, 56,
70, 87
Beman, Jehiel, 45
beneficent organizations, 68, 74–76,
93
Bicinia (Bicenter), Thronieve. See
Harris, Thronieve (Sophronia/
Phrone) Bicenter (Bicinia) Primus
Bishop, 5–7, 9
Black Yankees, xv, 170
blacks in Hartford. See also specific
topics
conflicts, 27–28, 37, 127–28, 131–32
Blackstone, John, 25, 35, 70
Blaikie, George, 188
Bliss, Lathrop, 35
boarders, 74, 91, 114
boarding out, 30, 43, 65, 142, 145
Boardman, Jennet, 38, 89
book publishing, 15, 49, 95, 166
Booth, Alfred, 132
Booth, Josephine, 132, 172, 176, 190
Brewster, Worthy, 70, 77, 79
Brooks, Phillips, 101, 180
Brown, Addie, 42, 43, 68, 74, 75,
78, 81, 107, 124, 135, 137–43,
145–60, 163, 175
"Addie Brown's Hartford," 81
churches and, 75, 155, 156
death, 176, 191
education and struggle toward
refinement, 140–41

erotic intimacy with women, 141
Henrietta Primus and, 135, 142,
145, 152
Holdridge Primus and, 140, 142,
144–45
Isabella "Bell" Primus and, 104,
144, 146, 151, 154–55, 158, 159
letters, 68, 72, 75, 77, 79, 88, 103,
105, 109, 110, 125, 130, 135,
136f, 138, 139, 141, 151, 153,
156, 159
Mehitable Primus and, 140, 143–45,
147, 149
Nelson Primus and, 140
overview, 191
Primus family and, 68, 81
and project to help former slaves
find their way in free society, 103
Raphael Sands and, 103, 138, 145,
149, 157–59
on race, 148–49, 156–58. See also
racism
Rebecca Primus and, xiii, xiv, 68,
72, 77, 79, 103, 109, 110, 125,
130, 135, 136f, 137–41, 151,
153–55, 158–59, 176
relations with Joseph Tines, 131,
141, 143–44, 151, 155, 159, 191
Sands family and, 103, 142, 145
Thomas Sands and, 79
work and employment, 42, 43,
145–48
cook at Miss Porter's school, 155
Brown, Ally, 138, 146
Brown, Henry "Box," 62
Brown, William Wells, 95–96, 100,
180
Buckingham, Gov. William A., 94, 152

California Gold Rush, 60
Holdridge Primus's experience,
60–63

Camp, George, 70, 173

Camp, Mary, 173

Carteaux, Christiana, 92

Champion, Bathsheba Jacobs, 75, 137, 171. *See also* Jacobs, Bathsheba

Champion, Emma, 179

Champion, Henry, 53, 55

Chapman, Helen Post, 167–68

Christ Before Pilate (painting), 184, 185

Christianity, 9, 25–27, 49. *See also* churches

slave views of, 9, 25, 27

churches. *See also* Baptist churches; Congregational churches; Episcopal churches

black, xvi, 21, 36, 41, 80, 169. *See also* African Methodist Episcopal (AME/A.M.E.) Zion Church; African Religious Society; Talcott Street Congregational Church

Hartford's first, 28, 37–38, 169–71, 173

segregated/separate and unequal seating, 20–21, 27, 32, 138

citizenship, full, 9, 193

civil rights legislation and, 80, 103, 171

Dred Scott v. Sandford and, 10, 129, 156

Fourteenth Amendment and, 115

goal of securing, xv, 3, 31, 32, 41, 68

military service and, 9, 27

Seaman's Protection Certificates and, 10

Civil Rights Act of 1866, 80, 129–30

Civil War, 24, 76, 95, 174

reasons for blacks not to enlist, 76–77

recruitment of black troops and 29th and 30th Regiments, 152–53

Twenty-Ninth (Colored) Regiment Connecticut Volunteer Infantry, 78

veterans as pensioners, 72, 74, 78–79

class and race, xiii, 36, 51, 97, 101–103, 131, 140, 155, 157, 168–70. *See also* middle class

class and cultural differences, 80, 81, 102–3, 109, 116–20, 127, 167, 169–71

Cleggett, Albert O., 71, 156, 170, 182–83

Cleggett, Clarissa, 75, 131

colleges for African Americans, 32–34. *See also* schools

colonization, 16, 27, 41, 49, 50, 52, 53. *See also* Hartford Colonization Society

Colt, Samuel, 165

Colt's Patent Fire Arms Manufacturing Company, 152, 158, 165

community formation, xiv–xvi, 20–22

black, 20–28

early leaders in, 9, 23–28

solidarity and, 23, 41, 159, 193f

Congregational churches, 5, 9, 20, 21, 27–28, 37, 50, 137–38. *See also* Talcott Street Congregational Church

Connecticut Anti-Slavery Society, 47

Cook (Cooke), Joseph, 24–25, 70

Cooper, Christopher, 34–35, 37

Cottrol, Robert, 16

Crandall, Prudence, 33f, 34, 41

crimes against blacks, 126, 127. *See also* sexual harassment; slavery

Cross, Frederick "Fred" O., 74, 77

Cross, Isaac, 50–51, 55, 74, 79, 156, 171, 182–83

Crowell, Margaret, 149, 150, 158

Crowell, Mr., 149

cultural identity. *See* Black Yankees;
     naming patterns; racial uplift
culture, xv, 8–10, 40, 67, 80, 117, 118,
     167, 171. *See also specific topics*
Cummings, Sarah, 155, 159
Custis, Henrietta Primus, 177, 186.
     See also Primus, Henrietta
Custis, Joseph, 145, 175, 177

Daniels, William W., 23, 24
*David Walker's Appeal to the Coloured
     Citizens of the World*, 26, 32, 99,
     244
Davis, Perry, 55, 71, 72, 131–32, 149,
     183
Dickson, Julia, 126–27
domestic service, 6, 37, 43, 147
double consciousness, 116, 157
Douglas, Chauncey, 71, 77, 78, 80
Douglass, Frederick, 10, 17, 41, 47,
     76, 126, 130, 190
Drayton, Paul, 41
Dred Scott v. Sandford, 10, 156
drunkenness, 25, 159
Du Bois, W. E. B., 116, 157

Easton, Hosea, 37–38, 41, 45, 50, 53,
     56, 156, 190
education. *See also* schooling for
     blacks; schools
  as key to racial uplift, 107
Edwards, Bessie, 195
Edwards, Edna, 195
Edwards, Isabella. *See* Primus, Isabella
     "Bell"
Edwards, Nellie, 178, 189
Edwards, William B., 183, 184, 186
  background, 177
  family, 178, 189, 195
  marriage to Isabella "Bell" Primus,
     104, 168, 177, 178, 183, 184,
     186

Ellsworth, Henry Leavitt, 15–16
Ellsworth, Oliver, 15
Ellsworth, William Wolcott, 15, 34,
     38, 52, 59
emancipation, 8, 10, 16, 36, 41, 46,
     112. *See also* abolition
Emancipation Proclamation of 1863,
     112, 122
emigration, 55. *See also* Garnet,
     Henry Highland; Mars, Elizabeth;
     Seymour, George; Washington,
     Augustus; Wilson, Henry M.
employment, 43. *See also* jobs held by
     blacks; labor market; occupational
     opportunities
Episcopal churches, 10, 91, 100–101.
     See also African Methodist
     Episcopal (AME/A.M.E.) Zion
     Church
equal rights, xv
  Addie Brown and, 158
  gender and, 130
  Rebecca Primus and, 130
  Reconstruction and, 171
equality, racial. *See also* citizenship; racial
     justice; racial uplift; social equality
  1835 riot and, 36, 37. *See also*
     riot(s): of 1835
  abolition, abolitionists, and, 16, 47,
     77, 167
  African Americans' doubts about
     achieving, 27
  black lodges and, 75
  churches and, 31, 32, 37
  community, activism, and, 68
  Declaration of Independence and
     the promise of, 27, 31
  doubts of the possibility, 27, 38, 55
  education as stepping-stone to, 67
  goal of and quest for, xv, 8, 20, 32,
     36, 37, 41, 55, 80, 158
  Hosea Easton and, 37, 38, 45

innate, 32
James Pennington and, 47, 49, 50
Jehiel Beman and, 45
slavery, racial mixture, and, 36
equals, promulgating the image of
    African Americans as, xvi

family, reliance on friends and, 99. *See
    also* networks
family members, separation of, xiii, 12,
    138–40
farming, 8, 11
fictive kinship, 149. *See also* virtual
    kinship
fires. *See* arson; San Francisco
    earthquake of 1906
Flagg, Benjamin, 35
Forten, Charlotte, 117–18
Forten, James, 118
Foster, Henry, 24, 38, 41, 49, 55, 58
Fourteenth Amendment, 115
Francis, George, 89–90
Francis, Justin, 78
fraternal organizations, 72, 74–75, 80
Freedmen's Aid Society. *See* Hartford
    Freedmen's Aid Society
Freedmen's Bureau, xiii, 102, 103, 110,
    112, 116, 123, 125, 127, 129,
    133, 143, 172, 175
Freedmen's Societies, 112, 173. *See also*
    Hartford Freedmen's Aid Society
Freeman, Alexander, 153
Freeman, Edwin C., 65, 71, 72, 99,
    117, 156, 168, 170, 173, 182–83
Freeman, Mason, 23, 34, 41
freedwomen brought North for
    employment, 102–103, 167
friends, reliance on family and, 99. *See
    also* networks
friendship between women, 81, 135,
    138–43. *See also* Brown, Addie:
    Rebecca Primus and

Fugitive Slave Act of 1850, 60, 65–66
fugitives, 57–60, 62, 167. *See also*
    Cook (Cooke), Joseph; Douglass,
    Frederick; Pennington, James;
    Underground Railroad; Williams,
    James

Gardner, William, 35
Garnet, Henry Highland, 41, 156
Garrison, William Lloyd, 24, 26,
    32–34, 40, 41, 47, 53, 66, 190
gender, xiii, 17, 26, 102, 109, 130,
    142–43. *See also* women
George Smith's Dye House, 146–47,
    150, 152, 154
Gibson, William, 119
Gilded Age, 163–64
Gillette, Francis, 166
Gillette, William, 166
Gilmore, Glenda, xv
gold in California. *See* California Gold
    Rush
Goldsborough, Asa, 20
Goodwin, Mary, 149
Graham, John T., 120
Grand United Order of Odd Fellows
    (GUOOF), 74, 75
Griffin, Farah, xiv, 125–26, 139, 141
Griffin, George, 166
Grimes, Leonard A., 100–101
Grimke, Charlotte Forten. *See* Forten,
    Charlotte
Guilford, Connecticut, 3–5, 7, 10,
    11, 14

Hamilton, Harriet, 110, 127
Hansen, Karen, xiv, 139, 141
Harris, Jesse Houston, 195–96
Harris, Sarah, 34
Harris, Thronieve (Sophronia/Phrone)
    Bicenter (Bicinia) Primus, 130–31,
    175, 177, 184, 186, 195

Hartford. *See also specific topics*
  1865 map of, 73f
  demographics, 67, 198. *See also*
    population of Hartford
  housing option for blacks, 51–52
Hartford Colonization Society, 26, 27,
  41, 49
Hartford Freedmen's Aid Society, 67,
  110, 123, 133, 153, 175
Hartford Freedmen's Society, 67, 175
Hawes, Joel, 20, 28
Hayes, King T., 169–70
Heehee, Julia, 175
helping tradition among blacks, 99,
  112
homosociality and homoeroticism. *See*
  same-sex loving friendship
Hooker, John, 58
human rights, 9. *See also* equal rights
humor, 104, 114, 115, 119, 125, 166
Humphrey, C. N., 60–62

industrial sector and new industries,
  165–66
inequality, 8. *See also* equality
  and emigration, 27
  in white churches, 31, 32
insurance companies, 166
Irish immigrants, 66, 102, 166

Jackson, Charles S., 154, 173
Jackson, John, 71, 77
Jackson, John H., 146, 157
Jackson, Lydia, 159
Jacobs, Aaron, 19, 22–24
Jacobs, Bathsheba, 19, 53. *See also*
  Champion, Bathsheba Jacobs
Jacobs, Emily "Em," 18, 19, 72, 75.
  See also Sands, Emily Jacobs
Jacobs, Esther, 19
Jacobs, James, 19
Jacobs, Jeremiah, 19, 72, 74, 139, 168

Jacobs, Mabel, 19
Jacobs, Mehitable Esther, 17, 19, 21,
  26, 28, 31, 38. *See also* Primus,
  Mehitable (Mehitabel) Esther
  Jacobs
Jacobs, Reese (Reece), 19, 21
Jerome, Elizabeth Gilbert, 89–90
job training. *See* colleges for African
  Americans
jobs held by blacks, 12, 23, 42, 66,
  74, 93–95, 148, 150, 173
Jocelyn, Simeon, 32–33, 40, 47
Johnson, Andrew, 103–4, 130
Johnson, Charles A., 50–51
Johnson, William, 26
Jones, Henry, 93, 97–99, 104, 142–43
Jones, Noble, 99
Jones, Pinkie, 99
Jones, Sylvie, 97, 99

Kellogg, Mrs., 146
kinship
  fictive, 49
  virtual, 68

labor market. *See also* employment;
    jobs open to blacks; occupational
    opportunities
  and slavery, 6. *See also* slavery
Lane, Martha, 129
Lane, Richard C., 129
lesbian intimacy. *See* same-sex loving
  friendship
Lewis, Edmonia, 92–93
Liberator, The (newspaper), 24, 75, 101
Lincoln, Abraham, 85, 122
Linsley, Malachi, 11, 12, 16
literacy rates, 66–67
Lloyd, Colonel, 126
lodges, fraternal, 72, 74–75, 80

Magira, Ishmael, 23–24

Magira, Nancy, 71
Magira family, 72, 159
Main Street, 15, 137f, 158, 164, 165f
Mars, Elizabeth "Betsy," 25–28, 46,
    55, 70
Mars, James, 9, 25, 45–47, 46f, 55,
    56, 59, 70, 190
Mars, John, 25, 55
Mason, William, 24
McEvers, John Wilfred, 188
Mendi. See *Amistad*
Methodists, 159. *See also* African
    Methodist Episcopal (AME/
    A.M.E.) Zion Church
middle class. *See also specific topics*
    black, xv, 32, 67–74, 80, 139, 193
    defense of the term, xv–xvi
    definitions and conceptions of, xv–
        xvi
    description of Hartford's, 67–70,
        139
    names of selected members, 70–71
midwives, 38, 42, 89
migrants, 66, 166, 169
    Southern blacks, 166–70, 171
military service. *See also* Civil War;
    Revolutionary War
    citizenship and, 9, 27
    racial prejudice and, 77
Miller, James A., 167
minstrel shows, 157–58
Miss Porter's School, 149–51, 155,
    157–59, 173, 175
missionaries, 49
Mitchell, Andrew, 71, 153, 168
Mitchell, Charles L., 101
Mitchell, Clara, 75, 101
Mitchell, Henrietta Primus Custis. *See*
    Custis, Henrietta Primus; Primus,
    Henrietta
Mitchell, Ralph, 71, 79
Mitchell, Theodore P., 186

Mitchell, Walter, 154
Mitchell, William, 71, 101
"mulattoes," 168, 169
Munckacsy, Mihaly, 184–85
music, 74, 75, 97, 98, 122, 154, 159,
    168

naming patterns, 6, 7, 9, 19. *See also*
    slaves: naming
Nat Turner rebellion, 32, 33, 42
Native Americans, xv, 15, 23, 36, 49
networks, 72, 111, 112, 128, 145,
    146, 154
    Primus family, 143, 171, 177, 179
New Haven, Connecticut, 32–33
Nott, Elizabeth, 142, 159
Nott, Henry, 55, 56, 71, 72, 142
Nott, James, 77, 159, 171, 173
Nott, Peter, 98, 99, 159, 171, 173

O'Brien, Hugh, 180
occupational opportunities, 163. *See
    also* employment; jobs open to
    blacks; labor market
occupations, xvi, 8, 51, 78, 80,
    114, 163, 198t. *See also specific
    occupations*
Oliver, Timothy, 60

Pacific (packet ship), 61–62, 183
Panic of 1819, 11
Panic of 1873, 171
Patterson, James, 50–51, 71, 170
patting (revival meetings), 118
Paul, Thomas, 77, 80
Peaster, William, 34–35
Pennington, Harriet Walker, 47, 109
Pennington, James W. C., 47, 48f, 49,
    50, 190
    education and, 47, 58, 170, 176
    as fugitive, 47–48, 57
    Hartford and, 47–52, 56–58, 76

Pennington, James W. C. *(continued)*
  life history, 47
  in New York, 58, 70, 76, 79
  personality, 47, 50
  publishing, 49, 109
  Rebecca Primus and, 47, 109, 176
  in Saratoga Springs, 173
  slavery and, 47, 57, 58, 76
  Talcott Street Church and, 47–49,
    109, 170
  Thomas Sands and, 79
  Underground Railroad, 57
  work and employment, 47–49, 52
  writings, 47
Pennington, Thomas Sands, 173. *See
  also* Sands, Thomas
Plato, Ann, 49, 97, 109
Plato, Benajah, 98, 99, 173
Pleasants, Mary Ellen, 188
Poble, Edward, 35
population of Hartford, 15
  black, 15, 22–23, 166–67, 198
  compared with that of other cities,
    21, 68, 112, 113
  growth in the, 166–67
Porter, Charles Ethan, 180–81
Porter, James A., 85, 87
Porter, Miss, 150–51, 173. *See also*
  Miss Porter's School
poverty
  family strategies and, 12
  taking in boarders and, 74
Prime, Amoretta. *See* Primus, Amoretta
  Prime
Prime, James, 91
Prime, Mary, 91, 97
Prime, Wealthy, 91
Primus, Amelia, 10–11
Primus, Amoretta Prime, 85, 91, 93,
  95–101, 105, 178, 179
Primus, Clara, 10–12, 24
Primus, Gad Asher, 10, 11

Primus, Ham, 10–12, 74, 190
Primus, Henrietta. *See also* Custis,
    Henrietta Primus
  Addie Brown and, 135, 142, 145,
    152
  birth, 38
  Civil War and, 152
  death and burial, 186–87, 189
  early life, 43, 47, 52, 61, 65, 89
  education, 47, 145
  Emily Sands and, 145
  family background, 38, 89
  finances, 145
  life history, 186
  marriages, 145, 186
  Rebecca Primus and, 130, 131, 135,
    145
  Smith's Dye House and, 152, 153
  work and employment, 43, 65, 147,
    152, 153
Primus, Holdridge, xv, 8–17, 28, 32,
    34, 36–37, 39f, 40–43, 48, 51,
    60–63, 65–66, 70, 72, 74, 79,
    144–45, 156
  Addie Brown and, 140, 142,
    144–45
  Amoretta Prime Primus and, 91
  Amos Beman and, 45
  Augustus Washington on, 53, 55
  birth, 10
  Charles Porter and, 180, 181
  Civil War and, 90–91
  death, 43, 181–83
  Ellsworth family and, 15–16, 28,
    38, 51
  estate, 183
  family, 11, 12, 89–91, 109, 131,
    145, 157, 178, 195
  family background, 3, 10–12, 45
  finances, 60, 95, 183
  Fugitive Slave Law and, 65–66
  Ham Primus and, 74, 190

Henry and Elizabeth Nott and, 142
Hosea Easton and, 37
James Pennington and, 48, 50
Leila Primus and, 144
Liberia and, 53, 55
Lloyd Seymour and, 74, 78–79
Mehitable Primus and, 17, 28, 31,
    32, 34, 37, 38, 42, 43, 51, 52,
    61, 63, 68, 72, 145, 172, 181
as mulatto, 168
Nelson Primus and, 89–91, 93, 95,
    181
obituaries, eulogies, and tributes to,
    181–82
overview, 181–83, 190
Pacific and, 61, 62, 183
Rebecca Primus and, 61, 140, 142
residences and properties, 60–61,
    72, 74, 172, 183
Talcott Street Church and, 28, 34,
    37, 41–42, 53, 66, 99, 170,
    181–82
voting rights and, 56
William Edwards and, 177
work and employment, 15–16,
    38–40, 39f, 42, 43, 51, 52, 60,
    62, 68, 170, 175, 178, 181, 182
Primus, Isabella "Bell," 104, 189, 195
Addie Brown and, 104, 144, 146,
    151, 154–55, 158, 159
birth, 48
death, 189
early life, 61, 65
education, 65
and the Jacksons, 146
Leila Primus and, 98, 104
marriage to Williams Edwards, 104,
    168, 177, 178, 183, 184, 186
Mehitable Primus and, 130, 144,
    176, 186
as mulatto, 168
as nanny, 98

Nelson Primus and, 88–89, 95–98,
    104, 105, 130, 177–78
Rebecca Primus and, 128, 144–46,
    175, 176, 178, 183, 184, 186
Primus, Leila
Addie Brown and, 144
birth and family background, 85,
    91, 185
death, 185
disability, 97–98, 179, 185
in Hartford, 98–99, 104, 130, 131,
    144, 175
Isabella "Bell" Primus and, 98,
    104
Nelson Primus and, 85, 91, 95–98,
    104, 130, 178, 185
Primus, Margetta, 11
Primus, Marietta, 10
Primus, Mary G. Wheeler, 179,
    184–88
death, 188
Primus, Mehitable (Mehitabel) Esther
    Jacobs, 144, 145, 156, 167, 175,
    181, 184, 190
Addie Brown and, 140, 143–45,
    147, 149
birth, 19
Charles Porter and, 180
Charles Thomas and, 133–34
class bias and, 103
competence, 42
death, 186
early life, 19, 20
Elizabeth Mars and, 26
Emily Jacobs Sands and, 72, 75, 173
family, 48, 75, 89
family background, 19, 22
Freedmen's Aid Society and, 123,
    153, 173
Holdridge Primus and, 17, 28, 31,
    32, 34, 37, 38, 42, 43, 51, 52,
    61, 63, 65, 68, 72, 145, 172, 181

Primus, Mehitable (Mehitabel) Esther
Jacobs *(continued)*
household management, 42, 43, 68,
72
Isabella "Bell" Primus and, 130,
144, 176, 186
Maria Stewart and, 26–27, 43
Mrs. Hall and, 112
as mulatto, 168
multiple roles, 42, 68, 72
naming of, 19
Nelson Primus and, 90–91, 95, 130
overview, xv, 42–43, 68
personality, 42–43, 144
Primus Papers and, 43
and project to help freedwomen find
work in the North, 103
racial uplift and, 31–32, 61, 63, 190
Rebecca Primus and, 72, 109, 117,
128, 131, 133–34, 143, 144, 176
residences and properties, 51, 52,
72, 172, 183
Talcott Street Church and, 28, 38,
42, 75
Thronieve Bicinia and, 130–31
whites and, 42, 43, 128, 173
women's sphere and, 42, 43, 74
work and employment
dressmaking and sewing business,
19, 27, 42, 72, 97, 147, 149,
176
as nurse midwife, 42
Primus, Nelson Augustus, 85, 107,
138, 144, 155, 157, 158, 163,
166, 171, 173, 177–78, 184–88
Addie Brown and, 138, 140
ambition, 88, 90, 91–92, 96, 105
Amoretta Prime Primus and, 105,
178
Amos Beman on, 87
Anti-Slavery Society and, 153

as artist in Boston, 81, 85, 87–105,
144, 175, 179, 180, 184, 185, 187
birth, 48
Charles Porter and, 180–81
Civil War and, 76
and class, 101, 102–103, 167
death, 189
discrimination and oppression
encountered by, 36
dress, 190
education, 65, 89, 90, 180
as artist, 88, 90, 91–92, 96, 105
family, 105, 186
family background, 11, 61, 65, 89
friends, 76–77, 98–99, 112
George Blaikie and, 188
George Francis and, 89, 90
Holdridge Primus and, 89–91, 93,
95, 181
Isabella "Bell" Primus and, 88–89,
95–98, 104, 105, 130, 177–78
on James Nott, 159
Laura Scott on, 188–89
Leila Primus and, 85, 91, 95–98,
104, 130, 178, 185
letters, xiii, 36, 76, 81, 86f, 87, 88,
130, 180, 190
Mary Wheeler Primus and, 179,
184–86, 188
Mehitable Primus and, 90–91, 95, 130
naming of, 10–11, 48
overview, 190
paintings, 137, 179–80, 184, 185,
188, 189, 195, plates 1–6
patent granted to, 180
personality, 188, 190, 191
photograph of, 191f
as "Primus of Boston," 187
Rebecca Primus and, 88, 105, 130,
131, 137, 140
in San Francisco, 187–89, 191f

in Seattle, 186
Southerners and, 167
William Brown and, 180
work and employment, 180, 190
Primus, Rebecca, 52, 88, 89, 97,
102–5, 107, 108f, 110–13,
116–17, 119–33, 135, 137–38,
139–43, 145–46, 150–51, 153,
155, 157, 158–59, 163, 167,
170–73, 175–79, 183–84, 186,
189–91, 195
Addie Brown and, xiii, xiv, 68, 72,
77, 79, 103, 109, 110, 125, 130,
135, 136f, 137–41, 151, 153–55,
158–59, 176
apparel and, 97, 118, 132–33,
190–91, 192f
birth, 38, 109
in Boston, 97
Charles Thomas and, 114, 115, 119,
124, 125, 129, 132, 134, 176–79,
183, 184
childhood and early life, 109
Civil Rights Act of 1866 and,
129–30
Civil War and, 77, 79
class identity, 81, 103, 109, 117, 167
classroom discipline, 120
death, 189–90
education, 47, 65, 109–10
family, 178, 179, 195, 196f
former slaves and, 81, 103, 116–18
Freedmen's Bureau and, 143
Henrietta Primus and, 130, 131,
135, 145
Holdridge Primus and, 61, 140, 142
homesickness, 130
Isabella "Bell" Primus and, 128, 144–
46, 175, 176, 178, 183, 184, 186
James Pennington and, 47, 109, 176
Joseph Tines and, 150

Josephine Booth and, 172
language skills, 138
legacy, 42–43
letters, 36, 107, 114–16, 130–32,
139, 143, 191
home weeklies, xiii, 107, 108f,
109, 133
marriage, 151, 177, 184
Mehitable Primus and, 72, 109, 117,
128, 131, 133–34, 143, 144, 176
Nelson Primus and, 88, 105, 130,
131, 137, 140
photograph of, 193f, 196f
racial justice and, 107, 109, 126,
130, 143, 176
racial uplift and, 63, 112
and racism, 11, 42, 128–29, 168, 171
Raphael Sands and, 158–59, 175
relations with whites, 128
religion and, 118–19, 127, 155
responses to racism, 36, 102, 107,
124, 126–29
in Royal Oak, 81, 88, 103, 105,
111f, 112–21, 123–26, 131–34,
159, 175–76, 191
Sarah Thomas and, 113, 115, 132
school for former slaves founded by,
81
school for girls opened by, 72
schoolhouse built for, 121–26, 175,
176
Talcott Street Church and, 37,
75–76, 109, 121, 130, 155,
158–59, 170, 176, 189, 191, 193f
Thronieve Bicinia and, 130–31
women's rights and, 130
work and employment, 109–10, 178
as schoolteacher, xiii, 47, 65, 89,
107, 109–10, 119, 120, 140,
177, 189. See also Royal Oak
writings, 49, 107, 109

Primus, Temperance Asher, 10, 11
Primus, Thronieve. *See* Harris,
    Thronieve (Sophronia/Phrone)
    Bicenter (Bicinia) Primus
Primus Institute of Royal Oak,
    Maryland, 125, 133, 189
Primus Papers, xiii, 43, 179, 183, 195
Primus timeline, 199–204

race mixture and amalgamation of
    races, 36. *See also* "mulattoes"
racial justice. *See also* equality
    Rebecca Primus and, 107, 109, 126,
    130, 143, 176
racial prejudice, 47. *See also* white
    supremacy
    abolition and, 68, 81
    Civil War, Reconstruction, and, 81,
    174
    military service and, 77
racial solidarity. *See* community
    formation
racial uplift, 112, 157, 167, 193
    active resistance and, 45
    Augustus Washington on, 53, 55
    churches and, 37
    doubts of effectiveness, 27, 38, 55
    education as key to, 107
    George Seymour and, 55
    goal of, 67, 77
    Hosea Easton on, 37, 53
    Mehitable Primus and, 31–32, 61,
    63, 190
    strategy of, 31–32
    theory/doctrine of, 112, 190
racism, 42, 171. *See also specific topics*
    individual black responses to
        Addie Brown, 156–58
        Amos Jerry Beman, 45, 47, 70
        Augustus Washington, 53 60
        Edward M. Bannister, 87–88
        Gad Asher, 6, 7, 9

        George Seymour, 55
        Ham Primus, 11, 61–62
        Holdridge Primus, 32, 36–37,
        39–40, 56–57, 190
        Hosea Easton, 37–38, 45
        James Mars, 45–47, 56, 59
        James Pennington, 47–48, 50, 57,
        76
        Jeremiah Asher, 8, 13, 20, 31, 32
        Mehitable Primus, 27, 42, 127–28,
        167
        Nelson Primus, 101, 102
        Rebecca Primus, 36, 102, 107,
        124, 126–29
    individual white responses to
        Helen Post Chapman, 167–68
        John Hooker, 58
        W. W. Ellsworth, 59, 167–69
Railroad Station. *See* Hartford Railroad
    Station
Randall, Benjamin, 55
Ray, Stephen G., 28
Reconstruction, 104, 133, 163, 171,
    174
refinement (culture), xvi, 67, 72, 140,
    155, 157
reform, xvi, 24, 32, 41, 80. *See also*
    State Temperance and Reform
    Society
Refugees, Freedmen, and Abandoned
    Lands, Bureau of. *See* Freedmen's
    Bureau
religion, 20, 21, 46–49, 67, 118–19,
    127, 155, 169. *See also* African
    Religious Society
respectability, xvi, 41, 67, 131, 157, 193
Revolutionary War, 6–9
riot(s). *See also* slave rebellions
    of 1835, 31, 34–38, 41
    Saint Patrick's Day riot in New
    York, 102, 166
Robbins, Thomas, 52

Robinson, Angeline, 171
Robinson, Jacob, 153
Rodney, John, 71, 74, 152
romantic female friendship. *See* same-sex loving friendship
Royal Oak, Maryland, 113f, 115. *See also* schools
  Charles Thomas in, 114, 115, 124–25, 176–78
  description and overview, 113
  Rebecca Primus in, 81, 88, 103, 105, 111f, 112–21, 123–26, 131–34, 159, 175–76, 191

Salvatore, Nick, xvi, 16
same-sex loving friendship, 81, 135, 138–43. *See also* Brown, Addie: Rebecca Primus and
San Francisco, 185–89
  Nelson Primus in delicatessen in, 188, 190, 191f
  Pacific and, 60–62, 65
San Francisco earthquake of 1906, 187f, 187–88
Sands, Bell, 103, 154
Sands, Emily "Em" Jacobs, 19, 72, 75, 103, 145, 147, 159, 173, 175. *See also* Jacobs, Emily
Sands, Raphael, 74, 139, 150, 172–73
  Addie Brown and, 103, 138, 145, 149, 157–59
  Bell Sands and, 103
  Emily Jacobs and, 103
  Jeremiah Jacobs and, 72
  life history, 173
  Rebecca Primus and, 158–59, 175
  Thomas Sands Pennington and, 79, 173
  work and employment, 72, 173
Sands, Sarah, 142
Sands, Thomas, 79, 103, 159. *See also* Pennington, Thomas Sands

Saunders, Lucinda, 122, 128, 153, 173
Saunders, Prince, 70, 122
Saunders, Roxanna, 70
Saunders, Thomas, 60, 70
Saunders, William, 24, 70, 144
schoolhouses, building, 50, 112. *See also under* Primus, Rebecca
schooling for blacks, antagonism toward, 34, 126–27
schools. *See also* colleges for African Americans; Miss Porter's school
  burning of black, 127
  for former slaves, 81, 110, 112–14, 116. *See also* colleges for African Americans; Primus Institute of Royal Oak; Royal Oak
  segregated, 34, 65
Schultz, Charles R., 61
Scott, Eva, 172
Scott, Isaac, 78, 79, 171–72
Scott, Laura Tooms, 188–89
segregated seating in churches, 20–21, 138
segregation, xv–xvi, 65, 128
  school, 34
Sellers, Charles, 10
seminaries, 34, 170
sexual harassment, 43
Seymour, George L., 55, 70
Seymour, L. Eugene, 173
Seymour, Lloyd, 55, 74, 77–80, 173
Sherman, Roger, 8
Shiloh Baptist Church, 169
shouting (revival meetings), 118–19
Sigourney, Lydia Huntley, 26, 27, 49, 110
Simpson, William, 92–93
slave narratives, 25, 46, 47, 157
slave rebellions, 32, 33, 40, 42
slave trade, 3–4, 14
slavery
  Christianity and, 9

slavery *(continued)*
    churches and, 36, 41, 60
    Civil War and, 76, 77, 80, 81
    in Connecticut, 3–6, 8, 19, 25, 31, 46
    court cases, 40–41, 59
    Georgia and, 126
    Hartford and, 14, 28, 31, 41, 59, 66, 76
    Holdridge Primus and, 3
    and inequality, 8, 17
    James Pennington and, 47–48, 57–58, 76
    legislation regarding, 6–8, 40–41, 59, 60, 65, 129. *See also* Emancipation Proclamation of 1863; Fugitive Slave Act of 1850
    national unrest over, 32, 36, 59–60
    in New England, xiv, 3–5, 9, 14, 36
    Northern, 6, 8
    Revolutionary War and, 6–7, 9
slaves
    freed, 7. *See also* Freedmen's Bureau; Freedmen's Societies; schools; schools: for former slaves
    church services of former slaves, 118
    first large-scale Northern migration of former slaves, 102, 103
    Rebecca Primus and, 81, 103, 116–18
    freeing of, 6–7. *See also* emancipation
    naming, 6, 70
    runaway, 57. *See also* Fugitive Slave Act of 1850; Underground Railroad
    treatment of, 6
Smith, James L., 58
Smith, John A., 38

Smith, Joshua B., 98
Smith, Venture, 6, 7, 9
Smith-Rosenberg, Carroll, 139
Smith's Dye House, 146–47, 150, 152, 154
social equality, 33, 36. *See also* equality
solidarity. *See under* community formation
sophistication. *See* refinement
State House, 14, 14f, 164f, 164–65
State Temperance and Reform Society, 49
Stetfield, Charles E., 92, 93
Stewart, James W., 26
Stewart, Maria W. Miller, 26–27, 43, 99
Stillman, Jacob, 62
Stowe, Calvin, 110, 166
Stowe, Harriet Beecher, 66, 110, 166. *See also Uncle Tom's Cabin*
suffrage, 31, 34, 56, 80, 115, 156, 171, 174
Swan, Prince, 24

Talcott Street Congregational Church, 22f, 55
    Addie Brown and, 75, 155
    Augustus Washington and, 52
    Charles Thomas and, 184
    founding, 21, 28, 46
    governing board, 99
    Henry Foster and, 38
    Holdridge Primus and, 28, 34, 37, 41–42, 53, 66, 99, 170, 181–82
    Hosea Easton and, 37
    James Mars and, 46
    James Pennington and, 47–49, 109, 170
    meetings, 36
    Mehitable Primus and, 28, 38, 42, 75

members, 49, 60, 66, 76, 156, 182, 191, 193f
pastors, 91, 170
Rebecca Primus and, 37, 75–76, 109, 121, 130, 155, 158–59, 170, 176, 189, 191, 193f
resolutions passed, 182
riots and, 34, 36, 41
slavery, abolitionists, and, 36, 60
Tappan, Arthur, 32–33
Tappan, Lewis, 40
temperance societies, 41, 72, 75, 80, 102, 159
Thomas, Charles N.
  death, 184
  early life, 114, 127
  Ernest Thomas and, 178
  finances, 178, 183
  in Hartford, 114, 176–77, 179, 183–84
  injury and disability, 178, 179
  Josephine Booth and, 132
  language skills, 134
  Mehitable Primus and, 133–34
  in Philadelphia, 179
  Rebecca Primus Thomas and, 114, 115, 119, 124, 125, 129, 132, 134, 176–79, 183, 184
  in Royal Oak, 114, 115, 124–25, 176–78
  Sarah Thomas and, 114, 176
  work and employment, 114, 124–25, 179, 183–84
Thomas, Ernest Primus, 178
Thomas, Rebecca Primus. See Primus, Rebecca
Thomas, Sarah, 114, 132, 176–77
Tines, Addie Brown. See Brown, Addie
Tines, Joseph, 176
  and Addie Brown's relations with women, 141, 143
Miss Porter and, 150–51
Rebecca Primus and, 150
relations with Addie Brown Tines, 141, 143–44, 151, 155, 159, 191
Tocqueville, Alexis de, 87
Tredwell, Mr., 94, 98
"triangle trade," 4
Trimble, Colonel, 156
Turner, Nat, 32–33, 42
Twain, Mark, 163, 166, 180
Twelfth Street Baptist Church (Boston), 99–100

Ulmer, Lizzie May, 180
Uncle Tom's Cabin (Stowe), 157
Underground Railroad, 47, 57–59, 100
Union Baptist Church, 169
uplift. See racial uplift

Vesey, Denmark, 32
virtual kinship, 68
voting rights, 31, 34, 56, 80, 115, 156, 171, 174

Walker, David, 26, 32, 99
Warburton Company, 60, 62
Warner, Charles Dudley, 163, 166
Washington, Augustus, 52–56, 60, 66, 70, 109
Wells, Harriet, 173
Wheatley, Phillis, 49
Wheeler, Henry T., 179
White, David, xiv, 9, 125, 189
white assumption of superiority, 50
white supremacy, 36, 57
whites. See also specific topics
  black attitudes toward, 16–17, 20–21, 101–3, 111, 124, 127–28
  blacks behaving differently in the presence of, 116

Williams, James H., 69f, 69–70, 74
Williams, Thomas, 59
Wilson, Henry M., 55
women. *See also* gender
    attitudes toward, 42–43
    books published by African
        American, 49

friendships between, 81, 135,
    138–43. *See also* Brown, Addie:
    Rebecca Primus and
women's agency, failure to recognize, 43
women's rights movement, 130
women's sphere, 42, 141. *See also*
    under Primus, Mehitable